China's Renaissance in Bronze

Robert D. Mowry

China's Renaissance in Bronze
The Robert H. Clague Collection of Later Chinese Bronzes 1100-1900

Phoenix Art Museum

Phoenix Art Museum
25 September 1993 – 30 January 1994

The exhibition is organized by the Phoenix Art Museum and is supported by Northern Trust Bank of Arizona.

Editors – Claudia Brown and Anne Gully
Design – Thomas Detrie
Photography – Craig Smith
Film Setting – Typography Unlimited, Inc.
Color Separations – American Color
Lithography – Prisma Graphic Corporation
Binding – Roswell Bookbinding

Cover – *Circular Gui-shaped Censer*, Hu Wenming, [12] detail

Library of Congress Cataloging-in-Publication Data
Mowry, Robert D.
China's Renaissance in Bronze: the Robert H. Clague Collection of Later Chinese Bronzes, 1100-1900. Robert D. Mowry.
    256 p   26.7 cm
    Includes bibliographical references.
    ISBN 0-910407-29-0
1. Bronzes, Chinese – Sung-Yuan dynasties, 960-1368 – exhibitions.
2. Bronzes, Chinese – Ming-Ch'ing dynasties, 1368-1912 – exhibitions.
3. Clague, Robert – art collections – exhibitions.
4. Bronzes – private collections – Arizona – exhibitions.
    I. Phoenix Art Museum.
    II. Title.
    NK7983.4.M69 1993   93-20881
    739.5'12 – dc20   CIP

Contents

Preface

MORE THAN EIGHT HUNDRED YEARS AGO, Chinese artisans set in motion a revival of bronze casting that would last until the twentieth century. Emulating the exquisitely cast ritual vessels from China's great Bronze Age, which began around 1600 BC, these artisans created superb works that echo the shapes and motifs of antiquity but infuse into them new patterns, new functions, and even new meanings. We are grateful to the Northern Trust Bank of Arizona for its support which enables the Phoenix Art Museum to explore this rekindling of the bronze tradition in the exhibition *China's Renaissance in Bronze: The Robert H. Clague Collection of Later Chinese Bronzes, 1100-1900.*

Within the past fifteen years, Robert H. Clague has become internationally known for his collecting of Chinese art. In 1980, the Phoenix Art Museum organized *Chinese Cloisonné: The Robert H. Clague Collection*, the Museum's first travelling exhibition of Asian art. That exhibition coincided with the founding of the Museum's Asian department and the appointment of its first curator of Asian art, Claudia Brown, who wrote the catalog for the exhibition. *Chinese Cloisonné* later travelled to fourteen museums in the United States and Asia. That collection of cloisonné enamels from the Ming (1368-1644) and Qing (1644-1911) dynasties is now a part of the Museum's permanent collection. In subsequent years, Robert Clague and his wife Amy were instrumental in founding the museum's Asian Arts Council, which has supported programs in Asian art, one of the museum's major areas of emphasis. In 1987, the Phoenix Art Museum organized *Chinese Glass of the Qing Dynasty: The Robert H. Clague Collection*, its catalog co-authored by Claudia Brown and Donald Rabiner, who was professor of art history at Arizona State University until his death in 1992. *Chinese Glass* opened in Phoenix and then travelled to Milwaukee, San Antonio and Tokyo; the collection is now permanently in the Hong Kong Museum of Art. The Clague collection of bronzes now offers an opportunity to investigate the intricacies of the bronze caster's art in a superb group of works dating from the Song (960-1279) through the late Qing dynasty.

The Phoenix Art Museum is very pleased that Robert D. Mowry has joined with our Curator of Asian Art, Claudia Brown, as co-curator for *China's Renaissance in Bronze*. As author of the present catalog, Robert Mowry, Curator of Chinese Art and Head of the Department of Asian Art at the Arthur M. Sackler Museum, Harvard University, brings his broad expertise in East Asian decorative arts, especially Chinese and Korean ceramics, to the examination and analysis of later Chinese bronzes. Both curators, working with Robert Clague, have created a superb exhibition and catalog.

Although museums and private collectors in this country have begun to acquire and display later Chinese bronzes in a limited way, the Clague collection is America's premier private collection in this long neglected field. Thus, first with Chinese cloisonné, then with Chinese glass and now with bronzes, Robert Clague has opened our eyes to the beauty of works hitherto neglected by museums and other private collectors and largely ignored by scholars. Robert Clague is not only a discerning collector, he is a pioneer who has legitimized not just one but three new fields of collecting and has thus inspired new areas of scholarly inquiry. By engaging the interest of museums and scholars in these areas he has had a tremendous impact on the study and appreciation of Chinese art.

James K. Ballinger
Phoenix Art Museum Director

Chronology

Shang   about sixteenth century BC – 1028 BC

Zhou   1027 – 221 BC
    Western Zhou 1027 – 771 BC
    Eastern Zhou   771 – 221 BC
        Spring and Autumn   722 – 481 BC
        Warring States   481 – 221 BC

Qin   221 – 206 BC
Han   206 – AD 221
Six Dynasties 221 – 589
Sui   581 – 618
Tang   618 – 907
Five Dynasties 907 – 960

Song   960 – 1279
    Northern Song 960 – 1127
    Southern Song 1127 – 1279

Yuan   1279 – 1368

Ming   1368 – 1644

Hongwu	1368 – 1398	Hongzhi	1488 – 1505
Jianwen	1399 – 1402	Zhengde	1506 – 1521
Yongle	1403 – 1424	Jiajing	1522 – 1566
Xuande	1426 – 1435	Longqing	1567 – 1572
Zhengtong	1436 – 1449	Wanli	1573 – 1620
Jingtai	1450 – 1457	Taichang	1620
Tianshun	1457 – 1464	Tianqi	1621 – 1627
Chenghua	1465 – 1487	Chongzheng	1628 – 1644

Qing   1644 – 1911

Shunzhi	1644 – 1661	Daoguang	1821 – 1850
Kangxi	1662 – 1722	Xianfeng	1851 – 1861
Yongzheng	1723 – 1735	Tongzhi	1862 – 1874
Qianlong	1736 – 1795	Guangxu	1875 – 1908
Jiaqing	1796 – 1820	Xuantong	1909 – 1911

Casting A Chinese Renaissance

URNING AWAY FROM THE BUDDHISM of the preceeding Tang dynasty, the government and intelligentsia of the Song espoused a newly resurgent Confucianism and initiated a Chinese renaissance. Embracing philosophy, music, and the arts, the movement drew its inspiration from the culture of the Bronze Age, that hallowed, formative era of Chinese history that gave birth to Confucius, Laozi, and many other honored cultural figures. Made from the Song through the Qing, the so-called later bronzes[1] are the most eloquent symbol of that renaissance. Cast through the lost-wax process[2] rather than through the piece-mold technique of antiquity,[3] they were produced in a manner very different from the archaic ritual bronzes upon which they were modeled; as censers, vases, and implements for the scholar's desk, they served functions unknown to their ancient models; in imitating the ancient bronzes' shapes and ornament, however, they forged a highly visible and symbolic link with the past.

During the Shang, Zhou, and Han dynasties, often called the great Bronze Age, the Chinese not only introduced bronze casting to northeast Asia but achieved a level of technical virtuosity unsurpassed even in modern times, producing exquisite bronzes that delight the eye and document early technological prowess. The classical culture associated with Bronze Age China came to a close neither because the art of casting was lost nor because iron displaced bronze,[4] but because that culture was transformed by the secularization of late Zhou and Han society, by the dissolution of empire, by the rapid growth of the Buddhist church following the collapse of Han,[5] and by the arrival of new goods and ideas through ever expanding trade over the fabled Silk Route.

Differences in religious practices led to the disappearance of many Shang ritual vessel shapes in the Western Zhou. During the mid- and late Zhou, increasing secularism bolstered by rising interest in philosophy[6] over religion prompted a further reduction in the number of ritual vessel shapes, so that by the Han the number of vessel types was limited indeed. In addition, sophisticated high-fired ceramics began to displace secular bronzes in well-to-do households during the Han. As the newly prosperous Buddhist church grew in the Six Dynasties,[7] and as the ranks of the faithful swelled to include even rulers and their families in the Central Plains, the heartland of Bronze Age culture, the need disappeared even for the limited number of bronze ritual vessel types inherited from the Han. The growth of Buddhism, combined with ongoing religious and intellectual change, thus closed the door on Bronze Age culture and its ritual vessels.

From Han through Tang, China witnessed ever increasing contact with the outside world, most importantly through the influx of luxury goods via the Silk Route.[8] As such goods became a part of daily life in wealthy and aristocratic circles, new industries arose in China to supply the market, producing, for example, gold and silver vessels. Potters quickly followed suit, imitating silver vessels in the newly invented white porcelain and appropriating decorative motifs from gold and silver pieces for their celadon wares. Perhaps copied from silver or glass imports, a few Tang ceramics even reflect influence from distant Greece and Rome. In addition, fabric designers readily incorporated Persian motifs into their silks, and musicians assimilated the *pipa*, or lute, and other foreign instruments into their orchestras.

Playing on a long-dormant but deep-seated suspicion of things foreign, a faction at court sought political advantage by initiating a series of persecutions against the Buddhist church in 845, confiscating property, destroying temples, and returning monks and nuns to lay life. The move ushered in a period of cultural self-examination that lasted well into the Song and that sought to define Chinese culture by separating the native from the foreign, always awarding pride of place to the native. As Buddhism waned, Confucianism reasserted itself, with renewed philosophical inquiry giving it the highly intellectualized framework that distinguishes it as Neo-Confucianism. Native musical instruments, especially the *qin* – the ancient zither that Confucius himself played – claimed primacy, relegating the *pipa* and other foreign instruments to professional entertainers. And on royal and aristocratic tables, refined, monochrome-glazed ceramics became the preferred wares, displacing, even if not replacing, gold and silver.

Antiquity served as the standard in identifying and defining things Chinese. Antiquarian interests fired an appreciation of Bronze Age antiquities, leading to the formation of collections of ancient bronzes and jades. Although works of painting and calligraphy had been collected at least since the Han and although serendipitous finds of ancient bronzes had always been considered auspicious, the systematic collecting of antiquities had to await the genuine interest in antiquity that came in the early Northern Song.

Ancient bronzes were no doubt prized at first as tangible bits of history – something that the Duke of Zhou or Confucius might once have held. Scholars quickly realized, however, that many ancient bronzes bear inscriptions and that the inscriptions constitute ancient documents of cardinal importance to historians and epigraphers. Finally, bronzes were accepted on their own merits as works of art. As historical documents, as works of art, and as relics of the hallowed past, archaic bronzes were eagerly collected by emperors, aristocrats, and well-to-do scholar-officials (who are often shown surrounded by them in paintings). Illustrated collection catalogs compiled during the Song served as models not only for later catalogs but for many later bronzes and ceramics.[9]

The literati not only collected ancient bronzes but used them as incense burners and flower vases on special occasions. Realizing that too frequent use of their prized antiquities would ruin them, they sought newly made vessels of similar shape and decoration in bronze and ceramic ware, encouraging both the renaissance in bronze and the taste for archaism that is a hallmark of later Chinese culture. In shunning the recent past in favor of the ancient, the people of Song generated a renaissance that found expression in philosophy, music, epigraphy, painting,[10] and the three-dimensional arts and that is akin in spirit to the Italian Renaissance.

Song bronzes – a generic term including works of copper, bronze, brass, and related metals – typically imitate the shapes of ancient bronzes, though their ornament derives from a variety of sources, from ancient vessels [catalog number 1] to more recent works in other media [2]. Thinly cast, Yuan bronzes often feature all-over diaper patterns resembling those in the borders of contemporaneous blue-and-white porcelain; new shapes appear to serve new functions [5] and old shapes accept modifications to fit new tastes [4, 6]. Non-imperial bronzes of the early Ming show a preference for surfaces with decorated areas contrasting with undecorated ones [7, 8, 43].

Imperially commissioned bronzes from the Xuande reign of the early Ming apparently ranked among the most exquisite of later bronzes, admired for their elegant shapes, sublime colors, delicate inlays and perfect casting. For reasons but little understood, virtually all such bronzes have disappeared, a situation lamented already by late Ming connoisseurs; seventeenth-century copies preserve something of their innovative style and elegance, however, and reveal that they were based as much on Song ceramics as on ancient bronzes [15, 16].

Except for those with gold or silver inlays, bronzes from the Song, Yuan, and early Ming almost always have decoration integrally cast with the vessel itself. From the mid-Ming onward, bronzes begin to rely on cold work (chasing and chiseling after casting) for their decoration [19, 50]. By the late Ming, the decoration on most bronzes was imparted through cold work [11, 13, 45-47]; from the late Ming on, some bronzes were not cast at all, but raised, or hammered, from sheet copper [12, 41]. Late Ming artisans expanded their range of sources for both shape and decoration to include contemporaneous lacquers, jades, porcelains, ivories, and cloisonné enamels; as a result, new, often playful, shapes and motifs appear [9, 13, 14], including many objects for the scholar's desk [44-49]. In the absence of dated inscriptions and archaeological data, such borrowings make the comparative method especially useful for dating.

Although literary records mention bronze casters, the tradition remains largely anonymous because so few bronzes are inscribed with their place of manufacture or maker's name. History has preserved a number of bronzes by the celebrated Hu Wenming of Yunjian (modern Songjiang, near Shanghai), two of which are in the Clague Collection [11, 12]. More bronzes bear the mark of Shisou than any other, including four in the Clague Collection [16-18, 55], but attributions to his hand remain unverifiable.

Often large [31, 37-39], Qing bronzes were cast as well as raised from sheet metal [41] or assembled from hammered components [26-29, 39]. Although they sometimes resemble those of Ming bronzes, the decorative schemes of Qing bronzes range from archaistic [37] to abstract [34-35], from formalistic [38-39] to naturalistic [26-29, 33, 56] and even eclectic [31-32]. Bronzes of the Kangxi period show a taste for a *yin-yang* pairing of complementary opposites [21, 32] and for abstract, gold-splashed decor derived from Xuande bronzes [34]; those of the Yongzheng and Qianlong eras reveal a preference for floral designs [27-29], archaistic dragons [37], and dragon-and-phoenix motifs [37-38]. Popular already in the late Ming, designs wishing the viewer wealth [27], marital happiness [56], and success in the civil service examinations [48, 57] became even more so in the Qing. Late eighteenth-century bronzes occasionally feature asymmetrical designs that represent a radical departure from tradition [40], whereas nineteenth-century ones espouse a new-found economy of material, substituting overlays of gold and silver for the more costly inlays of earlier centuries [42]. At their best, Qing bronzes show exquisitely finished surfaces unrivalled by those of other post-Tang examples [34, 37-39].

Select Bibliography
English-language References

Robert W. Bagley. *Shang Ritual Bronzes in the Arthur M. Sackler Collections.* Washington DC and Cambridge MA. 1987.

Noel Barnard. *Bronze Casting and Bronze Alloys in Ancient China.* Canberra and Tokyo. 1961.

W. Thomas Chase with the assistance of Jung May Lee. *Ancient Chinese Bronze Art: Casting the Precious Sacral Vessel.* Exhibition catalog. New York: China Institute in America. 1991.

Jerome Ch'en. 'Sung Bronzes: An Economic Analysis.' *Bulletin of the School of Oriental and African Studies.* Number 28. London. 1965. 613-26.

Dawn Ho Delbanco. *Art from Ritual: Ancient Chinese Bronze Vessels from the Arthur M. Sackler Collections.* Cambridge MA and Washington DC. 1983.

Wen Fong editor. *The Great Bronze Age of China: An Exhibition from the People's Republic of China.* Exhibition catalog. New York. Metropolitan Museum of Art. 1980.

Rutherford John Gettens. *The Freer Chinese Bronzes. Technical Studies,* volume 2. Smithsonian Institution, Freer Gallery of Art. Oriental Studies Number 7. Washington DC. 1969.

R. Soame Jenyns and William Watson. *Chinese Art: The Minor Arts (Gold, Silver, Bronze, Cloisonné, Cantonese Enamel, Lacquer, Furniture, Wood).* New York. 1963.

Rose Kerr. 'A Preliminary Note on Some Qing Bronze Types.' *Oriental Art.* New series 26. London. Winter 1980-81. 447-56.

Rose Kerr. *Later Chinese Bronzes.* Victoria and Albert Museum Far Eastern Series. London. 1990.

Rose Kerr. 'Metalwork and Song Design: A Bronze Vase Inscribed in 1173.' *Oriental Art.* New series 32. London. Summer 1986. 161-76.

Rose Kerr. 'The Evolution of Bronze Style in the Jin, Yuan and Early Ming Dynasties,' *Oriental Art.* New series 28. London. Summer 1982. 146-58.

Thomas Lawton, 'An Imperial Legacy Revisited: Bronze Vessels from the Qing Palace Collection,' *Asian Art.* Volume 1, number 1. Washington DC. Fall/Winter 1987-88. 51-79.

Thomas Lawton, *Chinese Art of the Warring States Period: Change and*

Continuity, 480-222 BC. Exhibition catalog. Washington DC: Freer Gallery of Art, Smithsonian Institution. 1982.

Max Loehr. *Ritual Vessels of Bronze Age China.* Exhibition catalog. New York. Asia Society. 1968.

Assadullah Souren Melikian-Chirvani. *Islamic Metalwork from the Iranian World, Eighth-eighteenth Centuries: Victoria and Albert Museum Catalog.* London. 1982.

Robert Poor, 'Evolution of a Secular Vessel Type,' *Oriental Art.* New series 14. London. Summer 1968. 98-106.

Robert Poor. 'Notes on the Sung Dynasty Archaeological Catalogs,' *Archives of the Chinese Art Society of America.* Volume 19. New York. 1965. 33-44.

John Alexander Pope, Rutherford John Gettens, James Cahill, Noel Barnard. *The Freer Chinese Bronzes. Catalogue.* Volume 1. Smithsonian Institution, Freer Gallery of Art. Oriental Studies Number 7. Washington DC. 1967.

Jessica Rawson. *Chinese Bronzes: Art and Ritual.* London. 1987.

Jessica Rawson. *Western Zhou Ritual Bronzes from the Arthur M. Sackler Collections.* Two volumes. Washington DC and Cambridge MA. 1990.

Jenny F.S. So. *Eastern Zhou Ritual Bronzes from the Arthur M. Sackler Collections.* Washington DC, forthcoming.

William Watson. 'Categories of Post-Yuan Decorative Bronzes,' *Transactions of the Oriental Ceramic Society.* Volume 46. London. 1981-82. 11-28.

William Watson. 'On Some Categories of Archaism in Chinese Bronze,' *Ars Orientalis.* Volume 9. Washington DC. 1973. 3-13.

Allied References

The Arts Council of Great Britain and the Oriental Ceramic Society. *Chinese Jade Throughout the Ages.* London. 1975.

William W. Atwell. 'International Bullion Flows and the Chinese Economy circa 1530-1650,' *Past and Present.* Number 95. Oxford. 1982. 68-90.

Helmut Brinker and Albert Lutz. *Chinese Cloisonné: The Pierre Uldry Collection.* Translated by Susanna Swoboda. Exhibition catalog. New York. Asia Society Galleries. 1989.

Claudia Brown. *Chinese Cloisonné: The Clague Collection.* Exhibition catalog. Phoenix AZ. Phoenix Art Museum. 1980.

Claudia Brown and Donald Rabiner. *Chinese Glass of the Qing Dynasty, 1644-1911: The Robert H. Clague Collection.* Exhibition catalog. Phoenix AZ. Phoenix Art Museum. 1987.

Claudia Brown and Donald Rabiner. *Clear as Crystal, Red as Flame: Later Chinese Glass.* Exhibition catalog. New York. China Institute in America. 1990.

John Carswell. *Blue and White: Chinese Porcelain and Its Impact on the Western World.* Exhibition catalog. Chicago. The David and Alfred Smart Gallery, University of Chicago. 1985.

J.P. Donnelly. *Blanc de Chine: The Porcelain of Tehua in Fukien.* New York and Washington DC. 1969.

Sir Harry Garner. *Chinese Lacquer.* London and Boston. 1979.

Basil Gray. 'Persian Influence upon Chinese Art from Eighth to Fifteenth Centuries,' *Iran.* Volume 1. London. 1963.

Basil Gray. 'The Influence of Near Eastern Metalwork on Chinese Ceramics,' *Transactions of the Oriental Ceramic Society.* Volume 18. London. 1940-41. 47-60.

Bo Gyllensvärd. *Chinese Gold and Silver in the Carl Kempe Collection.* Stockholm. 1953.

Clarence W. Kelley. *Chinese Gold and Silver from the Tang Dynasty (AD 618-907) in American Collections.* Exhibition catalog. Dayton OH: Dayton Art Institute. 1984.

Rose Kerr. *Chinese Ceramics: Porcelains of the Qing Dynasty, 1644-1911,* (Victoria and Albert Museum Far Eastern Series). London. 1986.

Chu-tsing Li and James C.Y. Watt editors. *The Chinese Scholar's Studio: Artistic Life in the Late Ming Period.* Exhibition catalog. New York. Asia Society. 1987.

Li Yihua editor. *Gugong zhen cang Kang Yong Qianciqi tulu* (Qing Porcelain of the Kangxi, Yongzheng, and Qianlong Periods from the Palace Museum Collection). Hong Kong. 1989 (in Chinese but with English captions).

Daisy Lion-Goldschmidt. *Ming Porcelain.* Translated by Katherine Watson. New York. 1978.

Max Loehr assisted by Louisa G. Fitzgerald Huber. *Ancient Chinese Jades from the Grenville L. Winthrop Collection in the Fogg Art Museum, Harvard University.* Cambridge MA. 1975.

Margaret Medley. *Metalwork and Chinese Ceramics,* number 2, Monograph Series. London. Percival David Foundation of Chinese Art, School of Oriental and African Studies, University of London. 1972.

Margaret Medley. *T'ang Pottery and Porcelain.* Boston. 1981.

Margaret Medley. *The Chinese Potter: A Practical History of Chinese Ceramics.* New York. 1976.

Margaret Medley. *Yuan Porcelain and Stoneware*. London. 1974.

Oriental Ceramic Society compiler. *Chinese Ivories from the Shang to the Qing*. Exhibition catalog. London. British Museum. 1984.

Percival David Foundation of Chinese Art compiler. *Imperial Taste: Chinese Ceramics from the Percival David Foundation*. Exhibition catalog. Los Angeles. Los Angeles County Museum of Art. 1989.

John A. Pope. *Chinese Porcelains from the Ardebil Shrine*. Washington DC. 1956.

Jessica Rawson. 'Song Silver and its Connexions with Ceramics,' *Apollo* Volume 120, new series number 269. London. July 1984. 18-23.

Jessica Rawson. *Chinese Ornament: The Lotus and the Dragon*. London.1984.

Mary Tregear. *Song Ceramics*. New York. 1982.

Suzanne G. Valenstein. *A Handbook of Chinese Ceramics*. Revised and enlarged edition. New York. 1989.

Michael Vickers editor. *Pots and Pans: A Colloquium on Precious Metals and Ceramics in the Muslim, Chinese and Graeco-Roman Worlds*. Oxford Studies in Islamic Art, number 3. Oxford. 1986.

Wang Shixiang and Wan-go Weng. *Bamboo Carving of China*. Exhibition catalog. New York. China Institute in America. 1983.

William Watson editor. *Pottery and Metalwork in T'ang China: Their Chronology and External Relations*. Colloquies on Art and Archaeology in Asia. Number 1. London. Percival David Foundation, School of Oriental and African Studies, University of London. Volume 1. 1970.

William Watson. *Tang and Liao Ceramics*. New York. 1984.

James C.Y. Watt. *Chinese Jades from Han to Ch'ing*. Exhibition catalog. New York. Asia Society. 1980.

James C.Y. Watt. *The Sumptuous Basket: Chinese Lacquer with Basketry Panels*. Exhibition catalog. New York. China Institute in America. 1985.

James C.Y. Watt assisted by Michael Knight. *Chinese Jades from the Collection of the Seattle Art Museum*. Seattle Art Museum. Seattle. 1989.

James C.Y. Watt and Barbara Brennan Ford. *East Asian Lacquer: The Florence and Herbert Irving Collection*. Exhibition catalog. New York. Metropolitan Museum of Art. 1991.

Ip Yee and Laurence C.S. Tam. *Chinese Bamboo Carving*. Exhibition catalog in two volumes. Hong Kong. Hong Kong Museum of Art. 1978 and 1982.

The Robert H. Clague Collection

1 Square Hu Vessel

with two loop handles and with *taotie* and interlaced dragon decor

Song dynasty, twelfth – thirteenth century
Cast bronze with cast decoration and a cast intaglio inscription in
bronze-script characters (*jinwen*) on the interior of the neck
47.6 centimeter height
Provenance: R. Strehlneck, London and Beijing; Gerald Krech, London
and New York
Clague Collection Number 235

THIS IMPRESSIVE FANGHU, OR SQUARE HU, rests on a well articulated square foot with rounded corners; constricting gently above
the foot, the walls rise to form the vessel's softly swelling body, terminating in a flat shoulder from which springs the modestly flaring square
neck. Strapwork moldings – the vertical ones with medial crests – divide the
surface of the ovoid body into four decorative panels; each round-cornered
panel extends from the midpoint of one face to the midpoint of the adjacent
one, wrapping around the vessel's corners. A tightly woven pattern of tiny
interlaced stylized dragons – sometimes called a silkworm pattern – enlivens
the decorative panels. Originally supporting moveable (but now lost) bronze
rings, two loop handles orient the vessel right and left, their curved tubular
lower halves issuing from the mouths of mythical animal heads. On the
lower half of the neck are two *taotie* masks, one each front and back, with
the bodies of the mythical beast continuing around the corners onto the
sides. Set against a finely cast *leiwen*, or squared spiral, ground, the lightly
modeled *taotie* masks lack vertical flanges, though their nose ridges echo
the medial crests of the vertical strapwork moldings below. The upper
half of the neck is undecorated, mirroring the plain foot and harmonizing
with the unornamented strapwork. A flat, low-relief band traverses the
otherwise plain base – at a level corresponding on the exterior to the top
of the constricted foot – in a 'handle to handle' orientation. The vessel
might originally have had a low, domed cover with a knob at its center.

   With its well ordered strapwork bands, this vessel recalls a style of
surface organization that appeared in the middle Western Zhou and then
enjoyed a measure of popularity in the late Western Zhou period, especially on *hu* vessels.[1] As exemplified by a pair of large covered *hu* vessels[2]
dating to the ninth or early eighth century BC, in the Charlotte C. and
John C. Weber Collection at The Metropolitan Museum of Art, New York,
typologically related vessels from late Western Zhou typically feature a
more elaborate strapwork pattern that divides the vessel surface into
eight decorative panels, that boasts a high-relief geometric ornament at
the crossing of its vertical and horizontal members, and that has flat bands
rather than the medially crested ones of the Clague vessel. Newly introduced in Song times, the crisply-defined flat shoulder of the Clague vessel
does not appear in *hu* vessels of the late Western Zhou, which characteristically exhibit elongated pear shapes with organically curving profiles.

   With its *taotie* masks on the neck and its interlaced dragons in the
body panels, the surface ornament on the Clague *hu* differs markedly
from that on Western Zhou vessels with strapwork decoration, which

occasionally display stylized birds but more typically feature relatively large-scale dissolved-dragon forms in rounded relief, the dragons set against a plain ground. The *taotie* mask – the most frequently encountered of all motifs on bronzes of the Shang dynasty – began to wane in popularity early in the Western Zhou period, and must be considered an anachronistic element on a vessel imitating a late Western Zhou style. Also anachronistic is the motif of tiny interlaced stylized dragons, which did not appear with frequency until a century or two later than the strapwork-decorated Western Zhou vessels that served as the primary model for the Clague *hu*'s surface decoration. During the Eastern Zhou period, the dragon interlace regularly occurred on both bronzes and jades,[3] especially those of the seventh through the third century BC. Interlaced dragon designs on bronzes cast earlier in that five-hundred-year period tend to exhibit a uniform height of relief,[4] but ones on vessels cast later in the period reveal considerable modulation in height of relief, the dragons' 'heads' and 'tails' often rising significantly above their bodies, clearly distinguishing one dragon – or 'plastic curl,' as Max Loehr termed them[5] – from the next.[6] The relatively even height of relief, the 'outlined' character of the individual dragons, and the arrangement of the dragons into horizontal rows suggest that vessels from the seventh to fifth century BC likely inspired the decoration of the Clague *hu*. In fact, the character and texture of the dragon interlace on the Clague *hu* relate closely to those on a *hu* vessel, probably of seventh-century BC date, in the Nezu Museum, Tokyo.[7]

Bronzes from the Song dynasty remain in sufficient numbers to illustrate that, when they wished, foundrymen were able to create deceptively faithful copies of Shang and Zhou vessels.[8] The simplified strapwork moldings, the new interpretation of the *hu* shape with a flat shoulder, and the combination of decorative elements in a fashion that would not have occurred in antiquity indicate that the Clague *hu* is not a direct copy of an early *hu*; rather, it is an archaistic vessel inspired by a variety of ancient bronzes, modified to create a new one. With its juxtaposition of utterly plain and highly textured surfaces, of rounded forms and angled corners, this vessel establishes a new set of happily resolved tensions, resulting in a stable, balanced, and very pleasing aesthetic.

Cast integrally with the vessel itself, an intaglio inscription in bronze-script (*jinwen*) characters appears inside the neck in four columns that read top to bottom, right to left. Although the inscription is legible only in part, due to its somewhat concealed placement, its unassertive casting, and its light patina, enough can be deciphered to ascertain that it reveals nothing of the vessel's date or circumstance of manufacture; rather, like the vessel itself, the inscription follows the form and style of inscriptions on bronzes from the Western Zhou era. The inscription seems to translate:

Bo Si(?) Hao made [this] *gui* [vessel] [for his] esteemed forebears [characters illegible/meaning unclear] to treasure. [May generations of] sons and grandsons forever value [and] use [it].

It remains uncertain whether the inscription was newly composed (in ancient style) when the bronze was made or whether it repeats one copied from a Zhou-dynasty vessel. Parts of a name, the first and third characters (Bo and Hao), occur frequently in inscriptions on Western Zhou bronzes, as do those of the last sentence, a standard component of most Western Zhou inscriptions. The inclusion of the character *gui* is curious, since the Clague vessel is clearly a *hu* rather than a *gui* (a two-handled, deep, bowl-like vessel that, in antiquity, was used for serving boiled grain, probably millet). The misnaming of the vessel suggests that the inscription was likely appropriated from an antique *gui* vessel, the designer either not recognizing the incompatibility of name and shape, or mistakenly assuming *gui* to be a generic name for 'ritual vessel.' Several characters appear to be incorrectly written, illustrating the difficulty in copying bronze script, a new field of scholarly inquiry at the time.

The *hu* – along with the *ding*, *gui*, *gu*, and *zun* – rank among the earliest antique bronze-vessel shapes revived in the Song. Popular in bronze, *hu*-shaped vessels were also produced in ceramic ware during the Southern Song period, especially in *guan* ware intended for the imperial court.[9] With their thick, concealing, opaque, grayish-blue glazes, *guan*-ware examples seldom have surface decoration but they typically possess hollow, cylindrical appendages at the neck reminiscent of those on Shang-dynasty bronzes [see discussion, 4].

In Song fashion, the vessel was made in four parts joined together after casting: body (including the foot), neck, and two handles. The small step at its base marks the lowest portion of the neck visible on the exterior; barely detectable on the exterior, the joining of neck and body is clearly indicated on the interior by a short lip on the bottom of the neck that projects downward into the body, anchoring the neck in place. (The need to secure neck to body might imbue the flat shoulder with a structural function aside from its aesthetic one.) Although the two pieces fit snugly together, technical analysis will doubtless reveal that long-term bonding of the two pieces relies more on a touch of applied molten metal than on mere physical tension. Pins anchor the handles in place, their flattened heads discernible on the interior of the neck; bits of applied molten metal reinforce the bond, securing the handles in place. Also in Song fashion, the decorative elements, taotie masks, leiwen patterns, and dragon interlaces, were integrally cast with the vessel parts and show minimal post-casting cold work (engraving, chiseling, or other techniques). The interlaced dragon designs were likely stamped into the wax used to prepare the mold for casting. The overall pattern of stamped designs was not tailored to the exact size and configuration of the decorative panels, however, with the result that the strapwork borders cut midway through design elements.

Strapwork moldings in combination with interlaced dragon designs on the body and taotie masks on the neck are typical features of Song-dynasty bronzes.[10] Reinforcing the attribution of this archaistic hu to the Song dynasty are its reliance on casting (rather than cold-working techniques) as the primary means of creating the decoration and the arbitrary relationship between the interlaced-dragon panels and their strapwork borders (resulting in the bisecting of numerous dragon elements). Unintended residues from casting, the extraneous traces of bronze that cloud parts of the dragon interlace, are also a feature of Song bronzes, attesting to the lack of extensive cold working.

The function of this bronze remains uncertain. One of the most persistent of ancient vessel types, the hu served as a wine storage jar during the many centuries of the Bronze Age, from the Shang through the Han dynasties. Made a thousand years later, the Clague hu could have been designed as a wine vessel for use in newly revived Confucian ceremonies, though it more likely served as a large vase. (The Southern Song guan-ware hu vessels mentioned above were almost certainly intended as flower vases, for example.) There is also the possibility that with its archaistic style and inscription the Clague hu was sold as an antique and brought joy to an unsuspecting collector[11] who assumed it to be from the golden age of Confucius (551-479 BC).

2 Cylindrical Zun-shaped Censer

with three anthropomorphic legs, with two ring-handle attachments, and with *leiwen* and stylized floral decor

Song dynasty, twelfth – thirteenth century
Cast bronze with cast decoration
13.0 centimeter diameter
Provenance: Dr Sidney Smith, Cambridge, England
Clague Collection Number 248

T HIS HANDSOME FLAT-BOTTOMED CYLINDRICAL CENSER rests on three evenly spaced legs in the form of kneeling male figures who bear the weight of the vessel on their shoulders. Their arms akimbo, the figures wear loose trousers secured at the waist and scarf-like upper garments that fall downward from the shoulders revealing their rather substantial bellies. Small tufts of hair crown their otherwise bald heads. A complex pattern of low-relief floral arabesques embellishes the exterior walls of the vessel (which taper ever so slightly near the top). Each of the three principal arabesques occupies a diamond-shaped panel framed by a double band of *leiwen* bounded by a relief bowstring line, the panels centered each above one of the anthropomorphic legs. Two half-panels of identical type fill the interstices, their corners touching at a point midway between adjacent legs. Two opposed *pushou*-mask escutcheons, each with a pendant fluted ring that originally had a free-turning bronze ring (now lost), appear one-third of the way down from the mouth. Narrow, undecorated bands encircle the vessel top and bottom, clearly demarcating the vessel's boundaries and bordering its decoration. The interior and base are plain.

The Chinese had burned incense at least as early as the Shang dynasty, and by Warring States and Han times had created specialized incense burners. Known as *boshanlu*, such censers usually had a cup-like container set atop a slender tubular stalk anchored in a small saucer-like basin that often had a coiled dragon on its floor; a perforated, conical cover in the form of a soaring mountain peak completed the composition.[1] As incense burned in the container, smoke emerged through the perforations in the cover, hovering like an enveloping mist about a mountain peak. Water in the basin not only afforded a measure of protection against fire, but completed the mountain-water symbolism that is emblematic of all nature, of *yin* and *yang*, of female and male [see 48].

The popularity of the *boshanlu* censer declined with the collapse of the Han. With the rise of Buddhism during the centuries following, two new types of censers appeared for use in Buddhist ceremonies: one type, which had a circular, bowl-shaped container and a long straight handle, was carried in processions, as indicated by wall paintings at Dunhuang and by illustrations in woodblock-printed books; the other type, which was for use on altars, as depicted in similar books and wall paintings, had an ornamented, circular, basin-like container that was surmounted by a tall, pierced, domed cover[2] which sat atop a ring of tall legs – usually five legs in the form of lion's claws. The late Tang and early Song periods witnessed the introduction of another censer shape: a vessel with a deep cup-like container resting on a flaring pedestal base and with a wide horizontal rim at the mouth.[3] Several variations on that shape evolved during the Song, some with naturalistic covers in the form of ducks, lions, and other animals.[4] The wide-lipped censers and those with naturalistic covers doubtless served both religious and secular worlds.

With the rediscovery of antiquity in the Northern Song, well-to-do Chinese began to collect ancient bronze vessels, appropriating *ding* tripods, *gui* bowls, and cylindrical-*zun* wine containers as incense burners and *gu* beakers and trumpet-mouthed *zun* vessels as flower vases on special occasions. The collectors of the Song and later periods realized that they were using the ancient vessels in ways very different from those for which they were made, and frequent purchase of the ancient bronzes could impoverish them, so they commissioned new censers in ancient styles, some in bronze and some in glazed ceramic ware.[5] By Yuan and early Ming times it was thought that vessels of bronze were best suited for the winter months and ones of ceramic ware for the summer ones, necessitating the alternation of bronze and ceramic forms with the rotation of the seasons.[6]

Like the previous *hu* vessel [1], this censer is an archaistic piece. The form derives from a three-legged cylindrical wine vessel of a type known as *zun* that was introduced late in the Warring States period and that flourished in the Han dynasty, with examples extant in bronze, jade, and ceramic ware.[7] (Song-dynasty antiquarians identified vessels of this type as *lian*, or cosmetic boxes, by which name they have generally been known until recent times; the inscriptions on two similarly shaped vessels of Han date excavated in the 1960s term them *zun* and show them to be 'warm wine' vessels.)[8] Typically set on legs in the shape of crouching bears, Han-dynasty *zun* occasionally rest on cabriole legs, though apparently not on ones of anthropomorphic shape, even though a few Eastern Zhou bronzes sit atop legs in the form of standing humans.[9] Han examples generally have two ring-handles suspended from animal-mask escutcheons. Ancient *zun* vessels range from unornamented to elaborately patterned; although the decorated ones embrace a variety of subject matter, from dragons amidst clouds to mountainous landscapes with ferocious beasts, floral arabesques do not figure among them. In looking to antiquity, the Song bronze casters who made this censer appropriated the general form of a Han-dynasty *zun* with its flat base, gently tapering cylindrical walls, *pushou*-mask handles, and three legs, but they altered the form of the legs and substituted a new decorative scheme.

The decorative scheme on the Clague vessel lacks prototypes in the archaic bronze tradition; in its taste for an all-over pattern that features floral motifs in panels surrounded by repeating design elements, however, it accords well with ceramic vessels produced late in the Southern Song and Yuan periods, especially jars and bottles with painted decoration produced at the Jizhou kilns in central Jiangxi province. The relics recently excavated from the Chinese merchant ship that sank off the coast of Sinan, Republic of Korea, in 1323, for example, include a small painted Jizhou bottle with two eight-lobed foliate panels set against a ground of scrolling feather-like foliage, one panel featuring a blossom and the other a motif of rolling waves.[10] Although such Jizhou ceramics did not serve as the direct inspiration for the present bronze censer, they provide a context for the elaborate patterning.

The exact source for the decorative scheme on this censer remains a mystery, since highly stylized, geometricized blossoms set in angular, diamond-shaped panels are not a feature either of ancient bronzes or of Song and Yuan ceramics. The design might well have been influenced by textiles or by architectural motifs,[11] but it might also have been sparked by details in Song-period woodblock-printed illustrations. The frontispiece to each of the seven scrolls of a *Lotus Sutra* printed about 1160, now in the collection of Rikkyō-an, a sub-temple of Daitoku-ji, Kyoto, Japan, depicts a Buddha surrounded by attendants, the Buddha seated on a lotus dais behind an altar on a paved terrace.[12] Set at a slight angle, the paving tiles in these frontispieces create a pattern whose overall effect bears a superficial resemblance to a compact but well defined *leiwen* ground. Each of the small tiles in the frontispieces sports a stylized flower head at its center, a reduced form of the paving tiles portrayed in Tang-dynasty woodblock-printed sutra frontispieces, such as that prefacing a text of *Diamond Sutra*,[13] printed in 868, recovered at Dunhuang and now in the British Museum, London, which portrays the Buddha seated on a lotus throne on a paved terrace in discourse with his disciple Subhūti and surrounded by attendants. The paving tiles illustrated in such frontispieces were based on actual ceramic tiles.

The diamond-shaped lozenges (excepting their *leiwen* borders) and the stylized blossoms on the Clague censer correspond closely to ornamental architectural tiles[14] and to the paving tiles depicted in the 868 *Diamond Sutra*. Even the arrangement of the repeating design elements on the censer suggests the layout of tiles, whether on a building wall or in a paved courtyard. Such similarities do not prove a relationship between bronze design and either architectural ornament or woodblock-printed books, but they suggest that the subject warrants further research, especially in light of the now well-documented influence of Yuan-dynasty woodblock-printed secular dramas on fourteenth-century blue-and-white porcelain from Jingdezhen.[15]

In antiquity, three-legged vessels were apparently intended to be oriented with their handles at right and left and with two legs in front and a single one in back;[16] as revealed in illustrations in contemporaneous woodblock-printed books, however, the convention had become misunderstood by Song times, with the result that such vessels were typically placed with handles right and left but with a single leg in front and two in back, an orientation that was followed for antique vessels as well as for newly made ones. This censer is thus properly placed with its two ring handles at right and left and with a single leg at the front center; that is the only position, in fact, that permits a symmetrical presentation of the vessel with a full floral panel centered at the front. This misunderstanding became accepted convention in later periods, so that tripod vessels made in the Yuan, Ming, and Qing dynasties, too, are properly oriented with one leg in front and the remaining two in back [compare 38].

The decoration on the Clague censer was integrally cast with the bowl portion and shows only minimal cold working. The legs and *pushou* masks were cast separately and affixed to the bowl, probably with applied molten metal. Traces of the bronze applied as a binder create a halo effect behind the heads of the crouching figures.

The integral casting of body and decoration points to a Song date for this censer, as does the minimal reliance on cold working. The arbitrary placement of the *pushou*-mask escutcheons in relation to the principal decorative motifs further suggests a Song date, recalling the relationship, or lack thereof, between the strapwork borders and the interlaced dragon patterns on the previous *hu* [1]. The possible relationship of the decorative scheme to design elements in Southern Song woodblock-printed sutra frontispieces also argues for an attribution to the Song, as do the rather thick walls and substantial weight. Finally, this censer is almost identical in size and overall shape – including tapering walls – to an undecorated Jun-ware censer on long-term loan to the Harvard University Art Museums, Cambridge, that is usually dated to the twelfth or thirteenth century.[17] Apart from decoration, the only difference between the two censers is that the Jun piece stands on cabriole legs and lacks *pushou*-masks.

3 Long-necked Vase

with two loop handles and with rolling wave decor

Song to Yuan dynasty, twelfth – fourteenth century
Cast bronze with cast decoration
8.9 centimeter height
Provenance: Dr Sidney Smith, Cambridge, England
Clague Collection Number 250

THIS MINIATURE *HU* HAS a compressed globular body resting on a short, lightly splayed foot. Hexagonal in section, the long, straight neck rises vertically, an intaglio ring at its base clearly distinguishing it from the body. An undecorated relief band sets off the vessel's mouth, accentuating the hexagonal shape of the neck and echoing the plain circular band that encompasses the lower edge of the foot. Their tops adorned with flattened *ruyi* heads and their bases anchored to corners between facets, two loop handles for the attachment of moveable bronze rings (now lost) appear at right and left, just above the midpoint of the neck. An all-over pattern of rolling waves in thread-relief lines covers the vase, the waves serving as a foil for vaguely defined shapes in slightly broader lines that are reminiscent of animals or birds. The inside of the short footring is plain, but the inset flat base, apparently original, reveals a design closely related to that on the body, a pattern of cresting waves with two butterfly-like shapes in broader lines set against them.

The shape of this miniature vase derives from the long-necked, bottle-like variant of the *hu* that was popular in both bronze[1] and ceramic ware[2] during the Han dynasty. Although this interpretation of the *hu* fell from favor after the collapse of the Han – replaced by a bottle type known as *baoping* that has an ovoid body, slender neck, and flaring mouth and that was perhaps introduced from India along with other paraphernalia associated with the Buddhist church[3] – it found renewed popularity during the Southern Song, as evinced by Longquan-celadon examples,[4] by ones in grayish-blue glazed *guan* ware,[5] and by Jizhou examples painted in under-glaze iron-brown slip.[6] Han-dynasty examples are apparently restricted to ones of circular section, but Southern Song ceramic examples include both circular and faceted ones, the faceted ones usually octagonal in section.[7] The Clague vessel's unusual combination of circular body and hexagonal neck is otherwise unknown among bronze and ceramic shapes of the Song and Yuan periods; it attests to the artists' enormous creativity and to their constant experimentation with shape and decoration to find the most aesthetically pleasing combination. In choice of shape, then, this *hu* draws on the classical Han *hu* bottle but, in faceting the neck, interprets it in a manner redolent of the Southern Song.

By the Southern Song, water had become an important genre of painting in its own right, usually presented as rolling waves, sometimes with whitecaps. Southern Song paintings on paper and silk occasionally feature cresting waves as their principal subject matter[8] and Southern Song ceramics from the Jizhou kilns sometimes carry patterns of rolling waves as their only decoration.[9] With their all-over wave patterns, thirteenth- and fourteenth-century Jizhou-ware vessels offer the closest ceramic parallels to the decoration on the Clague vase.

Bands of rolling-wave decoration had appeared on bronze vessels at least as early as the twelfth century, however, as indicated by the magnificent *hu*[10] in the Victoria and Albert Museum, London, whose dated inscription corresponds to 1173. In fact, the lowest two registers of decoration on the Victoria and Albert vase include birds and other animals set against a ground of tempestuous waves, perhaps the model for the designs on the Clague vase. In addition, the butterfly-like motifs on the base of the Clague vessel bear some resemblance to the designs in the third register of decoration (up from the bottom) on the Victoria and Albert vase, which are similarly set against a ground of rolling waves. The slight asymmetry of the decorative scheme also ties the Clague vase to bronzes of the Song and Yuan periods; on the Victoria and Albert vase, for example, an asymmetrically disposed motif inhabits the uppermost decorative register on the neck.[11]

The attention given the base also suggests a Song or Yuan date for this small *hu*. During the Song dynasty, for example, the potters at the Yue and Ru kilns went to great lengths to finish the undersides of their wares, glazing the bases – indeed, even the bottoms of the footrings – as carefully as they glazed the more visible upper surfaces.[12] Continuing this taste for meticulously finished detail, lapidary artists of the Yuan and early Ming periods typically embellished the bases of their jade vessels as exquisitely and elaborately as they ornamented the main surfaces.[13] In this regard as well, the Clague vase displays greater affinity to works of the Song and Yuan periods than to those of any other.

Although they might have been adapted from paintings on paper and silk, the wave patterns on Southern Song Jizhou wares might also have been inspired by decoration on Song bronzes, since the motif appears in bronze before it appears in ceramic ware. In addition, it is very likely that Song and Yuan bronzes were the source for the motif of auspicious animals set against churning waves that figures so prominently in early fifteenth-century porcelains[14] [compare 12, 21], since that theme was eschewed by artists painting on paper and silk.

4 Hexagonal Hu-shaped Vase

with two cylindrical appendages and stylized floral and diaper
pattern decor

Song to Yuan dynasty, twelfth – fourteenth century
Cast bronze with cast decoration
19.7 centimeter height
Provenance: Dr Sidney Smith, Cambridge, England
Clague Collection Number 247

P ROBABLY INTENDED AS A FLOWER VASE,[1] this elegantly profiled hexagonal vessel has a pear-shaped body set atop a short splayed hexagonal foot. Two hollow tubular appendages flank the slightly flaring neck, affixed at the neck's point of narrowest width. Relief vertical ridges at the corners emphasize the division of the vessel surface into six facets; the rounded edges of the ridges on the mid-portion of the vessel, which echo the contour of the gently swollen body, give way on the neck and foot to squared edges that better harmonize with the vessel's more insistently angular top and bottom. Thread-relief lines, spaced and configured to create narrow undecorated bands, divide the vessel into five horizontal registers, four on the vessel proper and one on the foot; intricate diaper patterns adorn the resulting thirty rectangular panels, contrasting with the unembellished vertical ridges and horizontal bands. From the top down, the first register includes upward-pointing isosceles triangles with curved sides, their interiors boasting a *ruyi*-head below and a comb pattern above, the triangles nestled amidst stylized flower heads (of different types) above and below; the second register displays diamond-shaped lozenges, each with an abstract flower at its center and a single *leiwen* in each corner; the tall third register features a pattern of small squares, each set on a corner point and each exhibiting a swastika at its center; the fourth register displays a pattern of tightly coiled *leiwen*, the pattern arranged so that the *leiwen* rest on their corner points; the narrow fifth register (the foot) repeats the design of the second register, as do the tubular appendages. The foot is hollow, its interior undecorated. A small section of the foot has been replaced, as has the flat base, bits of silvery solder at its edges attesting to its recent insertion. The original base was doubtless cast separately and inserted, like that on the previous miniature vase [3].

Because of the appendages at the neck, archaistic vessels of this type are often said to derive from the *touhu*, or pitch pot, a secular vessel used as the target in an arrow-throwing game popular from antiquity through the Qing dynasty [see 9]. Although bronze and ceramic vessels with squat globular bodies and elongated cylindrical necks with tubular appendages at their tops[2] do indeed derive from *touhu* vessels, vases of the sort seen here with organically flowing profiles were derived from ancient *hu* vessels, which during the Shang and Zhou dynasties were used for storing wine. *Hu* vessels from the Zhou dynasty typically have loop handles with free-turning rings [compare 1], but those from the Shang often have tubular appendages on the neck, set a short distance below the mouth, and are the clear, if distant, model for the Clague vase.[3]

Shang *hu* vessels are generally elliptical in section (with flattened sides); square ones, usually with rounded corners, and circular ones[4] predominated during the Western Zhou, while circular ones and square ones with angular corners found favor during the Warring States and Han periods.[5] Octagonal and decagonal *hu* vessels appear occasionally among the bronzes of the Warring States period;[6] hexagonal ones are virtually unknown.

This vase shows a kinship to ceramics of the late Southern Song and Yuan periods in the graceful interpretation of its shape, in the faceting of its body, in the division of its surface into horizontal registers, and in its preference for all-over decoration. During most of the Song dynasty ceramic vessels were circular or lobed in section, but in the Yuan a secondary, parallel taste emerged for polygonal vessels, evinced by several fourteenth-century blue-and-white octagonal bottles and jars from Jingdezhen[7] and by celadon-glazed octagonal vases from Longquan.[8] Such fourteenth-century ceramics usually claim all-over decoration; tall examples such as bottles, vases, and jars, characteristically have their decoration arranged in a series of thematically unrelated horizontal registers.[9] The lack of emphasis on one register as the primary band of decoration suggests that this bronze is typologically earlier than the fourteenth-century ceramics which almost always feature one register of decoration as the principal register, usually set off by its slightly larger size or more engaging subject matter. Indeed, a bronze *hu* with a dated inscription corresponding to 1173 in the Victoria and Albert Museum, London, reveals both that bronzes were already being divided into horizontal registers as early as the twelfth century and that such bronzes did not necessarily emphasize one register over another.[10] Given that many Yuan-dynasty ceramics derive their shapes from contemporaneous bronzes, the possibility thus exists that they also owe their horizontal registration to their congeners in bronze. Song and Yuan bronzes may well owe their horizontally sectioned surfaces to the organization of the decorative schemes on Shang bronze vessels of the Anyang phase.

The source of the decoration on this vase has yet to be pinpointed. The only motif that bears a clear relationship to that on archaic bronzes is the pattern of rising lappets in the topmost register, a pattern doubtless inspired by the triangular elements – sometimes meticulously rendered as cicadas – that appear in the uppermost register of many Shang bronzes.[11] Although the *leiwen* pattern in the fourth register certainly derives from the *leiwen* backgrounds on Shang and early Zhou bronzes, the *leiwen* pattern seldom, if ever, constituted a principal decorative motif in antiquity, and it was seldom, if ever, set on an angle, forced to stand on a single corner.

The diaper pattern in the second register seems to be a simplified version of that on the previous *zun*-shaped censer [2], while the swastika panels in register three resemble design elements found in architectural ornament, printed books, and carved lacquer. (An auspicious Buddhist emblem in East Asia, the swastika is also a symbol for the character *wan*, or 'ten thousand,' which further imbues it with auspicious meaning.) Perhaps textile patterns played a role in the creation of the all-over pattern on this bronze; equally possible is that Song and Yuan bronze casters simply created an eclectic new style of decoration for their vessels, turning sometimes to antiquity for inspiration, sometimes to contemporaneous works in other materials. In typical Song and Yuan fashion, the decoration of this vase was integrally cast with the vessel itself, showing minimal cold working after casting. The cylindrical appendages were cast separately and joined to the neck with applied molten metal when all elements were complete; the original base was most likely added in the same way [compare 3]. Although the previous *hu* and *zun* censer [1, 2] have relatively thick walls and are thus heavy in relation to their size – seemingly a feature of the best Song bronzes – the thin walls and light weight of this vase are far more typical of late Song and Yuan bronzes, as are the slightly less precise casting and the tiny clouds of bronze that mar the decorative scheme in a few areas. Also arguing for a late Song to Yuan date is the apparently arbitrary application of the decorative scheme to the surface of the vase, with the result that in the top register, for example, some of the rising lappets are centered while others are not, and yet others are cut through by the vertical ridge bordering the facet. The second register and the foot seem to lack any centering of the design at all; although the patterns in registers three and four seemingly fit their respective panels, the effect may be no more than an illusion created by very small repeating design elements that generally appear centered of their own accord and that do not cry loudly when bisected by borders. This lack of concern with centering and symmetry is a characteristic that finds precedent in the seemingly arbitrary placement of the *pushou*-mask escutcheon in relationship to the surface decor surrounding it on the previous *zun*-shaped censer [2], and in the arbitrary accommodation of the interlaced-dragon panels to their surrounding strapwork borders, with the result that the borders cut through elements of the dragon interlace, on the previous *hu* [1].

Setting aside art-historical analysis and argument, the most compelling reason for assigning this vase to the Southern Song or Yuan period[12] is its striking similarity to related pieces archaeologically recovered from datable sites. One of the closest such pieces is a hexagonal *hu* vessel[13] (with flat ear-like handles rather than cylindrical appendages) excavated from a Yuan-dynasty site in Inner Mongolia; excepting the attachments at the neck, the shape is almost identical to that of the Clague vase, its vertical faceting also accentuated by ridges at the corners. The excavated vase also has bands that divide its surface into five thematically unrelated horizontal registers. Although the decoration is not identical on the two vases, a related pattern of rising lappets appears in the uppermost register of each; in addition, the excavated vase has in its second register diamond-shaped lozenges, each with a tiny stylized flower head at its center, that are akin to those with swastikas at their center in the third register of the Clague vase. (Obviously from the same family of bronzes as the small *hu* excavated in Inner Mongolia, a hexagonal vase[14] in the Victoria and Albert Museum, London, also shares the same characteristics with the Clague vase, including a similar band of rising lappets at the top.) A second excavated piece – recovered from the same Yuan-dynasty site in Inner Mongolia as the previous hexagonal vase – is an elongated square *hu* vessel[15] (also with flat ear-like handles instead of cylindrical appendages); like the Clague vessel, it too has small ridges that set off the corners and narrow bands that section its surface into five horizontal registers. Though the decorative schemes of the two pieces are not identical, they are closely related in their reliance on small repeating design elements and in their placement of square elements on a diagonal so that they rest on their corners. At least two additional, though somewhat more distantly related, bronze pieces[16] were recovered from the remains of the Chinese merchant ship that sank off the coast of Sinan, Republic of Korea, in 1323 (and are thus datable to the early fourteenth century). One of the two *hu* vessels[17] from the Sinan ship find – with a flattened circular section and tubular appendages – has its decorative scheme divided into five registers, the wave-and-whitecap motif of the second register repeated on the foot, as the motif from the second register of the Clague vessel repeats on its foot. The taller foot and carefully centered decorative motifs in registers three and four of the Sinan vase distinguish it from the Clague piece, perhaps suggesting a different place of manufacture. This body of evidence amply confirms the Song to Yuan date of the Clague vase.

5 Hexagonal Incense-stick Holder

on an elaborate attached bronze stand, the holder with two ring
handles and with diaper pattern and stylized floral decor

Song to Yuan dynasty, twelfth – fourteenth century
Cast bronze with cast decoration
20.8 centimeter height
Provenance: Dr Sidney Smith, Cambridge, England
Clague Collection Number 225

T HIS UNUSUAL OBJECT COMBINES a four-legged hexagonal reservoir with a six-legged table-like stand to fashion a holder for a supply of incense sticks. Rounded ridges accentuate the corners of the faceted body, rising from the lower border of the reservoir to the top of the uppermost decorative register but not intruding into the unornamented band below the everted plain lip. Narrow but deeply cast indentations in the ridges generally correspond in placement to the encircling thread-relief lines that divide the body into three horizontal registers. An extra set of indentations appears on the vertical ridges at the midpoint of the top register of decoration, suggesting the appearance of bamboo stalks. At each side, right and left, on the uppermost decorated register, a low-relief stylized blossom overlaps the vertical ridge, serving as the visual support for a small loop from which hangs a moveable ring – the ring not cast but bent from a short section of bronze. Four curvilinear legs issue from the mouths of single-horned animal heads to elevate the open-bottomed hexagonal reservoir above its table-like stand. The legs at right and left are affixed to the reservoir's vertical ridges and appear directly below the ring handles; the other two legs are joined, front and back, at the center of the lowest decorated register. Intended to serve as the support for the incense sticks, the unembellished flat top of the hexagonal stand rests on eight small spacers that raise it above the stand's ornamental apron whose lower edge is bracketed; from the corners of the apron descend the six tapering, medially crested, s-curved legs that rest on the top edge of the continuous floor stretcher. The stand and the uppermost band of the reservoir are undecorated; the stand's stretcher and the reservoir's three main horizontal registers, however, are enlivened with complex diapering. The reservoir's uppermost decorated register exhibits an intricate pattern of diamond-shaped lozenges, each bordered by double bowstring lines and each displaying an abstract eight-petaled blossom at its center; the middle register includes a compressed pattern of tiny round and elliptical bosses that more or less line up in vertical columns (but not in horizontal rows) and that are interconnected by an elaborate network of fine thread-relief lines; the lowest register features a balanced but asymmetrical thread-relief scroll – presumably vegetal but perhaps inspired by the 'dissolved' animal interlaces on Eastern Zhou bronzes – that imparts a decided sense of movement. The continuous floor stretcher repeats the flower-in-the-square tile pattern of the topmost register. The interior of the reservoir and the underside of the stand are plain.

Called a *xiangtong* (literally, 'incense cylinder'), this implement would have been used with a censer, to hold a supply of incense sticks. For their studios and poetic gatherings, the literati favored rare fragrances that were often imported from tropical lands and that were usually prepared, depending on the material, in the form of powder, pellets, or splinters (as in a splinter of sandalwood); for daily use in scenting the home or in offering homage to household deities, however, incense sticks – often termed joss sticks – were traditionally used. Rarely, images appear in woodblock-printed books that include an incense stick holder vaguely of the type featured here, such as the illustration in the second *juan* of a 1608 edition of the secular drama *Jinjian ji* (The Brocaded Stationery) in the Beijing Library, that depicts a woman lighting a stick of incense before a seated image of the Bodhisattva Guanyin, a cylindrical incense-stick holder standing nearby on the altar, the ends of the incense sticks clearly projecting above its top.[1] The collection of the Victoria and Albert Museum, London, includes at least two bronze incense-stick holders with reticulated designs[2] that relate to the openwork elements in the lower portion of the Clague piece.

The attribution of this incense stick holder to the Yuan is fully justified by the similarity of its style to that of the previous hexagonal vase [4], whose late Song to Yuan date is confirmed by a wealth of archaeological data. The vessels share a taste not only for faceted bodies with accented corners but for bodies divided into horizontal registers ornamented with complex diaper patterns, some of which repeat from register to register, and some of which are asymmetrically disposed. Both vessels have thin walls, making them relatively light in weight for their size, and both have the dark brown patina associated with this group. Although both were cast in parts, later joined together, both claim integrally cast decoration that shows minimal cold working. Additionally both show the bits of bronze residue that slightly blur the decoration that are such telling features of late Song and Yuan bronzes. In addition, the diaper patterns in the top and middle registers of this incense stick holder are extremely close to those on a small, hexagonal bronze vase in the Victoria and Albert Museum, London, that has been dated to the Yuan dynasty on the basis of its similarity to a bronze vase excavated from a Yuan site in Inner Mongolia.[3] The diaper pattern in the top register is like the architectural ornament depicted in the *Han Palace*, a Yuan dynasty hanging scroll by Li Rongjin (active, first half fourteenth century) now in the National Palace Museum, Taipei.[4] The animal heads from whose mouths the four legs on the reservoir issue represent an early type, akin in style to the horned heads at the tops of ring handles on Song and Yuan bronzes [compare 6].

Lacking clear prototypes from antiquity, this incense holder shows less reliance on Bronze Age shapes than do many other Song and Yuan bronzes, a notable departure from classical Bronze Age taste being its combination of reservoir and table-like stand. Miniature bronzes had been mounted on bronze stands at least as early as the Northern Wei period,[5] their four-legged, square stands virtually identical in form to the bases of contemporaneous gilt bronze Buddhist sculptures. Whether the present incense holder represents a continuation of that tradition of mounted bronzes, or whether it represents a reinvention of the combination remains unknown. The closest parallels to the combination seen here occur among Yuan dynasty ceramics – especially *qingbai*, Jun, and Longquan-celadon wares which, perhaps under the influence of Song or Yuan bronzes, occasionally have a vessel set atop an integrally fired decorative stand in the form of a stool or table.[6] The excavations of the Chinese merchant ship that sank off the coast of Sinan (Republic of Korea) in 1323 have yielded a circular bronze *hu*-shaped incense stick holder with openwork decoration and with an elaborately pierced foot that resembles a small table or stand.[7]

The stands represented in such bronze and ceramic pieces compare with furniture of the day. In the graceful curvature of its legs, the elegant cusping of its apron, and the openwork articulation of its waist, the Clague vessel's six-legged table stand compares favorably with the small table depicted in the lower left corner of Liu Guandao's *Whiling away the Summer*, a late thirteenth-century handscroll in the Nelson-Atkins Museum of Art, Kansas City.[8] Both the strongly curled feet of the four upper legs and the continuous floor stretcher find counterparts on tables depicted in woodblock-printed books of the Yuan and early Ming periods.[9] Especially remarkable is the close kinship of the Clague vessel's table-stand to a small, red-lacquered, hexagonal table with inset Dali marble top (collection unknown) that Rosemary Scott has attributed to the Song dynasty;[10] related elements in the two pieces include the overall shape with its hexagonal form, the perforation of the waist with openwork designs, the cusping of the apron in a bracketed profile (similar to that seen about the rim of large, fourteenth-century, blue-and-white plates from Jingdezhen),[11] and the graceful curvature of the legs.

6 Long-necked Vase

with two ring handles and rolling wave and stylized bird decor

Song to Yuan dynasty, twelfth – fourteenth century
Cast bronze with cast decoration
23.6 centimeter height
Provenance: Dr Sidney Smith, Cambridge, England
Clague Collection Number 246

STANDING ON A SHORT, SPLAYED FOOTRING, this beautifully proportioned vase has a compressed globular body, of generally pear shape, whose upper walls gently constrict to form the tall neck, obscuring any division between body and neck. The thickened lip atop the almost imperceptibly flaring neck echoes the footring, harmoniously completing the vessel. Ring handles, their moveable bronze rings intact, appear at right and left, issuing from horned dragon heads affixed at the base of the decorative band at the top of the neck. Encircling the widest part of the body, the main band of decoration features two pairs of highly schematized confronting birds with long, scrolling tails set against a *leiwen* ground, a frontally set, fanged, feline mask separating the two birds of each pair. Four evenly spaced 'rising blades' enliven the shoulder and neck of the vase, one centered under each ring handle and one centered above each feline mask. Organized by narrow longitudinal bands into six vertical columns, *leiwen* patterns fill the rising blades, dissolving into an ogival comb-pattern at the top of each elongated triangular blade. A band of cresting waves embellishes the top of the neck, the whitecaps rising in slight relief above the wave ground, as the confronting birds and feline masks rise in slight relief above the *leiwen* ground in the main decorative register below. A narrow band of diagonally positioned *leiwen* sets off the midsection of the footring; the inside of the footring is plain, and the base is a modern replacement – silvery solder at its edges attesting to its recent insertion; for the original base that was most likely cast separately and inserted [see 3]. The function of this vase, like the function of many Song, Yuan, and Ming vessels, is difficult to determine; it might have served as a ceremonial vessel, though it might also have been a flower vase [compare 4], perhaps one of a pair of identical vases flanking a censer.

Like the miniature vase in the Clague Collection [3], this handsome vessel derives from the bottle-like variant of the *hu* – with long, straight neck and compressed globular body – that was popular during the Han dynasty and that was resurrected during the Southern Song period in both bronze and ceramic ware. The decorative scheme and ring handles distinguish this vase from Bronze Age examples, however, as do the slight flare of the neck and the organic flow of shoulder into neck, the lack of differentiation between neck and shoulder imparting a pear shape to the body. Thirteenth- and fourteenth-century ceramics from the kilns at Longquan and Jingdezhen (including both *qingbai* ware and porcelain with decoration in underglaze copper red) share the form of this bronze vase (including rings), underscoring the relationship between bronze and ceramics.[1]

The decoration on this *hu* takes its cue from antiquity, but combines elements old and new in a novel way. The birds – often called dragons but identified as birds by pointed beaks and curling crests atop their heads – in the main register derive from related creatures that often appear in a subsidiary band immediately above the principal band of decoration in bronzes of the early Western Zhou period.[2] The feline masks that separate the birds on the Clague vessel represent a reduction of the relief heads that typically separate birds, and sometimes dragons, in those same subsidiary bands on early Western Zhou vessels.[3] A typical feature of tall, slender vessels during the Shang dynasty, rising blades frequently appeared about the necks of ancient *gu* and *zun*;[4] despite the disappearance of the *gu* and the transformation of the *zun* into a sleekly styled urn with S-curved profile in early Western Zhou, the rising blade motif persisted, albeit in broader, squatter form with more emphatic decoration.[5] If the confronting birds on the Clague vase derive from those on early Western Zhou vessels, the elongated form and unassertive ornament suggest that its rising blades descend from ones on Shang bronzes;[6] even the pleasing alternation of plain and decorated areas on the neck and shoulder of this vase doubtless refers to the alternation of rising blades and unornamented areas on the flaring necks of Shang *gu* and *zun* vessels. Such rising blades (set against plain grounds) also appear on Song and Yuan ceramics, as seen in a thirteenth-century, trumpet-mouthed, *zun*-shaped vase from the Longquan kilns,[7] now in the Percival David Foundation, London. As documented both by this bronze vase and the large Song-dynasty *hu* in the Clague Collection [1], archaistic vessels of the Song and Yuan freely mix elements from different periods of antiquity in their decorative schemes.

They also add new elements, such as the ring handles and the wave pattern about the neck of this vase. More so than that on the miniature *hu* [3], the water pattern on this vase is virtually identical to that on thirteenth- and fourteenth-century slip-painted Jizhou ceramic vessels,[8] indicating a close link with Southern Song and Yuan ceramics. As Rose Kerr has pointed out, wave patterns on both Song-Yuan bronzes and painted Jizhou wares also find parallels in Song architectural decoration, as evinced by the stone reliefs depicting Buddhist figures against a ground of rolling waves carved on the walls of Chuzu-an hall at Shaolin-si (Shaolin Temple)[9] in Henan province, which was built in 1125. Cast separately and attached, the dragon heads from whose mouths the ring handles issue represent an early type, associated with the Song and Yuan dynasties, and thus differ from the lion and elephant heads that, while occasionally appearing on Song and Yuan bronzes, are a more standard feature of Ming and Qing ones.

The integral casting of decoration and body (with minimal cold working) establishes the twelfth-to-fourteenth century date of this vase, as does the low-relief decorative scheme with its relationship to features on contemporaneous ceramics. As noted in previous entries, the thin walls, relatively light weight, and dark brown patina are typical of this group of bronzes. Rose Kerr has dated a virtually identical vase in the collection of the Victoria and Albert Museum, London, to the twelfth to fourteenth century.[10]

The refined shape, elegant proportions, and symmetrical design set this vase slightly apart from related pieces of the same period [compare 2-6], as do the incorporation of plain surfaces and the more sensitive integration of the ring handles into the overall design scheme. The meaning of such differences, if any, is unclear, though vessels of this type herald the advent of the Ming style [see 7].

7 Pear-shaped Vase

with two ring handles and with rolling wave and *taotie* decor

Ming dynasty, probably fifteenth century
Cast bronze with cast decoration
33.0 centimeter height
Provenance: Dr Sidney Smith, Cambridge, England
Clague Collection Number 243

O RIGINALLY ONE OF A PAIR OF VASES that flanked a *ding*-shaped censer, this pear-shaped vase rests on a tall foot that rises in two stages, the lower stage with undecorated vertical walls and thickened rim, and the upper one with ornamented concave walls bordered by a narrow, relief ring at the top. The walls of the swelling body curve gracefully inward to form the neck and then reverse themselves, flaring outward and terminating in a short, vertical lip with thickened rim. The neck and lip configuration mirrors that of the foot, the symmetry lending dignity and stability to the shape. Ring handles – the rings square in section and issuing from the mouths of horned, maned, leonine heads – appear at right and left, framing the decorative band about the neck; the free-turning rings they once supported are now lost. Apart from the leonine handle mounts, decoration on this vase is limited to two bands, the primary one around the neck with a *taotie* mask on either side set against a ground of rounded *leiwen*, and the secondary one about the foot with undulating waves. The inside of the foot is plain and the inset base is a replacement for the original.

This vessel represents a Ming-dynasty transformation of the Bronze Age *hu* jar into a flower vase through a change in proportions and through a redefinition of the profile that includes the addition of a vertical lip echoing the footring. Though vases of this type clearly derive from Western Zhou *hu* vessels,[1] their exact source remains unclear since there are no ancient *hu* of identical profile. Wine storage vessels, Zhou-dynasty *hu* generally had covers that protected the contents and that completed the vessel aesthetically; lest it detract from the ornamented cover, the lip was seldom emphasized on ancient vessels, but the cover – more specifically, the handle crowning the cover – was typically shaped to resemble a small, inverted footring.[2] As flower vases, Ming-dynasty archaistic vessels had no need for a cover, so their designers were free to alter the appearance of the lip. It is likely that a Western Zhou covered *hu* inspired this vase and its congeners, the footring-like handle atop the cover serving as the model for the lip on later pieces.

The *taotie* mask in the upper band of decoration derives from masks on Shang and early Western Zhou vessels, but its ornamental flourishes and narrow, almost squinting eyes, readily distinguish it from Bronze Age examples. As mentioned in previous entries [3, 6], the wave pattern, seen in the band about the foot, lacks Bronze Age antecedents, but finds clear precedents in Song painting[3] and woodblock printing,[4] in Song architectural ornament,[5] in Song bronzes,[6] and in Song and Yuan Jizhou ceramic vessels with slip-painted decoration.[7]

As evinced by vertical, casting-mold seams that rise through the sides of both ornamental bands, the decoration on this vase was integrally cast with the vessel itself, thus maintaining continuity with Song and Yuan vessels in technique of execution. With the bulk of its surface undecorated, however, this vase exhibits the new, simplified style that is characteristic of early Ming, both in bronze and in blue-and-white porcelain[8]. Already apparent in a nascent stage of development in some Song-Yuan vessels [see 6], the new style eschews the exuberant, all-encompassing designs typical of the Song-Yuan phase of development [compare 3-5] in favor of a reserved, clearly focused design scheme.

The most easily discernible change in the presentation of the *taotie* mask is the substitution of a ground of tightly coiled spirals for the ground of angular, square-cornered *leiwen* – sometimes with interior patterns – of Song and Yuan vessels. Other newly introduced Ming features include the curly mane [compare 43] framing the leonine head that anchors each ring handle, and the emphatic foot, which is much taller than those of Song and Yuan bronzes. In a fashion characteristic of early fifteenth-century blue-and-white porcelain, the wave pattern emphasizes the undulating movement of the water rather than the breaking waves and whitecaps that figured so prominently in Song and Yuan ceramics[9] and bronzes [see 6]. Additionally, the ring handles now frame the decorative band, rather than arbitrarily intruding into it, and the bilaterally symmetrical organization (of both shape and decoration) dominates even more than in earlier vessels.

The attribution of this vessel to the early Ming period and the designation of its function as a vase rest on its similarity in shape to two identical (seemingly undecorated) bronze vases recovered in 1955 – along with a large bronze *ding*-shaped censer and a wealth of other goods – from a tomb dated to 1510 at Baima-si (White Horse Temple) near Chengdu, Sichuan province.[10] The excavation revealed that the pair of vases stood on a stone altar in the anterior room of the undisturbed, two-chambered tomb, flanking the *ding*-shaped censer; in depictions of similar arrangements of two vases and a censer in Yuan and Ming woodblock-book illustrations, such vases invariably hold flowers.[11] Like the Clague example, the excavated vases are of elongated pear-shape; each rests on a tall foot that rises in two stages and that is mirrored in the configuration of the neck and lip, exactly as in the Clague vase. The ring handles resemble each other on the Clague and Baima-si vases, especially the leonine heads from whose mouths the rings issue. The two Baima-si vases have moveable rings, confirming that the Clague vase doubtless once had such rings as well.

The funerary epitaph discovered in the tomb not only lists the tomb occupant's year of death as 1510, but states that he was a civil official, not to mention a confidant of the Prince of Shu[12] (modern Sichuan). Such circumstances indicate that bronzes of this type must have been held in high regard, especially since the censer and its accompanying vases occupied the place of honor on the stone altar.

8 Ceremonial Jue Vessel
with decoration of birds in flight

Ming dynasty, Tianshun period, dated 1464
Cast bronze with cast decoration and with three cast intaglio inscriptions
in standard-script (*kaishu*) characters, one inscription with a date reading
Tianshun banian zao
21.0 centimeter height
Clague Collection Number 258

KNOWN AS JUE, THREE-LEGGED, SPOUTED VESSELS of this type
were used as ritual wine vessels during the Shang dynasty, large
ones for warming the wine over a fire and small ones perhaps as
cups for drinking the heated wine. Like its Shang dynasty prototypes, this *jue*
stands on three slender, pointed legs, each triangular in section, that curve
outward near their points. The walls of the cylindrical, round-bottomed
container rise almost straight up, and then flare dramatically to form the
flattened, horizontally oriented spout arrangement at the top. Two small
posts with finials in the form of covered urns rise from the lip, midway
between the spout and its similarly shaped counterweight at the back.
Resembling a rolled metal edge, a cast lip encircles the vessel's mouth,
dipping slightly under the posts and thus underscoring the division between
spout and counterweight. Decoration is limited to a single band about the
cylindrical waist that features two pairs of long-tailed birds, one on either
side, set in relief against a ground of squared *leiwen*; each pair of confronting birds is shown in flight with wings extended and legs retracted.
Three intaglio inscriptions, each bordered by a single sunken line, appear
on the otherwise undecorated upper portion of the vessel, one under
each post and one at the back, opposite the spout.

Although this vessel clearly derives from Shang-dynasty *jue*,[1] its
shape and decoration set it apart from its Bronze Age models. A Shang-
dynasty *jue* (of the Anyang phase) virtually always has sturdy legs, for
example, and its flaring upper portion is usually so well proportioned to
its supporting cylindrical container that, despite its unusual, somewhat
asymmetrical form, the vessel appears balanced and stable. In addition, a
classical Shang *jue* typically has a vertically oriented strap handle at a
quarter turn from the spout, and its capped posts – probably used to lift
the vessel and its heated contents from the fire – tend to rise from the
base of the spout rather than from the midpoint of the lip. Characteristically
very short, inscriptions on Bronze Age *jue* usually appear inconspicuously
under the handle, never boldly positioned on the vessel's exterior.

For balance, a classical Shang-dynasty *jue* almost always has a triangular, winglike projection opposite its spout rather than the rounded form
seen on the present vessel. The rounded counterweight suggests that the
Clague vessel incorporates elements from both the classical *jue* and its close
relative, the symmetrical *jiao*,[2] a rare vessel type that has two matching
triangular spouts, similar in shape to the winglike projection that balances
the single spout of the standard *jue*. The bronze casters combined the
symmetry of the *jiao* with the spout shape of the *jue* in the Clague piece.

Decorated *jue* and *jiao* vessels from the Bronze Age almost always include one or another version of the *taotie* mask as decoration; since the *jue* and *jiao* disappeared as vessel types with the fall of Shang, extant examples almost never exhibit the long-tailed birds that rose to popularity during the succeeding Western Zhou period. Inspired by motifs on early Western Zhou bronzes,[3] the birds that embellish the Clague piece must be considered anachronistic on a vessel imitating a Shang shape. The bronze casters who made this piece were almost certainly unaware that their models for shape and decoration came from slightly different periods; the important point is that in creating archaistic vessels, artists were not compelled to mimic ancient vessels line for line, but were apparently free to combine shape and ornament in whatever manner seemed most pleasing and suitable.

The three inscriptions may be summarized as follows:

Side: At Huizhou-fu, the former Sub-prefect Zhang Xuan promoted Chen Xin, who is widely experienced, to be the tutor of Zhang Su.

Side: Liu Wei, an official of Chengxuan, Guangdong province.[4]

Back: Made in the eighth year of Tianshun [equivalent to 1464], supervised by Li Jing, crafted by Huang Shun.

Although *jue* vessels are virtually unknown among Song and Yuan ceramics and are comparatively rare among extant Song and Yuan bronzes, at least two early fourteenth-century bronze examples[5] have been recovered from the remains of the Chinese merchant ship that sank off the coast of Sinan (Republic of Korea) in 1323. However, in inaugurating his reign as the Hongwu Emperor (reigned 1368-98), Zhu Yuanzhang (1328-1398) – the first emperor of the Ming dynasty – ordered that *jue* vessels in white porcelain be used in sacrificial ceremonies, presumably on an altar in an ancestral temple,[6] after which the vessel became increasingly popular. *Jue* vessels in ceramic ware are well attested from the Ming dynasty,[7] as are ones in gold,[8] silver,[9] bronze, and even jade.[10] The collection of the Victoria and Albert Museum, London, includes a bronze *jue*, virtually identical in shape and decoration to this one, that bears four inscriptions, one of which is dated to 1465, just a year after this one, and another of which also mentions Liu Wei.[11]

It is assumed that bronze *jue* continued to be used as ceremonial wine vessels during the Ming dynasty – doubtless in Confucian ceremonies honoring ancestral spirits – unlike the *gui*, *ding*, and cylindrical *zun* vessels that were appropriated as censers, or the *gu*, *zun*, and *hu* vessels that were pressed into service as flower vases. The inscriptions suggest that this *jue*, like many Western Zhou bronzes and like the virtually identical *jue* in the Victoria and Albert Museum (see previous paragraph), might have been cast as a commemorative vessel, in this case, to record and commemorate the appointment of Chen Xin as tutor to Zhang Su. By the late Ming and Qing periods, however, kilns at Dehua in central Fujian province were producing porcelain versions (so-called blanc-de-Chine ware) of the *jue* that were probably used as secular cups for drinking wine and tea and, on occasion, as water-pouring vessels for the scholar's desk.[12]

Thanks to one of its inscriptions, this *jue* can be dated to a specific year (1464), a rare circumstance among later Chinese bronzes. The legs and posts were cast separately and added to the vessel, but the decoration and the three inscriptions were integrally cast with the vessel itself, the standard convention followed in creating vessels in the Song, Yuan, and early Ming periods. In typical fifteenth-century fashion, the majority of the vessel surface is unornamented, the decoration restricted to a single band about the waist [compare 7]. Also in early Ming fashion, the decorative scheme is bilaterally symmetrical, as is the positioning of the inscriptions; even the vessel has been interpreted in as symmetrical a manner as the limits of the shape allow.

9 Circular Touhu Pitch Pot

with four cylindrical appendages and with *taotie*, diaper pattern, and striding *chi* dragon decor

Ming dynasty, late sixteenth – first half seventeenth century
Cast bronze with cast decoration and with appliqué dragons
59.7 centimeter height
Clague Collection Number 263

CALLED A *TOUHU*, OR PITCH POT, this tall, imposing vessel served
as the target for the arrow-throwing game, popular from antiquity
through the Qing dynasty. The most striking feature of the vessel is
the arrangement about its mouth of four 'ears,' or cylindrical appendages,
that served as the actual targets of the game. Two of the four identically
shaped and decorated ears have their thickened rims at the same height
as the vessel's mouth; the other two stand a little lower, their tops reaching
the midpoint of the upper pair. The elongated, cylindrical neck boasts two
high-relief *chi* dragons striding about its midsection on a plain ground,
each with a tail segmented into three scrolling flourishes; the upper dragon
has its head turned to look straight up, while the lower one is positioned
to look straight down. Four wedge-shaped vertical flanges with rounded
outer edges segment the compressed globular body into four rectangular
compartments. Each flange falls midway between two of the appendages
at the top of the vessel; if the tubular appendages represent the four points
of the compass, the flanges would represent the points between. The wide,
tall base that supports the vessel rises in two stages, the lower one with
decorated inclined walls set atop a thickened footring, and the upper one
with decorated concave walls that spring from the flat shoulder atop the
lower stage. Apart from the *chi* dragons about the neck, the principal
decorative motif consists of four *taotie* masks set against grounds of
squared *leiwen*, one mask in each of the rectangular compartments around
the belly of the vessel. Diaper patterns and small *chi* dragons enliven the
remainder of the vessel. The uppermost decorative band, on the neck and
its four appendages, includes a row of coiled C-dragons in thread-relief,
while the lower portion of the appendages and the corresponding section
of the neck have a band of squared *leiwen* diapering set on a diagonal.
Diapering arranged in a *leiwen* meander embellishes the next section
down on the neck. The relief *chi* dragons occupy the central portion of the
neck, bordered at the top by a wide, relief band and at the bottom by a
rounded, relief ridge. A band of *leiwen* set on a diagonal, each *leiwen* with
a swastika at its center [see 4], decorates the lowest register of the neck.
Below the three steps surrounding the base of the neck, four descending,
leiwen-embellished lappets divide the shoulder into four compartments,
each compartment with a low-relief striding *chi* dragon that looks back
over its shoulder. Each small *chi* dragon is centered over a vertical flange;
each lappet is centered below a tubular appendage and above a *taotie*
mask. Divided into four compartments by relief vertical bands – with each
compartment centered on a flange – the concave walls of the upper

portion of the base are decorated with a *leiwen* pattern set on a diagonal, identical to that in the second register at the top of the neck. Two pairs of confronting *kui* dragons occupy the lower register of the base, an undecorated square space appearing between the faces of each confronting pair; a corresponding square space, perforated by a small round hole, separates the tails of the two pairs. The interior of the tall foot is undecorated; the flat base, apparently original, was inset, as indicated by the irregular traces of metal about its perimeter, applied molten to secure the base in place.

The arrow game was an aristocratic drinking game in which two contestants or teams threw arrows at the mouth of a *touhu* vessel;[1] the side that pitched the greatest number of arrows into the pot won and celebrated victory by serving penalty drinks to the vanquished. The game had been invented at least as early as the Eastern Zhou period, attested by its mention in the *Zuozhuan*[2] (Zuo Commentary on the Spring and Autumn Annals), attributed to Zuoqiu Ming, about sixth-fifth century BC; its complex rules and prescribed etiquette are set down in some detail in the *Liji* (Book of Rites), one of the Confucian classics.[3]

A Han tomb relief from Nanyang, Henan province, depicts two figures engaged in a game of *touhu* and an eighth-century painted leather guard from a musical instrument, now in the Shōsō-in, Tōdai-ji, Nara, is decorated with a group of gentlemen in a setting that includes a *touhu* vessel.[4] From the Song onward, the *touhu* pot and arrows were frequently depicted in paintings of scholars at their leisure.[5] The Song scholar-statesman Sima Guang (1019-1086) authored a treatise on the game entitled *Touhu xinge*, confirming continuing interest in the sport.

One of the earliest extant *touhu* vessels — an eighth-century bronze example preserved in the Shōsō-in — has a compressed globular body set on a splayed footring; two, narrow, tubular appendages with winglike, flaring lower edges flank its mouth, and a delicate floral pattern graces its surfaces.[6] The arrows that accompany the pot have round padded balls at the tip. According to the *Liji*, the arrows should be made of mulberry or zizyphus wood with the bark intact.

Like many Ming-dynasty pitch pots, the shape of this *touhu* derives ultimately from the long-necked, bottle-shaped variant of the *hu* that was popular in both bronze[7] and ceramic ware[8] during the Han dynasty [compare 3]. This general interpretation of the shape must have been standard by the Song dynasty, if small *touhu*-shaped flower vases in *guan* ware accurately reflect the appearance of contemporaneous bronze *touhu* vessels.[9]

The decorative style of *touhu* vessels varies with the period of manufacture, the only requisites being the long neck and the appendages, or ears, near the mouth; most such vessels have but two ears, though some, like the Clague example, have four. In most cases, the appendages are aligned vertically with the neck, but in a few rare cases they are set diagonally, at a forty five degree angle to the neck. The large size of the base on this vessel no doubt reflects an attempt to anchor the vessel (lest it be knocked over during a game of arrow pitching) as much as it reflects the Ming taste for tall, stepped bases.

The style of this *touhu* is very much that of the late Ming period. The segmentation of the vessel surface into numerous discrete compartments, here accentuated by ridges and flanges, is a late Ming characteristic, as is the tendency to establish a rule of form, then break it; here, for instance, the *chi* dragons playfully violate the otherwise strict bilateral symmetry of the overall design.[10] In addition, high-relief decoration first came into prominence during the late Ming period, as did the appliqué and cold-working techniques of decoration that were used to create the relief dragons on this *touhu*. Sometimes presented in pairs, playful, sinewy *chi* dragons with long snouts, bulging eyes, and curling tails were a favorite during the late Ming period, occurring both as decoration on vessels[11] and independently as brushrests [see 49]. Rose Kerr[12] has noted that long-necked, garlic-headed bottles with appliqué dragons were produced in white porcelain (so-called blanc-de-Chine ware) at the Dehua kilns in Fujian province from 1640 to 1680, a dating that is consistent with the late Ming attribution proposed for the Clague *touhu*.

The Clague *touhu* was cast as several separate pieces that were later joined together to form the finished vessel. The long neck was cast as a discrete unit, for example, and fitted into the globular body, as indicated by the lip at its base that projects downward into the body. Joined to the neck with a bit of applied molten metal, the four tubular appendages were also cast separately. The relief *chi* dragons encircling the neck were applied after the neck had been cast and the surrounding surfaces were carefully burnished to remove any trace of the applied bonding metal that might interrupt the design. Such finishing details as the dragons' claws and the linear designs on their tails were cold worked after application, a new technique of decoration. The *taotie* masks, *kui* dragons, and diaper patterns were integrally cast with their respective vessel parts, in the manner of Song, Yuan, and early Ming bronze vessels.

10 Circular Zun-shaped Vase

with foliated rim and with decoration representing Xu You and Chao Fu
with an ox set against a ground embellished with a crane, two pines,
rolling waves, and diaper patterns

Japanese; Edo period, probably first half seventeenth century
Cast bronze with cast decoration and appliqué three-dimensional figures
18.0 centimeter height
Provenance: Dr Sidney Smith, Cambridge, England
Clague Collection Number 245

OST LIKELY A FLOWER VASE, this *zun*-shaped vessel has at its base a plain, bowl-like body set on a decorated, splayed foot; its most dramatic features are the cusped, trumpet-shaped mouth that springs from the body's crisp, angular shoulder, and the free-standing figural group on the shoulder that comprises two gentlemen and an ox. The low-relief lines, descending from the eight indentations at the lip on both interior and exterior, segment the upper portion of the vessel so that it resembles an open blossom, the individual segments suggesting flower petals. The thickened mouth rim underscores the floral shape, its bracketed edge on the exterior complementing the indentations at the lip. The figural group includes two standing gentlemen facing the viewer, one each at right and left, with an ox between them; the ox strides toward the bearded gentlemen at the viewer's left, his course monitored by the man at the right who holds the rope fastened about the bovine's neck. The figures wear hats and long, flowing robes of the type usually associated with scholars; the gentleman on the left touches his left ear with his right hand. The *leiwen*-diapered background on the trumpet neck serves as a foil against which appear pictorial elements that create a backdrop for the figural group. A crane flies in the sky above the ox, for example, its wings outstretched, its legs and feet retracted. Below the crane and immediately above the ox is a three-legged stand from which hangs a gourd suspended by a string. A small hillock with a flowering orchid at its crest appears between the ox and the man holding the rope, the hillock firmly set on the narrow raised band that separates the neck from the shoulder of the vessel. A pine towers over the rope-wielding gentleman, its boughs spreading over several segments of the neck. A pine grows beside a rock at the back of the vessel. Beside the gentleman at the left a waterfall thunders downward, its origin a mystery, but its striated surface clearly the source of the undulating waves that engulf the vessel's shoulder. The lowest portion of the shoulder and the bowl-like body of the vessel are undecorated, harmonizing with the plain circular footring and the cusped mouth. The concave register around the splayed foot features rolling waves that mirror those on the shoulder. The inside of the foot is plain and the inset base, apparently original, is flat. The interior of the vase is undecorated, except for the thread-relief lines that descend from the cusps at the mouth.

The scene on this vase depicts the story of Xu You and Chao Fu, reclusive sages who, legend relates, were counsellors to the mythical Emperor Yao. When Emperor Yao suggested abdicating his throne in favor of Xu You, the latter declined and fled to a quiet place with a waterfall, where he washed his ears to remove from them any defilement they may have incurred through listening to such worldly temptation. His companion, Chao Fu, on hearing the reasons for Xu You's hurried ablutions, immediately washed his eyes and ears; noticing his ox drinking from the stream below the fall, he hastened to lead it away from the contaminated water. The legend further recounts that Xu You was accustomed to drinking water from the palms of his hands; noting this, a charitably disposed person gave him a gourd to use as a drinking cup. Xu You hung the gourd on the branch of a tree near his hut; since the wind whistling through it created a musical sound, however, he threw the gourd away, lest the pleasing sound remind him too much of the outside world he had rejected.[1]

The figures on the vase clearly correspond to those in the story, Xu You washing his ear with water from the waterfall, and Chao Fu leading his ox away from the contaminated stream rushing about the shoulder of the vessel. Xu You's gourd hangs not from a tree branch, but from an elegant, low-relief stand placed directly above the ox. Though not part of the story proper, the crane and pines suggest the wilderness setting and stand as symbols of the immortality often associated with reclusive sages.

Though its proportions have been radically altered, the basic shape of this vase finds its *locus classicus* in the *zun* wine vessels of the Shang dynasty, with their angular profiles and flaring necks.[2] Compared to Shang *zun* vessels, the body of this vase has been compressed, its shoulders flattened, and its neck elongated – not merely to create a stage for the figures, at it might first seem, but ultimately to create an elegantly attenuated vessel, as discussed below. Unknown in antiquity, the cusping of the mouth is a feature that rose to prominence in lacquer[3] and ceramic ware[4] during the Northern Song period but that did not gain currency in the more conservative bronze tradition until late in the Ming period, when greater liberties began to be taken in interpreting the revered shapes [see 32].

This bronze ranks among the most vexing in the Clague Collection in terms of attribution. Virtually identical pieces in other collections have been attributed not only to China but to Japan and even to Korea.[5] The present author contends that this vase was made in Japan, most likely in the seventeenth century, though he hastens to point out that others have assigned it to Ming-dynasty China with certitude.[6]

Although the story depicted on the Clague vase comes from Chinese mythology, it does not assist in determining the vessel's country of origin; with the revival of Chinese studies in seventeenth-century Japan, Chinese stories came into vogue among samurai officials, especially stories involving such Confucian themes as wise rulers, loyal subjects, and virtuous sages. In fact, due to the policies of the Tokugawa shogunate, such stories were more frequently depicted in Japanese art of the period than in Chinese art.

The attribution of the vase to seventeenth-century Japan rests on its similarity in shape and style of decoration to vessels produced in Japan early in the Edo period (1603-1868). Chinese vessels with long necks and flaring mouths typically have the body positioned at the midpoint of the vessel and set atop a tall base; in such pieces – whether bronze [compare 30, 32], jade,[7] or ceramic ware[8] – the neck and mouth may account for fully half the total height of the vessel, but seldom, if ever, do they claim as much as two-thirds of the total height, as they do here. Chinese vessels also tend to underscore the separation of neck from shoulder through an angular change in the profile, sometimes augmented by a relief band at the base of the neck; in this vase, the sweeping organic line that defines the neck springs from the vessel's angular shoulder, so that the raised band around the lower portion of the neck does not relate to any change in vessel profile. In addition, Ming and Qing interpretations of the *zun* vessel virtually always give it a rounded body, rather than a bowl-like body with an angular shoulder. The emphatic lip of this vessel is also unusual in the Chinese context, a thickened edge being more typical.

Anomalous in the Chinese tradition, all of the elements enumerated above are characteristic of Japanese bronzes of the Edo period. Japanese *zun*-shaped flower vases typically have a low-set, bowl-shaped body with an angular shoulder at the midpoint; springing from the angular shoulder, the soaring neck and trumpet mouth often account for more than two-thirds of the total vessel height. Edo-period vessels also frequently have a narrow raised band that encircles the lower portion of the neck which does not relate to any change in profile; they also often have emphatic rims.[9]

The most striking aspect of the decoration on the Clague vessel is its insistent frontal orientation. Although Chinese bronzes, jades, and ceramics of the Ming and Qing dynasties typically have decorative schemes that encircle the vessel, each vantage point usually affords an interesting and comprehensible view of the subject matter [compare 9]; seldom are Chinese pieces organized with such clear front/back orientation that the subject matter is recognizable from only one vantage point. Also most unusual from a Chinese point of view is the depiction of a waterfall without a source; in this case, the waterfall appears, *deus ex machina*, because the story requires it, even though there is no precipice, let alone a mountain, down which it can cascade. The circular motifs, apparently whirlpools, in the register of waves about the foot are curious in a Chinese context, since wave patterns on Chinese bronzes tend to feature either undulating waves [see 7] or breaking waves with whitecaps [see 6]; the circular motifs on this vase do, however, find kindred forms in the wave pattern on an eighteenth-century Japanese bronze vase recently published by Michael Goedhuis.[10] Also very unusual from a Chinese point of view is the presentation of several pictorial elements – the crane and pine trees, in particular – such that they cross the borders formed by the thread-relief lines that descend from the cusps at the lip, spreading across several of the petal-like segments. Chinese artists tend to respect borders, establishing them to emphasize the form of the vessel and to relate the decorative schemes they frame to that form. When Chinese artists violate their carefully established borders, as they occasionally do in the late Ming period, they do it in a playful but self-conscious manner for calculated visual effect [see 9]; usually limited to one discrete unit of the decoration, such breaking of form in the arts of late Ming seldom involves the overall design scheme, as it does here. In these characteristics, also, the Clague vase corresponds more to Japanese art of the Edo period than to Chinese art of the late Ming and Qing periods.

Though most likely made in Japan, this vase was inspired by a Chinese original, probably of late Ming date. The late Ming witnessed a vogue for vessels with high-relief decoration, sometimes in combination with diaper patterns [see 9]; carried to Japan, such vessels no doubt inspired the present piece. The Japanese imported large quantities of both ceramics and bronzes during the Song, Yuan, and Ming periods, prizing the bronzes as vases and censers for use in the tea ceremony.[11] Included in the present exhibition, this vase illustrates the close relationship between later Chinese bronzes and at least one family of Edo-period Japanese bronzes.

11 Circular Covered Incense Box

with orchid and *lingzhi* fungus decor against a diapered ground

Hu Wenming (active late sixteenth – early seventeenth century)
Ming dynasty, late sixteenth – early seventeenth century
Cast bronze with cast and cold-worked decoration, inlaid silver wire, gilding, and an incised intaglio mark in seal-script (*zhuanshu*) characters
reading *Yunjian Hu Wenming zhi* in a rectangular cartouche on the base
7.3 centimeter diameter
Clague Collection Number 239

ACH CLAIMING A STRAIGHT, VERTICAL, OUTER WALL, a curved cavetto, and a flat face, the two halves of this small, circular, covered box mirror each other. The decorative scheme on the cover features a growing orchid with twin blossoms and a *lingzhi* fungus with two branches. Gilded, the decorative elements rise in low relief against a ground of hexagonal diapers with double-Y markings on their interiors, the diapered ground worked in ungilded but darkened metal. A narrow, raised border separates the central medallion from the gilded walls of the curving shoulder. The outside vertical walls of both cover and box have a single band of linked squared *leiwen* inlaid in silver wire in a plain ground. On the box, the gilded walls of the cavetto curve downward to the ridge-like footring that encircles the wide, flat base. The rectangular mark in the center of the base has six intaglio seal-script characters in two columns; a single sunken line borders the mark, the gilded ground of the mark contrasting with the otherwise plain base. The interior of both box and cover are undecorated. With its cover removed, the box exhibits an in-curving lip – cast separately, inserted, and anchored with a touch of molten metal – that echoes the curve of the cover, that assists in securing the cover in place, and that is designed to protect the contents of the box from gusts of wind. Thick cast walls make the box heavy in proportion to its size.

Called a *xianghe* (literally, 'incense box' in Chinese), this small covered box was a container for powdered incense and was originally part of a set of bronze incense implements. (Although some circular covered boxes served as receptacles for cinnabar seal-paste, boxes with in-curving lips were almost invariably for incense, especially bronze ones in the Hu Wenming tradition.) By the Yuan and Ming periods, the five implements of the incense set comprised a censer, a small covered box for containing the incense, a flat-bowled bronze spoon, a pair of chopstick-like bronze tongs, and a vase for holding the spoon and tongs when not in use. The spoon was used in preparing the bed of ash – preferably from wood of the *wutong*, or firmiana, tree – in the censer to receive the incense, and the tongs were used in manipulating the incense within the censer. Although only one complete bronze incense set is known to have survived intact from the Ming – now in the Royal Ontario Museum, Toronto – such sets often appear in paintings and in decorative arts motifs of the period.[1]

The incised intaglio mark on the base of this box has six seal-script characters in two columns reading *Yunjian Hu Wenming zhi* (Made [by] Hu Wenming [of] Yunjian), indicating that the box was made by the most famous bronze caster of the late Ming period. History records little about the life of Hu Wenming,[2] except that he was famous for his bronzes (especially his censers) and that he worked in Yunjian (modern Songjiang, also called Huating, about twenty miles southwest of Shanghai), an affluent center in southern Jiangsu province long associated with the arts[3] and with metal working. Hu Wenming's dates of birth and death remain unknown, but two of his vessels bear dated inscriptions, one corresponding to 1583 and the other to 1613, indicating that he was active during the reign of the Wanli Emperor. Marks on several other bronzes reveal that they were made by a son, Hu Guangyu,[4] who perhaps inherited the workshop or succeeded his father as proprietor. Though details about the Hu family are scarce, biographical dictionaries mention two Ming gentlemen, surnamed Hu, whose two-character given names include 'Wen' as the first syllable: Hu Wenbi (dates unknown, but *jinshi*, 1517), who served as an official in the Zhengde and Jiajing reigns;[5] and Hu Wenhuan (dates unknown, but active in the late sixteenth century), a bookseller in Hangzhou who published an abridged version of Cao Zhao's *Gegu yaolun* in 1596.[6] The similarity of names could be coincidental, since the character 'Wen' is both common and appropriate as a given name, but it could also indicate a familial relationship, perhaps as brothers or as first cousins. Further research on these individuals might shed light on the Hu family, if not on Hu Wenming himself. Although the passage of time has obscured the circumstances of his life, Hu Wenming remains one of the few Chinese bronze casters whose name is known and who can be associated with specific works in this otherwise largely anonymous craft tradition.

History remembers Hu Wenming best for the articles he produced for the scholar's studio: brushpots, *ruyi* scepters, hand warmers, flower vases, and especially incense paraphernalia – censers, incense boxes, vases, spoons, and tongs. His works comprise two groups, those in cast bronze, such as this incense box, and those in raised copper, such as the Clague Collection censer [see 12]. Virtually all of his works have colorful surfaces, achieved through parcel gilding in the hammered copper pieces and through parcel gilding, inlays of gold and silver, or a combination of both in the cast bronze ones. Many of his pieces draw upon Shang and Zhou bronzes for their shapes – *gu* beakers and trumpet-mouthed *zun* vessels for flower vases, and *gui* bowls and cylindrical *zun* vessels for censers; in addition, they often employ archaic *taotie* masks as decoration. Lacking archaic prototypes, other vessels, such as the present incense container, feature more naturalistic decoration that accords well with that seen on jade and lacquer pieces of the period.

Perhaps containers for cosmetics, small, circular, covered boxes appear among the repertoire of Han-dynasty silver[7] and may have served as the model for the symmetrical gold and silver boxes from the Tang[8] and Song[9] dynasties, the distant ancestors of the present incense container and its congeners. The two halves of such Tang and Song boxes usually mirror each other in shape, often having vertical walls, rounded corners, and flat or lightly domed covers; both halves usually are decorated, often with a floral arabesque – sometimes inhabited by a variety of animals and birds – set against a ring-punched ground. Ceramic imitations of the gold and silver boxes appeared in the Tang period[10] and rose to popularity in the Song.[11] Typically undecorated, covered boxes in Ding ware usually follow their gold and silver models very closely in shape; Yue and Yaozhou examples, by contrast, often add a short footring to the box and a boldly carved design of parrots or scrolling flowers to the cover.[12] Probably inspired both by Tang gold and silver boxes and by Song ceramic ones, small decorated incense boxes became a standard feature of the Ming jade[13] and lacquer[14] traditions. With *leiwen* borders on its straight vertical sides and with a carved floral design set against a patterned ground on its broad flat face, a small red-lacquer covered box in the Avery Brundage Collection, Asian Art Museum of San Francisco, represents the type of lacquer box that must have served as the immediate prototype for the Clague box.[15]

Although orchids and *lingzhi* fungi do not figure among the motifs depicted on Tang gold and silver boxes, a variety of floral motifs, often set against a diapered ground, embellishes the Ming lacquer and jade boxes that served as the model for this family of bronze incense boxes.[16] A plant long associated with immortality,[17] the *lingzhi* fungus frequently appeared in painting and decorative arts of the Ming dynasty. The orchid gained prominence as a subject of Chinese art during the Yuan dynasty, in the paintings of Zheng Sixiao[18] (1241-1318); a symbol of the cultivated gentleman, it remained popular through the Ming dynasty.[19] Although Hu Wenming occasionally imitated the ring-punched backgrounds of Tang-dynasty gold and silver in his work [see top and bottom registers of 12], the clear source for the patterned background on this incense container is the *leiwen* ground of Shang and Zhou bronzes, as filtered through the textured grounds of Song and Yuan bronzes [see 4-6] and through the ornamental diapering of Ming lacquers. The same Shang and Zhou bronzes provided the *leiwen* band that encircles the sides of the box; although occasionally used as borders in earlier times on both bronzes[20] and ceramics,[21] *leiwen* began regularly to be used as borders only in the Ming.

The juxtaposition of naturalistically rendered floral group and diapered ground, a combination that finds exact parallels in contemporaneous jades,[22] lacquers,[23] and textiles,[24] signals the late Ming date of this incense container, as does the new-found reliance upon lacquerware models. The weight of this container also indicates its late Ming date, since the box is much heavier in proportion to its size than the thin-walled vessels of the Song and Yuan periods [compare 4-6]. In addition, with its gilded surfaces and its *leiwen* borders inlaid in silver wire, this box reflects the late Ming popular taste for bright colors.[25] Although parcel gilding had been used in the decoration of Ming copper and bronze vessels at least since the Xuande period, earlier pieces lack the visual force of late Ming examples.

Apart from the identifying mark, the naturalistic floral motif that combines two different plants and the straight, vertical sides of the relief elements distinguish the style of this box as that of Hu Wenming, as do the hexagonal diapers embellished with double-Y markings[26] and the gilding of both relief elements and unembellished backgrounds. Also typical of Hu Wenming's work is the reliance upon cold working to create both relief decoration and diapered ground, the technique imbuing the decorated surfaces with the clarity and precision of carved lacquer. In this piece, for example, both box and cover were cast, though the mark was incised, the diapering struck with a hammer and punch (which accounts for its sharpness), and the relief decoration sculptured with a hammer and chisel (which accounts for the relief elements' straight, vertical sides and for the series of telltale chisel marks). Although the *leiwen* borders were inlaid through the traditional method of fitting silver wires into prepared recesses, the gold overlay was most likely effected through the use of mercury, or parcel, gilding. In this technique, the areas to be gilded would have been painted with an amalgam of powdered gold and liquid mercury after casting and cold working were completed, and then the vessel would have been heated lightly. As the mercury evaporated, it left behind a thin but even layer of gold. Since the layer of gold is thin, it wears away easily.

The six-character, seal-script mark on this incense container is similar in content and calligraphic style to those on other works by Hu Wenming.[27] Although the corpus of Hu Wenming marks exhibits too much variation for all to be from the same period, let alone the same hand, marks on vessels whose styles allow a credible attribution to the late Ming period show sufficient consistency to relate them to a single workshop. Hu Wenming marks were incised rather than struck with a die, even on cast pieces, so that even apparently genuine marks reveal more variation than might be expected on items from a single workshop. It must be emphasized, however, that fewer than one hundred pieces bearing a Hu Wenming mark have so far come to light; since the workshop was in operation for at least thirty years, as proved by the two dated censers of 1583 and 1613, and probably much longer, some variations in style may have more to do with chronology than with authenticity, especially if different craftsmen were entrusted with responsibility for adding marks. Because the marks were incised, it is also theoretically possible that some genuine but originally unmarked pieces bear spurious marks added at a later date.

The range of shapes associated with Hu Wenming's work clearly indicates that his primary clients were members of the scholar class. Obviously very popular in their day, his works did not necessarily meet the aesthetic standards of the most discerning critics of the time, however; in his *Zhangwu zhi* of 1637, for example, the erudite connoisseur and cataloger of taste Wen Zhenheng (1585-1645) termed Hu's censers vulgar[28] – presumably because of their bright colors and newly invented, fanciful designs that had little, if anything, to do with antiquity. Even so, Wen recommended Hu's incense tongs,[29] as did the humble scholar Tu Long (1542-1605) who, among others, composed a treatise on incense.[30] Such assessments convey insight into the rarefied world of literati taste in the late Ming period; more important in the present context, however, they confirm Hu Wenming's historicity and demonstrate that he was not only active in the Wanli period, but well known by that time.

12 Circular Gui-shaped Censer with two loop handles and with fanciful sea animal (*haishou*) and rolling wave decor

Hu Wenming (active late sixteenth – early seventeenth century)
Ming dynasty, late sixteenth – early seventeenth century
Raised copper with cold-worked decoration, with traces of gilding, and
with an incised intaglio mark in seal-script (*zhuanshu*) characters reading
Yunjian Hu Wenming zhi in a rectangular cartouche on the base
17.5 centimeter diameter
Clague Collection Number 209

MOUNTED ON A LIGHTLY SPLAYED, CIRCULAR FOOT, this *gui*-shaped censer of raised copper has a circular bowl whose walls gently constrict to form the neck, and then flare slightly to define the mouth. Attached cast bronze handles appear at right and left; decorated with a projecting spur at the bottom, and with flame-like tufts of fur and ring-punched texturing along their sides, the ring handles issue from the mouths of maned mythical animal heads. Originally gilded, plain relief bands divide the vessel surface into three horizontal registers, each with low-relief decoration set against a textured ground. Encircling the swollen belly of the censer, the principal band features six fanciful sea creatures, or *haishou*, arranged in two symmetrical groupings, on a ground of rolling waves, each wave comprising three, four, or five concentric arcs, as space allows; breakers appear on either side of the handles and at the bottom of the register, while raised circular dots, seemingly randomly placed among the waves, suggest sea foam. A *feiyu*,[1] or flying fish-dragon, rises upward in the center of each side, occupying the place of honor and standing as the principal decorative emblem. On one side, the long-snouted, single-horned, fish-tailed *feiyu* looks toward its proper left, its outspread feathered wings resembling those of a bird, its stout body resembling that of a fish. Flanking the *feiyu*, two hoofed quadrupeds, each shown in profile, gallop toward the center of the register; the winged equine on the (viewer's) right, probably a *haima* (literally, 'sea horse'), gazes directly ahead at the *feiyu*; the wingless equine-like animal on the left, perhaps a *qilin* (due to its seemingly cloven hooves), looks over its shoulder, towards it tail. Although the central *feiyu* on the other side of the censer also has a long snout, a bipartite fish tail, and a scale-covered body, it differs from the first in having a two-pronged horn, a lithe, dragon-like body, and wings resembling those of a bat; it also varies from the first in having a two pairs of fins – a caudal pair and a ventral pair under the wings – and in looking toward its proper right. Two striding, maned, lion-like animals with carefully detailed spines flank the *feiyu*, each shown in three-quarter view from above and each looking inward toward the awesome fish-dragon; the hornless, *ruyi*-nosed creature on the viewer's left might be a lion [*shizi*; compare 43], while the single-horned, fox-snouted one on the right might be a *baize* or a *bixie*.[2] Wisps of flame emanate from all six animals, signaling their extraordinary powers. On both faces of the censer a bird flutters on either side of the *feiyu*, separating the benevolent creature from its attendants. The top register of decoration has two pairs of highly stylized, confronting birds, one pair on either side of the censer; the butterfly-like motif that appears above each *feiyu* separates the crested, long-tailed birds of each pair. A stylized floral scroll encircles the foot, its ten blossoms, each with four heart-shaped petals, evenly spaced. Ring-punched patterns enliven the grounds of the top and bottom registers. The rectangular mark in the center of the base has six intaglio seal-script characters arranged in two columns; a single sunken line borders the mark, the gilded ground of the mark contrasting with the otherwise plain base. Undecorated except for traces of gilding, the wide lip and footring complement the heavily decorated vessel. The interior is plain, except for the band of gilding at the lip, though its blackened walls faintly echo the decoration on the exterior, the result of cold working. Since the vessel was hammered from a sheet of copper, rather than cast, the foot is hollow, its contours and depressed ring fully visible on the interior.

The incised mark on the base reads *Yunjian Hu Wenming zhi* (Made [by] Hu Wenming [of] Yunjian), indicating that this censer, like the previous covered box [11], was made by Hu Wenming, the most famous bronze caster of the late Ming period. Identical in content and closely akin in style to that on the covered box, the mark on this censer gives every indication of authenticity, and it compares favorably with those on other pieces believed to be genuine works by Hu Wenming.[3] As the covered box typified the style and technique of manufacture of his cast vessels, this censer exemplifies Hu's works in hammered copper.

This censer clearly owes its shape to handled *gui* vessels from the late Shang or early Western Zhou period.[4] A vessel for serving offerings of boiled grain, probably millet, the *gui* is a deep, handled bowl mounted on a splayed circular foot. The archaic *gui* vessel spawned many jade[5] and ceramic[6] imitations in the Song, Yuan, and Ming dynasties that were used as incense burners. Especially popular in *guan*, *ge*, and Longquan celadon ware, Song and Yuan ceramic examples seldom have decoration, relying instead on tautness of form and beauty of glaze for aesthetic appeal; in addition, such ceramic censers usually have flattened handles in the form of stylized fish or dragons and their proportions usually differ from those of the present censer. The similarity of this censer's shape, proportions, and handles to those of archaic bronze *gui* suggests that Hu Wenming drew upon the form of Bronze Age vessels rather than upon Song or Yuan ceramic interpretations in creating his censers.[7]

Although the *taotie* mask was the most common decorative motif on Shang-dynasty *gui* vessels, and confronting birds the most frequently used motif on those of the early Western Zhou, some Bronze Age *gui* vessels have plain surfaces, while others include such non-representational decorative schemes as lozenges, bosses, or vertical ribbing; none, however, illustrates a scene of imaginary animals frolicking over waves. The origin of the creatures pictured on the Clague vessel and its congeners[8] is uncertain, though they may have been picked from an illustrated version of the *Shanhai jing* (Classic of Mountains and Waterways), a late Zhou text on geography, or, as Schuyler Cammann has suggested, from the Natural History section of the *Sancai tuhui* (Illustrated Compendium of the Three Powers), a famous encyclopedia.[9] Ferocious as they appear today, such beasts were no doubt considered auspicious omens during the Ming dynasty.

Birds and other animals had been paired with rolling waves in the decorative arts at least since Han times. A variety of 'sea animals' cavort on the backs of Tang bronze mirrors, and dragons, fish, and ducks appear against a chased design of stylized waves on the floor of a seventh- to early eighth-century silver bowl[10] in the Nelson-Atkins Museum of Art, Kansas City, and dragons emerge from waves in two, tenth-century Yue ware vessels in The Metropolitan Museum of Art, New York – a ewer with alternating parrot and dragon-and-wave roundels[11] and a large bowl with three dragons on its interior.[12] A variety of birds and animals (including a monkey) frolic amidst waves on a twelfth-century bronze jar[13] in the Victoria and Albert Museum, London [compare 3], though the animals do not enjoy the same assertive presentation as those on the Clague censer. As reflected by the huge black-jade wine bowl of 1265 in the Round Fort, Beijing, the repertoire of *haishou*, or sea animals, had expanded by the Yuan dynasty to include dragons, horses, pigs, deer, rhinoceri, and conches, all set over billowing waves.[14] The bird-winged *feiyu*, or flying fish-dragon, had also made its appearance by Yuan or early Ming times, as illustrated by a magnificent openwork plaque in translucent white nephrite in the Seattle Art Museum.[15] James Watt notes that the Yuan dynasty witnessed the assimilation of a number of Tibetan motifs into the repertoire of Chinese art and also the modification under Tibetan influence of a number of traditional Chinese motifs, with the result that many Chinese mythical animals, including the *feiyu*, came to be depicted in Tibetan style with feathered wings.[16]

During the early Ming period, the *feiyu* entered into the repertory of imperial motifs, as shown by its double appearance (with small, bat wings) on one of the carved stone panels[17] recovered from the site of the banqueting hall of the imperial palace in Nanjing, built by the Hongwu Emperor in the late fourteenth century. Though not common in the Ming, the *feiyu* occurs from time to time on porcelains from the fifteenth, sixteenth, and early seventeenth centuries, with examples known from the Xuande,[18] Chenghua,[19] Jiajing,[20] Wanli,[21] and Tianqi[22] reigns. Such vessels from the Wanli period usually present the *feiyu* as the principal decorative motif, surrounded by a variety of other sea creatures, all set against a ground of roiling waves. The decorative scheme on the Clague censer is especially close in both style and content to porcelain vessels from the Wanli period with *feiyu* decoration.

The exact meaning of the *feiyu* is unclear, except that it is an auspicious beast whose appearance heralds the arrival of good fortune. Although James Watt has suggested that the *feiyu* represents the transformation of the carp into a dragon as it leaps the falls at Longmen[23] [compare 57], wings are not traditionally mentioned as attributes of the carp-dragon in that story, however helpful they might be in assisting the carp to ascend the falls. Without commenting on the meaning of the motif, Schuyler Cammann points out that according to the *Ming shi* (Official History of the Ming Dynasty) robes with *feiyu* patterns were worn by palace attendants beginning in the Yongle reign, and that according to later references, they were also bestowed on ministers of state and worthy courtiers.[24] Given its auspiciousness and its at least quasi-association with officialdom, the *feiyu* must have held strong appeal for scholars, especially ones aspiring to enter official ranks, and for families with sons preparing for the civil service examinations.

Like the principal band of decoration, the floral scroll encircling the censer's foot seems to have been borrowed from contemporaneous ceramics, perhaps from the border of a blue-and-white vessel. The decoration in the uppermost register, however, derives from antiquity and features two pairs of highly schematized confronting birds with long, scrolling tails. The birds, often called dragons but identified as birds by tails, beaks, and crests, evolved from related creatures that often appear in a subsidiary band immediately above the principal band of decoration in bronzes of the early Western Zhou period.[25] The butterfly designs that separate the birds on the Clague vessel represent a reduction and transformation of the relief heads that typically separate birds, and sometimes dragons, in those same subsidiary bands on early Western Zhou vessels. Hu Wenming and his son frequently incorporated such butterfly-like motifs into their bronzes, often as legs on cylindrical incense burners;[26] such whimsical transformations of antique designs held a special appeal during the late Ming. The formalized pattern of waves was appropriated from contemporaneous lacquer, while the ring-punched grounds of the top and bottom registers of the handles were drawn from Tang silver.

By Ming times, the *taotie* and certain other creatures from antiquity were generally understood to be ferocious beasts of such insatiable appetite that they consumed their own bodies; that understanding explains the curious handles on Hu Wenming censers, which often take the form of a fanciful animal head swallowing its own fur-covered body.[27] The column of stylized vertebrae along the outer edge of the handle confirms the identification of the ring as an animal's body.

Unlike the previous incense box [11], this censer was not cast but hammered from a sheet of copper, in the manner that a silversmith might raise a vessel from a sheet of silver. Entirely cold worked, the decorative elements stand in slight relief above their textured grounds, many of them surrounded by a sunken outline whose beveled outer edge makes the relief appear much higher than it actually is. The decoration was worked only from the exterior on this thick-walled vessel, with no hammering on the interior to raise the relief elements; the interior is thus smooth and plain, with only faint echoes of the exterior's decorative scheme. The principal ornamental elements may have been struck with an intaglio die to define their general form and raise their relief, but their interior drawing and finishing details were chased and chiseled with a variety of burins, points, and punches, as were the formalized wave and ring-mat grounds. Among extant censers with closely related designs, none has identically executed motifs, revealing both the extent of the cold working and the attention paid to each vessel. Attached with rivets (whose heads are visible on the interior), the cast bronze handles find exact counterparts on other vessels,[28] indicating that their molds were no doubt prepared from standard models kept in the workshop. Only traces remain of the gilding that originally covered the lip, footring, handles, relief elements, and raised bands between registers. Applied through the mercury-gilding process [see 11], the layer of parcel gilding was extremely thin and thus readily subject to wear; having disappeared from the raised areas, the remaining gold appears largely in the hollows of the design.

If the decorative scheme with its two *feiyu* and other sea creatures dates this censer to the Ming dynasty, the theme having first appeared in Yuan or early Ming times and having virtually disappeared by the early Qing,[29] its similarity in style to a Wanli-marked blue-and-white porcelain bowl[30] in the National Palace Museum, Taipei, places it solidly in the late Ming. The taste for bright, contrasting colors also signals its late Ming date, as do the interest in narrative – even the handles tell stories – and the delight in visual puns and playful ambiguities, especially ones with classical overtones,[31] so that the 'butterfly' in the top register can also be read as the face of a bat, as the head of a *lingzhi* fungus, and, of course, as the stylized head of a feline (from an archaic bronze).

The mark (with its late Ming seal-script characters) on the censer's base identifies the artist as Hu Wenming, as do the use of an all-over decorative scheme created solely through cold-working techniques and the juxtaposition of raised motifs and textured ground. Especially typical of Hu Wenming's style is the combination of antique elements – the *gui* form, the handles, and the birds in the top register, for example – with contemporaneous ones drawn from porcelain, jade, and lacquer, such as the *feiyu*, sea creatures, and undulating waves in the principal register, and the floral scroll in the lower one. Unusual in the hammered works of other artists, the thick walls of this censer are a standard element of Hu Wenming's raised copper vessels; they impart the substantial weight that is such a consistent feature of his works [compare 11].

13 Circular Covered Incense Box

with *chi* dragon and *lingzhi* fungus decor against a diapered ground

Ming dynasty, sixteenth – early seventeenth century
Cast bronze with cast and cold-worked decoration
7.0 centimeter diameter
Clague Collection Number 254

THE TWO HALVES OF THIS CIRCULAR COVERED BOX are similarly shaped. The cover has a broad flat face with rounded edges that turn downward to form the short straight sides; continuing the straight lines of the cover, the walls of the box descend and then curve inward at the bottom to meet the low ring that circumscribes the wide, shallow, countersunk base. An incised line defines the narrow, undecorated lip at the edge of both box and cover. The cover sports low-relief decoration comprising two salamander-like *chilong*, or *chi* dragons,[1] shown from above, enmeshed in a pattern of scrolling *lingzhi* fungi. Their bodies echoing the vessel's curvature, the *chi* dragons stride forward, each turning its head toward the center of the cover to stalk its companion. Two symmetrically arranged stalks of branching *lingzhi* fungus occupy the center of the cover; each *chi* dragon grasps one stalk of the auspicious fungus in its mouth and each places its proper left front paw on a branch of the other stalk. Each *chilong* has a single horn, a mane divided into two tufts, a carefully articulated spinal ridge from which emanates a wisp of flame, and a bifurcated tail whose symmetrically curled ends blend harmoniously with the *lingzhi* scrolls and spiraling wisps of flame. One following the other, two *chi* dragons stride around the sides of the box, each shown from above and each bearing a branch of *lingzhi* fungus in its mouth. The branches of fungus do not scroll, but project forward, separating the head of one *chilong* from the tail of other. Similar to those on the cover, each *chilong* has a broad, flat snout, a single horn, a mane (undivided in this case), a dorsal ridge with a curling wisp of flame, and a bifurcated tail with elegantly coiled tips. Each *chilong* marches forward, its head turned slightly to its proper left, its extended right front paw firmly planted for the next step. On both box and cover, the broad, unembellished areas of metal that make up the *chi* dragons and *lingzhi* fungi contrast with the background, which is textured with an incised pattern of formalized flower designs. The countersunk base is undecorated, as are the interior surfaces of the box and cover.

Like the Hu Wenming covered box [11], this incense container derives ultimately from the small gold and silver covered boxes that rose to popularity in the Tang, though it finds its closest parallels in the small jade and lacquer boxes that were favored in the Ming. A small, white jade box by Lu Zigang, thought to date to 1561 and now in the Bei Shan Tang Collection, Hong Kong, has the same shape as the Clague box, with its straight sides, rounded corners, broad, flat face, and countersunk base encircled by a raised ring.[2] Also dating to the late Ming, a small carved red-lacquer box in the Florence and Herbert Irving Collection, shares the Clague box's size, shape, and proportions, and its narrow, undecorated lip, though it has a different decorative scheme.[3]

The decorative scheme on this box also comes directly from carved lacquer, with only minor modifications. A Song or Yuan circular covered box in the Avery Brundage Collection, Asian Art Museum of San Francisco, and another in the Florence and Herbert Irving Collection, are carved with a design of two *chi* dragons on their covers.[4] Shown from above and enveloped in scrolling clouds, the striding *chilong* turn their heads to look at each other, each bearing a small sprig of *lingzhi* fungus. Retaining the main components of the design, the Clague box eliminates the scrolling clouds, replacing them with *lingzhi* fungi of increased size and with the formalized patterns created by the *chi* dragons' long tails and curling wisps of flame. In typical late Ming style, the Clague box makes the design readily comprehensible by arranging it in a strictly symmetrical fashion and by segregating the principal motifs from the background, texturing the latter and raising the former in slight relief, a technique already introduced into lacquer in the fifteenth century, as shown by a small covered box carved with a design of two lions playing with a brocaded ball,[5] in the National Palace Museum, Taipei. Although scrolling clouds adorn the sides of the Irving box, two *chilong* ornament those of the Brundage box, again providing the prototype for the Clague box.

The *chilong* enjoyed an ancient lineage in China, appearing at least as early as the Warring States period and finding widespread popularity in the Han, especially as decoration on jades.[6] With the decline of interest in things foreign in late Tang and the renewed interest in antiquity in early Song, the *chilong* experienced a renaissance, finding a home in the ornament of bronzes, lacquers, ceramics, and jades,[7] from Song through Qing.

Although the convention of dragons, birds, and felines biting themselves dates at least to the Warring States period,[8] that of animals bearing auspicious plants originated much later, probably in the Tang. The animals in the inhabited vine scrolls on Tang mirrors and on Tang gold and silver pieces sometimes bite their encircling stalk, for example, and a shallow Tang silver bowl – excavated in 1970 from an eighth-century site at Hejiacun, near Xi'an – features on its floor a design of two confronting lions, each grasping a floral scroll in its mouth.[9] Though not a frequently occurring motif, small jade sculptures representing animals bearing branches of auspicious plants begin to appear in increasing numbers in the Song and Yuan periods, as witnessed by a jade deer holding a branch of *lingzhi* fungus (Victor Shaw Collection, Hong Kong), a jade phoenix with a branch of fruiting peach (Guanfu Collection, Hong Kong), and a jade fish with several stalks of lotus (excavated from a Jin-dynasty site).[10] By the Ming dynasty, the theme had gained widespread popularity, with numerous and varied animals, all seemingly domesticated and well trained, clutching stalks of auspicious plants.[11]

Apart from its similarity to late Ming lacquer and jade boxes, the symmetry of the design and its clarity of presentation establish the late Ming date of this incense box, as do the subject matter and the combination of low-relief decor and highly textured ground. With their playful attitudes and their strongly articulated spines that continue well into their tails, the *chi* dragons are closely akin in style to one that graces a white jade plaque excavated in 1966 from the Wanli-period tomb of Zhu Shoucheng[12] and to those that embellish the top and bottom of the bamboo aromatics container carved by Zhu Ying (Zhu Xiaosong; active, late sixteenth – early seventeenth century) recovered from the same tomb.[13] Popular in ceramic ware already by the Yuan dynasty,[14] the formalized flower diapers that texture the background of the Clague box appear frequently in the works of Hu Wenming.[15] Also signalling the late Ming date of this box is its reliance upon cold working to create both relief decoration and diapered ground, the technique recalling that of Hu Wenming [see 11]. Thick-walled, both box and cover were cast, though the diapering was incised and the relief decoration sculptured with a hammer and chisel, which accounts for the relief elements' impeccably straight, vertical sides and for the chatter marks along their edges. It is probable (as it also is with the cast works of Hu Wenming) that the principal decorative motifs were cast in relief but that definition of form and articulation of detail were accomplished through cold working.

14 Circular Covered Incense Box with lion decor

Ming dynasty, Wanli period (1573-1619)
Hammered and turned copper with decoration inlaid in silver wire and
with a mark inlaid in silver wire in standard-script (*kaishu*) characters
reading *Da Ming Wanlinian zhi* on the floor
4.8 centimeter diameter
Clague Collection Number 240

O F HAMMERED COPPER, this small circular covered incense box comprises two similarly shaped halves. Additionally, the box has a short vertical lip soldered to its inner edge to receive the cover and a small circular depression in the center of its underside that serves as a base. Box and cover are fully decorated on their exteriors and partially embellished on their interiors with linear designs inlaid in silver wire. Shown from above, five striding lions grace the cover, a single one in the center surrounded by the four others arranged in a ring. Its body curled to echo the cover's curvature, the lion in the center grasps the tail of its nearest companion in the outer ring; most lions in the ring clutch the tail of the preceding one, so that the design spirals outward. The silver-wire inlays not only describe the lions' form but show off their windblown manes and fur-tufted spines. Scrolling branches of auspicious *lingzhi* fungus complete the design. The box is similarly decorated, but with four lions instead of five, a single one in the center encircled by a ring of three. At the center of the cover's interior is a bouquet comprising a spike of narcissus with two blossoms and four leaves, a sprig of *ruyi*-headed *lingzhi* fungus, and a section of jointed bamboo stalk with three clusters of leaves, all outlined in silver-wire inlay. The otherwise undecorated interior of the box has at its center a mark of six *kaishu* (standard-script) characters inlaid in silver wire in two columns.

Small boxes with identically shaped and decorated tops and bottoms, even lacking a lip or foot to distinguish box from cover, appear among the limited corpus of Han-dynasty silver.[1] Though such a Han-dynasty box could have surfaced in Ming times to be copied in bronze at the request of a late Ming antiquarian, it is likely that this covered box descends ultimately from Tang gold and silver boxes, sharing the same immediate ancestors in jade and lacquer as the previous incense boxes [11, 13].

Unlike the tiger, which was native to China (at least in some species) and which had figured prominently among the motifs of Chinese art since the Bronze Age[2] – with a white tiger emblematic of the west in Chinese directional symbolism at least by Han times – the lion is a relative newcomer to Chinese art, introduced from India during the Han dynasty as part of the rich visual imagery that accompanied Buddhism. As the Buddhist church became established, its Chinese followers had increasingly numerous occasions to see representations of lions, since, in the Indian manner, a pair of the noble beasts typically flanked the Buddha's throne – especially in depictions of the Buddha Śākyamuni, the Lion of the Śākya Clan – and since, according to the canons of Buddhist iconography, the lion was the proper mount for the Bodhisattva Mañjuśrī (Chinese, Wenshu Pusa), the Bodhisattva of Transcendent Wisdom. Both its continuing presence in Buddhist art and its appearance as decoration on a variety of foreign luxury goods imported from afar over the fabled Silk Route sustained Chinese interest in the lion in succeeding centuries. Under these dual influences, depictions of lions came to grace a variety of secular goods during the Tang dynasty, appearing not only on the decorated backs of bronze mirrors[3] and in the inhabited vine scrolls of gold and silver objects but independently as sculptures in marble[4] and ceramic ware.[5] Lions also appear as the principal decorative motif on some Tang silver vessels, such as the shallow silver bowl – excavated in 1970 from a mid-eighth-century site at Hejiacun, near Xi'an – that features two confronting lions on its floor, each lion grasping a floral scroll in its mouth.[6] By the late Song and Yuan dynasties, lions were often shown at play, sometimes with a brocaded ball,[7] a theme that commanded great popularity in the decorative arts of the Ming and Qing, from lacquer and jade to ceramics and bronze. Interspersed with sprigs of *lingzhi* fungus and grasping each others' tails [compare 13], the lions on the Clague box are very much in the late Ming mode.

The floral motif on the inside of the cover reflects a genre of painting – cut branches set against an unembellished background – that arose in the Southern Song period, as seen in a small painting by Zhao Mengjian (1199 - about 1267), now in the National Palace Museum, Taipei; in ink on paper, the album leaf represents one branch each of pine, bamboo, and blossoming plum, the so-called 'Three Friends of Winter,' arranged to form a bouquet.[8] Also by Zhao Mengjian, a handscroll in ink on paper portraying a bed of flowering narcissus plants,[9] now in The Metropolitan Museum of Art, New York, represents the ancestor of the narcissus designs that ornament a number of Ming lacquer and jade covered boxes,[10] and thus the distant ancestor of the narcissus on the cover of the Clague box. Deriving ultimately from Song painting, floral bouquets remained a popular feature of Ming decorative arts, those of the late Ming characteristically including a branch of *lingzhi* fungus. Many late Ming lacquers display a flowering sprig or blossoming cut branch,[11] and a white jade plaque in the Chih-jou Chai Collection, Hong Kong, reliably attributed to the late Ming period, features a motif of narcissus, bamboo, and *lingzhi* fungus,[12] providing a context for the design on the interior of the Clague box cover.

First appearing about the sixth century BC, China's earliest inlaid bronzes were typically decorated with inlays of copper and semiprecious stones (usually turquoise and malachite) arranged in angular patterns;

perhaps influenced by painted lacquers of the day, those of the fourth and third centuries BC are characterized by fluid scrolls, usually inlaid in sheet silver or gold. Popular well into the Han dynasty, examples from the late Bronze Age share a taste for geometric designs, inlaid in sheet gold and silver and occasionally in semiprecious stones, that emphasize ornament over description.[13] With the revival of interest in antiquity during the Song came a renewed fascination with inlaid bronzes, archaic as well as newly made. The dating of inlaid bronzes made during the long period from Song through Qing remains one of the most vexing problems in the study of later Chinese bronzes.

Fortunately, this box carries a mark on its floor reading *Da Ming Wanlinian zhi* (Made [during the] Wanli era [of the] Great Ming), indicating that it was made during the reign of Zhu Yijun (1563-1620), who ruled as the Wanli Emperor (reign 1573-1620). The calligraphic style – as manifested in the characters for *wan* and *li*, in particular – is identical to that in an artist's inscription, or *biankuan*, dated to 1612 on the side of a jade seal excavated in 1969 from a Ming tomb near Shanghai,[14] confirming the authenticity of the inscription and thus the Wanli date of the box. Standard on imperial porcelains, genuine Ming reign marks are rare on later bronzes, though spurious ones abound. The mark thus sets this modest incense box apart as a special piece, all the more important because it documents the use of silver-wire inlay in the late Ming, alongside the better known inlays in sheet gold and silver.

The decorative style of the box includes not only the all-over patterning and bird's-eye view but also the reliance on relatively wide lines for description and the incorporation of numerous short, noncontinuous lines that add a staccato effect, increasing the sense of compositional movement, often a goal in late Ming scenes of animals and figures. Qing-dynasty examples, by contrast, tend to feature sparser designs described with long, continuous lines of narrower width; the effect is usually one of quiet equilibrium [compare 17, 18].

In late Ming fashion, this piece was completely cold worked [compare 12], the box and cover hammered from a sheet of copper; cut from a sheet of copper, the narrow lip was soldered into place. The decoration was inlaid by hammering silver wire into prepared channels – presumably channels with edges slightly undercut to hold the inlay in place – that were cut into the copper after the box and cover had been shaped.

15 Circular Gui-shaped Censer
with two handles in the form of stylized dragons and with *taotie* decor

Ming to Qing dynasty, seventeenth century
Cast bronze with decoration inlaid in silver wire and in sheet silver, with
induced surface color, and with a cast mark in thread-relief standard-
script (*kaishu*) characters reading *Da Ming Xuandenian zhi* in a recessed
rectangular cartouche on the base
7.9 centimeter diameter
Clague Collection Number 203

CHINA'S RENAISSANCE IN BRONZE

RISING FROM THE SMALL CIRCULAR FOOT, the thick walls of this heavy but sleekly styled circular *gui*-form censer expand rapidly to form the swollen body, constrict to shape the neck, and then flare gently to define the mouth. In the form of stylized, scale-covered dragons (or possibly fish) facing upward, the integrally cast handles divide the censer into two halves. Four glowering *taotie* masks stare out from the censer, one on each side and one centered under each handle. Long curvilinear lines inlaid in silver wire describe the basic features of the masks, inlaid discs of sheet silver representing the irises and pupils of the eyes. Undecorated areas act as unifying shields, pulling together the features of the masks, while symmetrically placed *leiwen* elements suggest a background. Inlaid in silver wire, continuous *leiwen* meanders between bowstring lines border the top and bottom of the censer, a plain band distinguishing neck from body and another separating body from foot. The plain but deeply sunken base has at its center a cast mark in six thread-relief *kaishu* (standard-script) characters arranged in three columns within a recessed rectangular cartouche. The interior of the censer is undecorated. Chemically treated after casting to achieve its warm rust-brown surface, the brass-colored metal shows on the underside of the footring and in areas of the lip where the skin has worn thin.

Despite its six-character Xuande mark, this censer dates to the seventeenth century; in this case, the mark reflects the censer's derivation from early Ming bronzes of the Xuande period. After receiving some 39,000 catties (about fourteen and five-eighths tons) of copper as tribute from the King of Siam in 1427, the Xuande Emperor – Zhu Zhanji (1399-1435), the fifth emperor of Ming, who ruled as the Xuande Emperor (reign 1426-35), commissioned the production of thousands of bronzes in 1428 for imperial altars and for the various offices and halls of the palace.[1] The Emperor ordered his officials to study both Song ceramics and Song-dynasty illustrated catalogs of antiquities in designing the vessels to insure fidelity to antiquity.[2] The Emperor and his ministers would have preferred to use original Bronze Age vessels as models, but since the imperial collections had been dispersed or destroyed with the fall of Northern Song in 1127 and of Southern Song in 1279, the court had little choice but to turn to representations of antique vessels in ceramic ware and in such illustrated collection catalogs as *Kaogu tu* (Pictures for the Study of Antiquity) of 1092 by Lü Dalin (1046-1092) and *Xuanhe bogu tulu* (Xuanhe Album of Antiquities) of 1123. The reliance upon Song ceramics as models brought a surpassing level of refinement to Xuande bronzes – evident, according to late Ming and Qing connoisseurs, in their elegant shapes, pleasing colors, and exquisite casting – with the result that they were widely copied in succeeding centuries.[3] Since virtually all of the thousands of original Xuande imperial bronzes have now disappeared – except, perhaps, for small, largely unpublished groups that remain in the Beijing and Taipei branches of the Qing palace collection and thus have more claim than most to authenticity, at least in terms of provenance – copies and imitations afford a measure of insight into the celebrated world of Xuande bronzes.[4]

Cast in the seventeenth century, this censer numbers among those imitations. Like the *gui*-shaped censers of the Xuande period, this censer derives ultimately from Bronze Age *gui* food-serving bowls [compare 12], though its form reflects the strong imprint of Song-dynasty *guan* and Longquan ceramic censers,[5] the models on which the Xuande censers were based. The organic profile and the yoke-shaped handles in the form of dragons with arched backs and with heads and tails that project beyond their anchoring posts attest to the Song ceramic connection; the sleek styling, by contrast, discloses the more immediate descent from Xuande bronzes,[6] or, more likely, from replicas of them.

Although it preserves the general form of a Xuande bronze, this censer is a free interpretation rather than a literal copy of such a piece. The 1526 edition of *Xuande yiqi tupu* (Illustrated Catalogue of Xuande Sacral Vessels) includes woodblock-printed illustrations of several *gui*-shaped censers of similar form;[7] the bronzes in the illustrations have handles identical in shape to those on the Clague censer, but they have a larger footring and a less dramatic profile. The illustrations thus reveal Xuande censers to be closer to Song-dynasty ceramics than to the Clague censer in their proportions, but perhaps intermediate between the two in sleekness of design. The elegant but mannered form distinguishes the Clague censer from Xuande-period examples and dates it to the seventeenth century. Although Xuande bronzes are said to be heavy in relation to Song-Yuan bronzes [see 2-6] and to early Ming non-imperial bronzes [see 7, 8], the thick walls and relative weight of this censer also find more parallels among the cast bronzes of the late Ming and early Qing [compare 11, 13] than they do among the few bronzes credibly attributed to the Xuande period.

According to late Ming and Qing connoisseurs, beauty and variety of surface color ranked among the most prized characteristics of Xuande bronzes.[8] Descriptions range, among others, from jadeite green, mulberry purple, and ripe crab-apple red to hibiscus yellow, date red, and chestnut and wax-tea brown. Other bronzes apparently had mottled surfaces dappled with azurite blue, malachite green, cinnabar red, or lacquer black, perhaps in imitation of ancient patinas. Decoration included designs – probably *taotie* masks – inlaid in gold and silver as well as splashes of gold dispersed over the surface like snowflakes or drops of rain [see 34, 35], the gold preferably the color of the peaches of immortality. Some colors may have been applied to the surface with a binder, but most were doubtless achieved through a variety of chemical and thermal treatments. Like the shape, the warm russet brown surface color signals the direct descent of the Clague censer from Xuande bronzes. Although the color would seem to correspond to one of the Xuande browns – perhaps chestnut or wax-tea brown – its fidelity to the original remains unknown. Whether or not the early Ming model for the present piece included a *taotie* mask also remains unknown, but the interpretation of the mask, like the interpretation of the vessel itself, reflects seventeenth-century taste. The emphasis on ornamentation over representation – without the staring eyes, for example, the motif would hardly be recognizable as a *taotie* mask – indicates the seventeenth-century date of manufacture. The complexity of the design, seen in the use of four *taotie* masks rather than the traditional two and in the detailing of the scales on the handles, also attests to the censer's seventeenth-century date. In addition, the mask's florid style – evident, for example, in the circuitous path of the lines that describe the nose – is characteristic of the seventeenth century, as is the reduction of the *leiwen* ground to little more than a passing reference.

The six-character mark on the base reading *Da Ming Xuandenian zhi* (Made [during the] Xuande era [of the] Great Ming) asserts that this censer was made during the Xuande period. Since the style clearly dates the censer to the seventeenth century, the mark must be regarded as spurious, as must the vast majority of Xuande marks on later bronzes. Renowned for its exquisite porcelains, lacquers, and bronzes, the Xuande period and its reign mark came to symbolize quality in the decorative arts, tempting later artists to furnish their wares with Xuande marks, even when the pieces clearly were not in Ming, let alone Xuande, style.

Tradition[9] holds that genuine Xuande bronzes may have a reign mark discreetly placed on the underside; that the characters of the mark should rise in relief and may appear within a rectangular cartouche; that the mark may comprise two, four, or six characters reading, respectively, *Xuande*, *Xuandenian zhi*, or *Da Ming Xuandenian zhi*; that, depending upon the number of characters, the mark may be written in one vertical column (two or four characters), in one horizontal row (four or six characters), or in three vertical columns of two characters each (six characters); and that the calligraphy of the mark should be in either small-seal-script (*xiaozhuan*) characters or standard-script (*kaishu*) characters in the powerful but balanced style of the early Tang calligrapher Ouyang Xun (557-641). As in all genuine marks on works from the Xuande period, the character *de* (second graph in the name Xuande) should omit the horizontal stroke at its center – the stroke that ordinarily appears between the 'four' and 'heart' elements in the dictionary form of the character.

In content and calligraphic style, the mark on the Clague censer answers to the above criteria – as, however, do the majority of Xuande marks, genuine as well as spurious, since the general characteristics of such marks are well known. Although the mark on this censer resembles those on genuine Xuande-period porcelains[10] and those on several bronze censers in the Palace Museum, Taipei, that have some claim to authenticity,[11] subtle points of style distinguish it as an imitation, for example: in genuine marks, the stroke that sweeps downward and to the right in the character *da* is usually longer than the stroke that sweeps downward and to the left; in the character *ming*, the vertical stroke at the left edge of the 'moon' element usually projects further downward than the bottom of the hooked vertical stroke at the right, and the 'sun' radical is typically smaller in proportion to the character as a whole than in this example; in the character *xuan*, the horizontal stroke between the 'roof' radical and the 'sun' element is usually shorter than the top of the 'sun' element, and the character as a whole is usually slightly more attenuated than is the case here. The differences are subtle indeed; just as this censer reflects the designer's familiarity with Xuande bronzes, the mark reveals his acquaintance with Xuande marks.

16 Circular Censer

with two handles in the form of stylized dragons and with *taotie* decor

Ming to Qing dynasty, seventeenth century
Cast bronze with decoration inlaid in silver wire and in sheet gold and silver,
with induced surface color, with a cast mark in thread-relief standard-
script (*kaishu*) characters reading *Da Ming Xuandenian zhi* in a recessed
rectangular cartouche on the base, and with a second mark inlaid in silver
wire in clerical-script (*lishu*) characters reading *Shisou* also on the base
13.3 centimeter diameter
Clague Collection Number 214

RESTING ON THREE SMALL CABRIOLE LEGS, this deep-bowled circular censer has a large flat base from which the almost vertical walls rise and then flare outward at the top. The integrally cast platform-like base projects well beyond the wall's perimeter, providing visual support for the bowl. Separately cast and attached at either side with rivets, the handles take the form of stylized *kui* dragons marching upward toward the lip; their backs arched, the dragons have snouted heads and florid tails that project beyond the posts for attachment to the vessel. A frontal *taotie* mask embellishes each side of the vessel, its nose, mouth, and body described by *leiwen* bands inlaid in silver wire, its eyebrows, horns, and selected other details inlaid in sheet gold and silver. A classic *leiwen* meander between bowstring lines borders the top of the mask while a row of interlocked T's sets off the bottom. Inlaid in silver wire, a band of undulating forms resembling waves but probably representing clouds encircles the lip. A double row of semi-linked cloud heads in the form of inverted C-scrolls surrounds the convex edge of the base. Enclosed by a ring of stylized clouds, an inlaid spiral coils outward on the bulbous portion of each cabriole leg. Around its periphery, the underside of the base has a wide unembellished ring that circumscribes the broad, shallow well and that receives the integrally cast legs – which overlap both the underside of the base and its extended convex edge. At the center of the otherwise plain, flat, countersunk well is a cast mark in six thread-relief *kaishu* (standard-script) characters arranged in three columns in a recessed rectangular cartouche, the ground of which has been darkened to enhance the legibility of the characters. Inlaid in silver wire, a second mark in *lishu* (clerical-script) characters also appears on the base, its two characters appearing one above and one below the cast mark's central column. The interior of the bowl is undecorated, as are the backs and bottoms of the legs. The surface of the bronze was chemically treated after casting to color it a warm rust-brown.

The Xuande mark, the warm rust-brown color, and the relationship to Song ceramic forms indicate that this seventeenth-century censer imitates an early Ming bronze of the Xuande period [compare 15]. In fact, illustrations of several vessels of this general type appear in the 1526 edition of *Xuande yiqi tupu* (Illustrated Catalogue of Xuande Sacral Vessels), albeit with simpler bases and with handles of a different type.[1] One of several new shapes that appeared in the Ming, vessels of this cauldron-like form lack clear antecedents; eclectic rather than radically new, the form draws elements from the bronze and ceramic traditions, combining them in a new and novel fashion. Since the Song imperial collection of antiquities disappeared with the fall of the dynasty, the Ming officials charged with responsibility for designing the thousands of bronzes commissioned by the Xuande Emperor in 1428 did not have access to original Bronze Age vessels as models; instead, they based their designs on representations of archaic vessels in Song ceramics and in Song-dynasty woodblock-printed collection catalogs. Through whimsy, misunderstanding, or circumstances now forgotten, reliance on such indirect sources occasionally resulted in fanciful interpretations of the ancient forms, a phenomenon that might explain the unusual appearance of the present censer.

With its deep bowl, vertically inclined walls, and flaring lip, the basic form recalls a Shang or early Western Zhou *yu*, a food-serving vessel akin to the *gui* but having a deep bowl with steeply pitched straight walls rather than the *gui*'s bulbous bowl with expanding and contracting profile.[2] On rare occasions the *yu* may have legs,[3] though, like the *gui*, it typically sits atop a ring foot; in addition, the *yu* never has a platform base and it seldom has vertically oriented handles.

The distinctive base derives not from the bronze tradition, but from the Song ceramic tradition. Narcissus-bulb bowls in imperial Ru[4] and *guan*[5] ware, for example, have steeply inclined walls that spring from a similar, if less exaggerated, platform-like base with rounded edges; the undersides of such bases reveal a wide, unornamented ring that receives the legs and that surrounds a broad, flat, slightly sunken, central well, exactly as in the present censer. Despite such correspondences, Ru and *guan* bulb bowls lack handles, have elliptical rather than circular bodies, have four cloud-head feet rather than three cabriole legs, and have shallow bowls with short sides rather than deep bowls with tall sides.

Popular in Zhou and Han times, cabriole legs support a variety of Bronze Age vessels.[6] Antiquarian interests sparked the use of cabriole legs in Song ceramics, especially for Ru, Ding, and *guan* ware censers modeled on ancient cylindrical-*zun* wine vessels.[7] Though they could thus have been drawn from either ancient bronzes or Song ceramics, the cabriole legs on this censer likely came from the ceramic tradition, along with a base borrowed from Ru or *guan* ware.

Dragon-form handles of the type on this censer have no precedent among ancient bronzes, but their forebears grace Song-dynasty *guan* and Longquan censers of *gui* shape.[8] Large and meticulously articulated, the handles are considerably more elaborate than the abstract dragon-form handles on Song ceramics. In interpretation, the formalized, square-snouted *kui* dragons find parallels in the strapwork dragons that ornament the tops of most Kangxi-period white-jade plaques of Lu Zigang type[9] and in the dragon roundels that embellish Kangxi beehive-shaped water pots.[10] The exact relationship of these handles to the decorative arts of the Kangxi period remains uncertain, however, as these dragons are more complex than those on Kangxi ceramics and jades. Since they show affinities to works in the Kangxi style and since they are quite different from those on similarly shaped vessels illustrated in *Xuande yiqi tupu*, the handles on this censer may be Kangxi-period replacements for lost originals. If, on the other hand, the handles are original and thus contemporaneous with the vessel, perhaps their dragon forms anticipate those of the Kangxi period. Though unusual, the censer's form is not unique; a close relative – a censer with identically shaped bowl and base (but with different legs, handles, and decoration) – was recently published with an attribution to the seventeenth century.[11]

Like many late Ming and Qing bronzes, this censer was chemically treated after casting to produce its warm, russet surface color, a fashion begun in the Xuande period [compare 15]. The rust-colored ground provides the perfect foil for the fanciful *taotie* masks, which, on this censer, are unusual in having their noses and mouths described by curvilinear bands of inlaid *leiwen* scrolls rather than by bands of sheet gold or silver or by a series of lines inlaid in silver wire. Though without direct classical antecedents, the use of *leiwen* scrolls to describe the mouth and nose recalls the so-called 'dissolved' *taotie* masks that occasionally appear on late Shang bronzes.[12] Such 'dissolved' *taotie* masks lack a unifying shield or escutcheon to draw the parts of the mask together, thus allowing the mouth, nose, eyes, and other features to float against the ground as flat, low-relief bands, each band carrying a single row of *leiwen* scrolls. The mannered form of the *taotie* masks points to a seventeenth-century date of manufacture for this censer.

The fine-line *taotie* mask on a cast-bronze, *ding*-shaped censer in the British Museum, London, has eyebrows inlaid in sheet silver in the same forked convention as on this censer, not to mention related horns and identically shaped *leiwen* coils.[13] The presence of a two-character mark on its base reading *Xuande* has led to the censer's attribution to the early fifteenth century, but, like the Clague piece, it must date to the seventeenth; the similarity in the style of the inlaid decoration suggests that both pieces came from the same workshop. Lacking authentic Xuande examples, these imitations, and the one in the previous entry, shed light on the sophisticated forms of early fifteenth-century imperial bronzes.

The cast six-character mark on the base reading *Da Ming Xuandenian zhi* (Made [during the] Xuande era [of the] Great Ming) asserts that this censer was made during the Xuande reign (1426-35) of the Ming dynasty. The style clearly dates the censer to the seventeenth century, however, so the mark must be regarded as false. Like that on the previous censer [15], the mark corresponds to traditional descriptions of marks on Xuande bronzes and, generally, it compares in style and content to imperial marks on ceramics of the Xuande period; subtle points of style distinguish it as an imitation, however, in the same manner that other points identify the mark on the previous censer as spurious.

Reading *Shisou*, the two characters inlaid in silver wire on the base of this censer are an artist's mark claiming authorship for Shisou, an elusive figure who seems to have escaped the notice of his contemporaries, so that the dates and places of his birth and death are unrecorded, not to mention the details of his life; even the proper rendering of his name is disputed, some maintaining that the two characters represent a surname (Shi) and a single-character given name (Sou), and others arguing that they constitute a two-character *hao*, or sobriquet, meaning 'Old Man of the Stone.' Tradition asserts that Shisou was a Buddhist monk active at the end of the Ming dynasty and that 'Shisou' is a religious name, his family and given names having been lost to history. He is said to have excelled in craft-ing inlaid bronzes, his works of such refinement that they captured the imagination of the literati and thus came to be produced almost exclu-sively in shapes appropriate for the scholar's studio. Tradition further states that he signed his works discreetly on the base with the two-character signature *Shisou* in either seal script (*zhuanshu*) or clerical script (*lishu*), the calligraphy always elegant and stately.[14]

Numerous later bronzes bear Shisou marks, including four in the Clague Collection [16-18, 55]; in fact, the mark appears on far more works than that of Hu Wenming [11, 12] or any other known bronze caster. As tradition asserts, pieces with the Shisou mark are virtually always items for the scholar's studio; even small sculptures, usually of the Bodhisattva Avalokiteśvara (Chinese, Guanyin pusa), sometimes display the Shisou mark [55]. In cast bronze rather than raised copper, Shisou-marked pieces invari-ably have linear decoration inlaid in fine silver wire, the decoration occa-sionally embellished with a few judiciously placed bands of sheet silver or gold, as in the present censer. Sculptures usually restrict their fine-wire inlays to garment edges, enlivening the remainder of the robe with an elegantly simple pattern of drapery folds. The bronze surfaces range in color from rust brown to gunmetal gray and even to dark brown (in the case of sculptures), though gunmetal gray is characteristic [see 17]. Although works with the Shisou mark thus show a certain homogeneity, they exhibit far too much variation for all to be from the same period, let alone from the same individual artist.

The problem of Shisou ranks among the most perplexing in the history of later Chinese bronzes. History records a variety of miscellaneous details about numerous bronze casters, including ones for whom works cannot be located today, yet it records almost nothing about Shisou, whose corpus of 'signed' works is the largest of all. If Shisou was indeed active in the late Ming period, it is curious that his works are not mentioned in such standard treatises as Wen Zhenheng's *Zhangwu zhi* (Superfluous Things) of 1637 and Tu Long's *Xiangjian* (A Commentary on Incense) or *Wenfang qiju jian* (A Commentary on Articles for the Scholar's Studio). Lacking documentation, perhaps tradition erred, assigning Shisou to the late Ming when, in fact, he lived in the Qing. Perhaps Shisou was born in the closing years of the Ming, but rose to fame in the Qing, after the celebrated Ming chroniclers of taste had died (Tu Long in 1605, Wen Zhenheng in 1645).[15]

In clerical-script (*lishu*) characters inlaid in silver wire and placed discreetly on the base, the Shisou mark on the Clague censer conforms to the traditional description of such marks and it resembles those on numerous other vessels. The combination of Shisou and Xuande marks – supposedly representing periods two centuries apart – is a rare, though perhaps not unique, phenomenon;[16] it does not augur well for the authenticity of the Shisou mark. This censer and its cousin in the British Museum, mentioned above, represent a continuation – or possibly a revival – of the Xuande bronze tradition; while it is entirely possible that Shisou began by imitating Xuande inlaid bronzes, it is unlikely that his mature 'signed' works would perpetuate such a conservative manner. The Shisou mark on this censer is probably a later addition.[17] Many Shisou marks were no doubt added surreptitiously, to antiques and to newly made items, to increase their salability.

Traditionally it is considered that works with the Shisou mark range in date from the late Ming period to the modern era and that in a relative sense, 'early' works have complex decorative schemes sometimes ornamented with carefully placed bands of sheet gold or silver whereas 'late' ones feature simple designs in wire inlay only.[18] Thus, this censer would be classified as an 'early' work, though the censer's actual relationship, if any, to an individual named Shisou has yet to be established.

A recently published *gui*-shaped censer with the six-character mark of Hu Wenming attests to the production of cast bronzes with inlays in both silver wire and sheet gold and silver in the late Ming;[19] similar though not identical in style, the Hu Wenming censer supports the attribution of the Clague piece to the seventeenth century. Should information ever come to light that confirms the authenticity of the Shisou mark on the Clague censer, the relationship of the piece to a marked Hu Wenming censer will assist in establishing Shisou's period of activity.

Without hard evidence – even basic information about his dates of activity and the characteristics of his style – attributions to Shisou's hand cannot seriously be considered; the term 'Shisou manner,' however, can meaningfully be used as a generic term to designate those later bronze studio implements with fine-line decoration inlaid in silver wire.

The collection of the National Palace Museum, Taipei, includes a Qianlong-period porcelain censer with cabriole legs and with a bowl identical in shape to that of the Clague censer, the piece entirely covered with a mottled rust-brown glaze imitating bronze.[20] Pyrotechnical displays of skill, such trompe l'oeil ceramics were made in imitation of a variety of materials – jade, marble, bronze, lacquer, and wood, to name but a few – in the eighteenth and nineteenth centuries merely to delight and to amuse. Intended for the palace, such imperially marked Qianlong-period ceramics were typically modeled on earlier pieces rather than upon contemporaneous ones, indicating that the form of the Clague censer was considered 'old' by the eighteenth century. The model for the censer might have been a Xuande bronze, though it might also have been a late Ming or early Qing imitation, like the present piece, mistaken for an original. The porcelain censer has animal-head handles at either side, like one pictured in *Xuande yiqi tupu*, confirming the relationship to Xuande bronzes; significantly, it also has a wide, unornamented ring encircling the periphery of the base.

17 Small Square Hu Vessel
with two ring-handle attachments and with *taotie* decor

Qing dynasty, probably eighteenth century
Cast bronze with decoration inlaid in silver wire, with induced surface
color, and with a mark inlaid in silver wire in clerical-script (*lishu*)
characters reading *Shisou* on the base
13.4 centimeter height
Clague Collection Number 224

A FTER CONSTRICTING TO SET OFF THE DIMINUTIVE BASE, the walls of this handsome *fanghu*, or square *hu*, expand to shape the bulging body and then reverse themselves, the shoulders sloping inward to form the neck; a short, vertical lip set atop the gently flaring neck echoes the low foot. Cast separately and attached with rivets, handles in the form of stylized elephant heads appear at the base of the neck at right and left; the wear in the inlay below the handles confirms that the elephants' curled-under trunks once supported moveable rings, now lost. Each side of this *fanghu* sports three *taotie* masks inlaid in fine silver wire, a principal mask on the swollen body with subsidiary masks above and below. Large C-horns dominate the principal masks; representing the pupil, a small, non-concentric circle within the iris distinguishes the eyes of the principal masks on this vase. A band of interlocked T's borders the lip, mirroring a similar band on the foot. Treated after casting, the exterior has assumed an understated, gunmetal gray surface (with earthen undertones) that harmonizes with the silver inlays. Their golden brown surfaces untreated, the interior of the vessel and the underside of the foot are plain, though the deeply recessed, flat base bears a two-character mark in *lishu* (clerical script) inlaid in silver wire.

The two-character mark asserts that this small vase was made by Shisou, the elusive late Ming or Qing craftsman who reputedly excelled in producing silver-inlaid bronzes for the scholar's studio. Lacking reliable evidence about his style and dates, Shisou's authorship neither can be confirmed nor refuted. It should be noted, however, that this vase not only corresponds to the traditional description of Shisou's style [compare 16], it typifies the work associated with his name. Though not so elegant in its calligraphic style as some Shisou marks,[1] the two clerical-script characters inlaid on the base of this vessel are of the type virtually always associated with Shisou-manner bronzes. Probably a water container for the scholar's desk, this small vase derives from a late Bronze Age *fanghu* wine jar; in fact, its elongated pear-shaped body signals its descent from a Han-dynasty example[2] rather than from the high-shouldered Warring States version.[3] The artist of this vase streamlined its form by moving the handles upward to the base of the neck, by substituting a low, platform base for the tall, angular foot of late Bronze Age examples, and by integrating the small base into the organic flow of the vessel's profile. Even the flattened, windswept elephant-head handles reflect the streamlined style, their vertical stripes echoing the outlines of the C-horns that crown the *taotie* mask below. The vase finds counterparts in lacquerware from the late Ming and early Qing periods, such as the black lacquer *fanghu* vase with decoration inlaid in mother-of-pearl in the Florence and Herbert Irving Collection;[4] with its conventional *pushou*-mask handles and tall, vertical foot set off from the body, however, the Irving vase likely dates several decades earlier than the Clague bronze.

The elephant-head handles are a charming feature of this vase. Apparently native to China, elephants captured the imagination of the Shang people, who used their ivory tusks as a material for carving and who occasionally represented them on their bronzes, even basing several famous ritual wine vessels on the elephant's bulky form.[5] Oracle bone inscriptions from the time also include a character for 'elephant,' the ancestor of the character in use today. Overzealous hunting led to the disappearance of the elephant by Zhou times, so that it seldom appears in the arts of the Warring States and Han periods. The Buddhist church reintroduced the elephant to Chinese art in the early centuries of our era, as it introduced the lion [see 14]. While the lion was considered the proper mount (*vahana*) for the Bodhisattva Mañjuśrī (Chinese, Wenshu pusa), the elephant – in particular, a six-tusked, white elephant – was regarded as the appropriate vehicle for the Bodhisattva Samantabhadra (Chinese, Puxian pusa). In addition, the Buddha's mother, Queen Maya, dreamt that at the moment of her son's conception a small white elephant entered her side. An emblem of royalty in India, the elephant played an important role in Buddhist symbolism and came to hold an important place in East Asian Buddhist art. Although the elephant appears in Chinese Buddhist painting, in Tang-dynasty wall paintings at Tunhuang, for example, and although it occasionally turns up in the inhabited vine scrolls on Tang silver,[6] it never garnered the same widespread popularity as the lion in the secular arts. Beginning in the Song and Yuan periods, however, the taste for ornament led designers of both bronzes[7] and ceramics[8] occasionally to fashion handles in the form of elephant heads, their trunks supporting decorative rings. Although the handles on this vase resemble feline heads, the triangular ears and flattened, almond-shaped eyes identify them as elephant heads.

The decorative scheme on this vase continues the trends, noted in seventeenth-century works [compare 15], toward ornamentation and complexity, increasing the number of masks on each face to three and presenting the masks in a florid style but without *leiwen* backgrounds. In addition, the decorative scheme introduces a note of playful ambiguity, such that the central mask on each side can be read in two ways: as a single, frontal *taotie* mask and as a pair of large-eyed, parrot-beaked birds seen in profile. Disconcerting in a frontal mask, the eyes with their off-center pupils encourage the reading of the motifs as confronting birds. Even the principal *taotie*'s unusually shaped (and seemingly mustachioed) upper lip can be read as wings associated with the avian heads. With this double entendre, the vessel cleverly refers to two prominent decorative motifs from high antiquity, *taotie* masks from the Shang and birds from the early Western Zhou. Although Chinese artists had created items for the scholar's studio in the form of visual puns that could be read two ways at least since the mid-Ming,[9] such liberties probably were not taken with the *taotie* mask until the Qing. In like manner, the upper mask on the handleless sides can also be read in two ways: as a single, frontal *taotie* mask and as a pair of confronting, bovine-like *kui*-dragon heads; in this case, the added crescent within the eye favors the reading as two confronting *kui* dragons. On the other two sides, the elephant heads have been so well integrated into the overall design that the inlay work surrounds and borders them and complements their shapes. The band of interlocked T's that embellishes the lip of this vase recalls the similar band at the base of the *taotie* mask on the previous censer [16]; the band at the bottom of this vase has shorter stems.

Tradition would assign this vase to the early to mid-Qing period, based on its all-over decorative scheme inlaid solely in fine silver wire[10] [see discussion, 16]. The absence of securely dated comparative material renders precise dating impossible, but the attenuated form with its elegant profile and well integrated base finds a counterpart in a small Dehua *fanghu*-shaped vase of the eighteenth century.[11] The exquisite craft favors an eighteenth-century date, as does the playful interpretation of both the masks and the elephant-head handles. The masks resemble those on Qianlong-era jades, the resemblance especially cogent because of the elimination of the *leiwen* ground. Following standard Ming convention, the previous vessel [16] furnishes each border with a different ornamental design; with its interlocked T's at top and bottom, however, this vase embraces the eighteenth-century taste for formalized borders in recurring patterns. The previous vessel also reveals its seventeenth-century origins in the use of a concentric circle within the iris to represent the pupil of the eye; as noted above, the off-center placement of the pupils in the principal masks of the present vase reflect eighteenth-century whimsy.

18 Long-necked Circular Vase
with angled shoulder and with bamboo, rock, and bat decor

Qing dynasty, eighteenth – nineteenth century
Cast bronze with decoration inlaid in silver wire and with a mark inlaid in
silver wire in clerical-script (*lishu*) characters reading *Shisou* on the base
11.0 centimeter height
Clague Collection Number 219

S TANDING ON A SMALL CIRCULAR FOOT, this diminutive vase has a cylindrical body whose walls expand ever so gently at its top to receive the angled shoulder; a tall, subtly flaring neck rises from the shoulder's crown, a relief rib clearly segregating neck from shoulder. Three raised ribs encircle the neck a third of the way up from its base. The body of the vessel features a scene of bamboo growing beside a rock, the simplified design inlaid in silver wire against an unembellished ground; the shoulder features four bats in flight, their wings spread, their heads pointing upward. Its silver inlay now partly missing, a single bowstring line borders the lower edge of the cylindrical body, while another highlights the central rib on the neck. The flat, shallow base has at its center a mark reading *Shisou* in two *lishu* (clerical-script) characters; inlaid in silver wire, the mark is large in proportion to the base. The surface color is that of aged but untreated bronze, though the possibility of enhancement after casting is not ruled out. Although the artisan who made this bronze has exercised every effort to convey the impression of integral casting, the rib at the top of the shoulder no doubt conceals the join of a separately cast neck and body.

Like those on the two previous vessels [16, 17], the mark on this vase claims it to be the work of Shisou, the putative late Ming craftsman re- nowned for bronzes elegantly inlaid with designs in silver wire. Although the technique of this vase accords with conventional descriptions of Shisou's work, the assertiveness of the rather large mark would seem at odds with traditional descriptions of his signatures as refined and stately. In the Shisou manner, this vase is no doubt later than the previous two pieces and per- haps dates to the late eighteenth or nineteenth century.

The Chinese had produced small bottles and vases in a variety of shapes since remote antiquity, but most such bottles of pre-Qing date have round or pear-shaped bodies rather than cylindrical ones with angled shoulders.[1] During the Song dynasty, the *guan*, Ru and Longquan kilns introduced a family of larger ceramic bottles with long necks, straight sides, and flat or angled shoulders[2] that might have served as the distant model for this bronze; such Song-dynasty bottles lack the dramatic profile of this vase with its long, ribbed neck, however, and they have flat or gently inclined shoulders rather than the steeply pitched, bowed variety seen here. In fact, it was only in the Qing that small bottles for the scholar's table began to appear in quantity in both bronze and ceramic ware. In that context, this bronze would find parallels, though not exact counter- parts, among the small vases of the so-called 'eight objects for the writing table' that soared to popularity late in the Kangxi period.[3] (Crafted in porcelain, the 'eight objects' include a seal-paste container, a brush washer, water coupes of two varieties, and small vases of four different shapes; connoisseurs have traditionally favored those with peachbloom glaze.) Of the four vase types standard among the 'eight objects,' two have elongated necks and one has relief ribs at the base of the neck;[4] one of the long-necked vases also has an inclined shoulder. The shape thus argues for a date no earlier than the eighteenth century for this small vase.

Thanks to praise showered upon it by Confucius, bamboo came to be admired for its resilience, standing as a symbol of uprightness and strength-in-weakness.[5] Because it retains its leaves the year round, even during the cold winter months, bamboo was also regarded as an emblem of strength in the face of adversity. In addition, bamboo was thought to mirror the virtues of the *junzi*, or Confucian gentleman, so it was the perfect symbol for the literati,[6] and thus an appropriate motif for items destined for the scholar's desk, such as this small water container.

The association of ink bamboo painting with the literati began in the Northern Song with such masters as Su Shi (1037-1101) and his distant cousin, Wen Tong (1018/19-1079). In bamboo these artists found an ideal vehicle for the expression of feelings through descriptive but highly calligraphic brushwork. Ink bamboo rose to prominence during the early Yuan in the works of such painters as Zhao Mengfu (1254-1322) and Li Kan (1245-1320), and had become a fully established idiom by the closing years of the dynasty; such paintings typically represent a clump of bamboo growing beside a rock, the clear ancestor of the scene depicted on this vase. In the Ming and Qing periods this interest in bamboo not only led a number of artists to specialize in bamboo painting but also sparked the desire for scholars' accoutrements crafted in bamboo[7] [compare 31].

Popular as the subject of painting on paper and silk since Song times, bamboo did not find a role as a principal motif in the decorative arts until the Qing dynasty,[8] though it had occasionally appeared alongside other plants, especially as one of the 'Three Friends of Winter,' since the Yuan and early Ming[9] [see 14]. With clusters of three leaves branching from a stalk composed of a single line, the bamboo has been depicted in a very direct fashion on this vase; its unostentatious presentation contrasts with the more complex treatment of the bamboo on a Shisou-marked ink stick stand in the Victoria and Albert Museum, London, in which leaves overlap and in which the sections of the bamboo stalk are individually outlined.[10]

Seldom depicted before the Qing, the bat is another motif that became ubiquitous in the decorative arts of late imperial China.[11] Its popularity stems not from any ancient classical associations but from a coincidence involving the pronunciation of its name, *fu*: in Mandarin Chinese, the characters for 'bat' and 'good fortune' are homonyms, having exactly the same pronunciation, but different written form.[12] With the Qing fascination with symbols, the bat appeared in the decorative arts with increasing frequency as a rebus, or visual pun, wishing the viewer 'good fortune.' The same cultural phenomenon that gave rise to the *taotie* masks on the previous vessel that can be read in two different ways [17] has here expressed itself in a penchant for puns and rebuses.

Although vessel shape and decorative style both indicate a Qing date for this vase, precise dating remains elusive. In relative terms, the simple decorative scheme, the direct, unpretentious drawing, the lack of formal borders, and the willingness to leave a large proportion of the surface undecorated suggest that this vase is later than the previous example. Since an attribution to the eighteenth century has been proposed for the previous example, perhaps an attribution to the eighteenth to nineteenth-century period would not be inappropriate for this one.[13]

19 Circular Foliate Censer with lotus decor

Ming dynasty, second half sixteenth century
Cast bronze with cast and appliqué decoration and with cold-worked details
11.4 centimeter diameter
Clague Collection Number 237

UNUSUAL AMONG MING BRONZES, this lobed, circular censer was cast in the form of a flower, its six lobes suggesting overlapping petals. The censer's most striking feature is its base, which is as beautifully and meticulously decorated as its sides; cast in the form of a mallow blossom, the base has six petals whose tips fold over on themselves and whose S-curved profiles impart a sense of rotary motion to the design. Imitating petals, the comma-shaped lobes on the side of the censer spring from the flower on the base and grow upward in a swirling fashion, culminating in the horizontal, elliptical forms that represent petal tops. The lobes' surfaces are inclined; each petal top is higher at its (proper) right than at its left, the gradation in height suggesting the petals' overlap. Bowed forms along the tops and bottoms of the lobes represent petal edges folding over on themselves, exactly as on the base. A collar of chrysanthemum petals encircles the base of the short, vertical neck, the round tipped petals enclosed by relief outlines. Cast separately and attached with pins, a lotus spray graces each relief lobe, the spray including a blossom in the center, a bud at the right, and a leaf in profile at the left. Bound with a ribbon a short distance below the bouquet head, three cut stalks follow the median line of each lobe to the base. The lightly mottled surface has assumed a warm reddish brown hue, perhaps naturally, perhaps through treatment after casting.

This censer derives ultimately from a dish whose walls were shaped to resemble flower petals; originating in Tang gold and silver, dishes with petaled walls soared to popularity in Song and Yuan lacquer and ceramic ware. An early example, a silver gilt cup stand excavated from a Tang-dynasty site at Xi'an, Shanxi province, has its rim shaped to resemble a blossom, its six petals radiating outward from the central well;[1] although the straight-sided petals do not overlap, their upper edges fold over on themselves, in the same manner as those on the present censer. Ceramics[2] and lacquerwares[3] began to incorporate mallow-petal forms into their walls in the Song dynasty, sometimes imparting an S-curve to the petal edges to suggest overlapping and perhaps also to suggest motion. By the fourteenth century the mallow blossom was appearing with great frequency in both architecture and the decorative arts.[4] In fact, the blossom on the base of this censer resembles in form ones that embellish the Juyong Gate outside Beijing,[5] a structure dedicated in 1345; although the flowers differ in detail – the Juyong Gate blossoms have elaborate outlines and their petals do not fold over on themselves – their unusual tripartite centers are virtually identical. In delicacy of interpretation, the mallow blossom on the base of this censer recalls the flowers on Ming carved lacquerware.[6]

By the Yuan and Ming periods, fashion dictated that ceramics, jades, and lacquers, not to mention works in a variety of other materials, be well finished on their undersides; in fact, the finest works of the day often display bases as intricately finished as their more readily visible upper surfaces, even works in jade and lacquer.[7] The exquisitely finished flower on the base of this censer finds its closest counterparts in the related flowers that sometimes ornament the bases of works from the mid-Ming period. Produced during the second half of the sixteenth century, a carved red lacquer bowl, formerly in the collection of Sir Harry Garner, London, has a flower at the center of its base, the blossom with twelve overlapping petals;[8] and a late sixteenth-century cloisonné basin, formerly in the Clague Collection and now in the Phoenix Art Museum, has a flower at the center of its broad base, the elaborate blossom with two tiers of overlapping petals, seven in the inner ring and nine in the outer one.[9] Such pieces permit an attribution to the second half of the sixteenth century for this censer.

Native to China, the lotus, which decorates the walls of this censer, was celebrated in the ancient poetry of the *Shijing*, or Book of Songs, but its appearance in the visual arts had to await the coming of the Han, when it was occasionally depicted in pictorial tiles, especially ones from Sichuan province.[10] Even so, it was only with the rise of the Buddhist church in the early centuries of our era that the lotus became a staple of Chinese art. A symbol of the church and its teachings,[11] the lotus figures prominently in Buddhist art, appearing in altar vases, in the hands of bodhisattvas, in the borders surrounding images of deities, and, most conspicuously, in the form of the bases on which deities stand or sit. In the secular arts, the lotus was regarded as an emblem of purity and perfection. One of the 'flowers of the four seasons,' the lotus symbolizes summer, standing alongside the peony, chrysanthemum, and plum, which symbolize, respectively, spring, autumn, and winter. In addition, the lotus also symbolizes the seventh month in the Chinese calendar (generally corresponding to August in the Western calendar) and the mallow, whose form the censer imitates, stands for the ninth month (corresponding to October).

The lotus had been introduced into mainstream secular arts by the Southern Dynasties period, appearing occasionally as decoration in fifth- and sixth-century celadon vessels from the Yue kilns;[12] by the Tang dynasty, the lotus frequently appeared on articles of gold and silver,[13] and by the

Song, it had become the most popular decorative motif on ceramic ware.[14] During the Xuande reign of the Ming dynasty, a lotus spray was featured as the principal decorative motif on a series of large blue-and-white dishes; their cut stalks tied with a ribbon, the bouquets include a bud, a blossom, a seed pod, and a leaf, representing a complete cycle of life.[15] The lotus bouquets on the early fifteenth-century blue-and-white porcelain dishes are presumably the direct inspiration for the bouquets applied to the lobes of the Clague censer, especially since early Ming porcelains were already highly prized by the sixteenth century. In addition, secular artists of the sixteenth century included the lotus among their depictions on paper and silk, as in the brilliantly colored handscroll of lotuses by Chen Shun (1483-1544) in the Nelson-Atkins Museum of Art, Kansas City,[16] and such specialists in the art of flower arranging as Zhang Chou (1577-1643?), the well known late Ming collector/connoisseur/critic of Chinese painting, advocated its inclusion in certain types of arrangements.[17]

In typical mid- and late Ming fashion, the artist employed both casting and cold-working techniques in creating this censer. The vessel was integrally cast with its floral base, relief lobes, chrysanthemum collar, and short neck. The lotus bouquets were cast separately and attached with rivets, the rivets' flattened heads visible on the interior. Minor finishing details were engraved after casting – the veins in the petals of the mallow blossom on the base, for example, and the veins in the leaves, buds, and blossoms of the lotus bouquets.

20 Rectangular Fangding-shaped Censer

with four cabriole legs and two twisted-rope handles and with eight
auspicious emblems (*bajixiang*) decor

Ming dynasty, late sixteenth – early seventeenth century
Cast bronze with cast decoration with cold-worked details and with a cast
thread-relief mark in standard-script (*kaishu*) characters reading *Da Ming
Xuandenian zhi* in a recessed rectangular cartouche on the base
8.3 centimeter width
Clague Collection Number 204

O F RECTANGULAR FORM with rounded corners and convex sides, this small censer stands on four cabriole legs. A loop handle in the form of three intertwined filaments resembling twisted rope rises from the flattened lip of each short side. A narrow raised band with ten hemispherical bosses borders the top of the censer; an identical one surrounds the base. The censer's bulging sides sport the 'Eight Auspicious Emblems,' or *bajixiang* – wheel, conch shell, canopy, umbrella, flower, covered jar, double fish, and endless knot – arranged with one emblem in the center of each side and one on each rounded corner. At the center of the otherwise plain, flat base is a cast mark in six thread-relief *kaishu* (standard-script) characters arranged in three columns in a recessed rectangular cartouche, the ground of which has been darkened to enhance legibility. All elements of the censer were integrally cast, with only minimal cold working after casting.

Like two censers previously discussed [15, 16], this censer and the five following ones [21-25] bear marks claiming they were made during the Xuande reign of the Ming dynasty. All six censers in this group have the standard Xuande mark reading *Da Ming Xuandenian zhi* – except number 25, whose mark reads *Da Ming Xuandenian zao* – arranged in three columns of two characters each. Although each mark incorporates the basic Xuande conventions discussed in entry fifteen, each includes elements that betray its later origin. The two censers previously discussed were very likely inspired by Xuande censers or copies of them; the present examples, by contrast, are far enough removed in style from Xuande bronzes that they must be regarded as fanciful interpretations: some doubtless descend from the Xuande tradition through a series of intermediate copies or through woodblock-printed illustrations in such catalogs as *Xuande yiqi tupu*; others are hybrids, combining elements from Xuande bronzes with elements from other traditions; yet others are simply fabrications with little, if any, connection to the Xuande tradition, except the mark. A late sixteenth or early seventeenth-century work, the present censer falls into the category of hybrids, drawing its bosses and twisted-rope handles from Xuande bronzes but its shape and decorative scheme from other sources.

The shape of this censer derives ultimately from a square *ding*, or *fangding*, a rectangular cauldron which, during the Bronze Age, was used for boiling grain.[1] *Fangding* from the Shang dynasty virtually always have angular corners, but ones from the Western Zhou sometimes employ rounded corners.[2] Although circular *ding* of Western Zhou date occasionally rest on cabriole legs, *fangding* of the period stand on columnar legs whose height typically approximates that of the vessel's body. Though this censer descends from classical models, its squat proportions, cabriole legs, and decorative scheme distinguish it as a work of the Ming dynasty.

The 1526 *Xuande yiqi tupu* depicts three rectangular censers with angular corners and one covered *fangding* with rounded corners and cabriole legs.[3] Although it might descend from the covered *fangding* with rounded corners or from a type not illustrated – since *Xuande yiqi tupu* illustrates only a selection of all the different Xuande shapes – the Clague censer, with its short legs, bulging sides, and squat proportions, reflects a late Ming interpretation of the shape. The bosses and handles definitely derive from Xuande bronzes, however, as evinced by depictions in *Xuande yiqi tupu* that show *li* tripod censers with rope-like handles[4] and low, circular censers with convex sides bordered top and bottom by a band of bosses.[5]

Though used only infrequently in antiquity, rope-like handles have an ancient lineage in China, stretching back to the Neolithic era as attested by the white earthenware ewers of vaguely zoömorphic form produced on the Shandong peninsula between 2400 and 2000 BC by potters of the Longshan Culture.[6] Bail handles imitating twisted rope sometimes appear on Shang-dynasty wine vessels,[7] and loop handles resembling twisted rope occasionally grace Zhou-dynasty *ding* and *li* tripod food vessels,[8] the certain, if distantly removed, *locus classicus* for the handles on this censer. Although only a few Song and Yuan ceramics[9] have rope-like handles, they are standard fare on Yuan bronzes,[10] as witnessed by those recovered from the Chinese merchant ship that sank off the coast of Sinan, Republic of Korea, in 1323. As noted above, *Xuande yiqi tupu* reveals that twisted-rope handles were used during the Xuande period, though it does not establish whether they were inherited from Yuan bronzes or adopted from ancient vessels (perhaps via depictions in Song catalogs). Reflecting the far-reaching influence of Xuande bronzes, Ming and Qing censers in cloisonné enamel[11] and Dehua porcelain[12] (so-called blanc-de-Chine ware) sometimes have rope-like handles, paired, in most cases, with the elegantly streamlined body types associated with Xuande censers.

Although they sometimes appear as the principal decoration on Bronze Age vessels,[13] bosses first found popularity as border decoration in the narcissus-bulb bowls and flowerpot basins produced by the Jun[14] and Longquan[15] kilns in the Song, Yuan, and early Ming periods. Jun ware basins typically have their bosses set in a band, suggesting that they are the likely source for the bosses on Xuande censers and, thus, for those on the Clague censer. Uncommon on early Ming porcelains from Jingdezhen, bosses occasionally appear on mid- and late Ming blue-and-white wares, usually as border decoration,[16] providing a late Ming context for the Clague censer.

The 'Eight Auspicious Emblems,' or *bajixiang*, ornament the sides of this censer.[17] Popular in the Ming and Qing periods, the motif was introduced to Chinese art from Tibetan Buddhism during the Yuan dynasty; it appears occasionally on Jingdezhen porcelains and Longquan celadons of the day.[18] Best known as an ornamental motif in the decorative arts, the 'Eight Auspicious Emblems' were also fashioned independently as small sculptures in porcelain, gilt bronze, and cloisonné enamel[19] for placement on Buddhist altars or in three-dimensional Buddhist *mandalas* (cosmological diagrams). Although they vary considerably in Yuan-dynasty depictions,[20] both the emblems constituting the motif and their order of appearance had been standardized by Ming times as follows:

> wheel (*lun*) symbolizing the Wheel of the Law (*falun*) and thus the Buddha and his teachings
>
> conch shell (*luo*) symbolizing majesty, felicitous travel, and the voice of the Buddha
>
> canopy (*chuang*) symbolizing spiritual authority, reverence, and purity
>
> umbrella (*san* or *gai*) symbolizing royal grace
>
> flower (*hua*) symbolizing truth, purity, and creative power
>
> vase or jar (*ping*) symbolizing eternal harmony, abundant blessings, and ultimate triumph over birth and death
>
> double fish (*yu*) symbolizing fertility, abundance, conjugal happiness, and protection against evil
>
> endless knot (*jie*) symbolizing longevity, eternity, and receipt of the Buddha's assistance.[21]

Even though the emblems and their order were prescribed by the Ming, their styles changed over time, providing clues vital for dating. The emblems on the Clague censer correspond exactly to those on Wanli-period blue-and-white porcelains, confirming its late sixteenth- or early seventeenth-century date.[22] In particular, the wheel, with its eight spokes oriented toward the points of the compass, is identical to those on Wanli porcelains. The flower is the lotus, which was regularly used until the late seventeenth century after which it was often replaced by a peony [compare 22]; in Wanli fashion, the lotus is presented as an eight-petaled 'foreign lotus,' or *fanlian*, a stylized flower whose jewel-shaped center is exposed and whose pointed petals have the characteristic interior drawing seen in the Clague example.

Qing-dynasty representations of the 'foreign lotus' tend to have both a greater number of petals and a longer stalk with several leaves.[23] In Wanli fashion, the jar is interpreted as a *guan* with a lotus-leaf-shaped cover, a *pushou*-mask handle on its shoulder, and a ring of bosses around its base. In Qing-dynasty examples, the jar tends to be ornamental rather than utilitarian, having a distinct footring as well as surface decoration[24] [compare 22]. One of several umbrella types, the jeweled umbrella first appeared during the Yongle era but remained popular throughout the Ming and Qing; the fashioning of the tops of the umbrella and the canopy to resemble a lotus leaf – thus making them harmonize with the lotus blossom and with the cover of the *guan* jar – also points to a late Ming date for this censer. In addition, the Clague censer follows late Ming fashion in setting the emblems against an unembellished background, omitting the fluttering ribbons associated with eighteenth-century representations [compare 22] and the floral scrolls typical of nineteenth-century depictions.

It remains uncertain whether Xuande censers were ever ornamented with the 'Eight Auspicious Emblems.' Logic would argue that they were not, since such censers were supposedly modeled on Song aristocratic ceramics and on representations of archaic bronzes in Song catalogs, neither of which carried the 'Eight Auspicious Emblems' motif. In addition, *Xuande yiqi tupu* does not picture any bronzes with the *bajixiang* motif nor does *Xuande dingyi pu* list any with a motif so named. Still, *Xuande dingyi pu* mentions,[25] and *Xuande yiqi tupu* illustrates,[26] censers decorated with *siddham* (auspicious Buddhist syllables written in an Indic script), indicating that Xuande censers were sometimes embellished with Buddhist motifs; in addition, Xuande blue-and-white porcelains[27] occasionally depict the 'Eight Auspicious Emblems,' so it is possible, even if unlikely, that Xuande bronzes might have featured them as well. Wen Zhenheng's comment in his *Zhangwu zhi* of 1637 that bronze censers with *bajixiang* decoration are vulgar and thus to be avoided in the scholar's studio[28] indicates that such items were both plentiful and popular by the early seventeenth century.

21 Covered Rectangular Censer

with two lion-head handles and with decoration of imaginary beasts against waves, the cover with dragons and phoenixes amidst clouds

Qing dynasty, Kangxi period (1662-1722)
Cast bronze with cast decoration, with cold-worked details, and with a cast thread-relief mark in standard-script (*kaishu*) characters reading *Da Ming Xuandenian zhi* in a recessed rectangular cartouche on the base
15.8 centimeter diameter
Provenance: Dr Sidney Smith, Cambridge, England
Clague Collection Number 244

T HE BOWL OF THIS COVERED RECTANGULAR CENSER rests on a
rectangular foot with rounded corners, the angled lower portion of
the foot with a panel of descending lotus petals, the constricted
upper one with a plain vertical wall. The sides of the bowl rise steeply
from the flat floor to the short, undecorated lip that flares and then resolves
itself in a flat rim that supports the cover. Attached with rivets on the
short ends of the bowl, separately cast handles in the form of lion heads
with curly manes and *ruyi*-shaped noses originally clutched moveable
rings, the butts of the now-lost rings secured in the deep circular recesses
at the ends of the lions' mouths. A tall, rectangular, domed cover with
openwork decoration completes the censer; the cover's walls rise vertically
from the unpierced, skirt-like lip and then turn inward to culminate in the
large, centrally placed, hollow knob whose openwork walls are integral with
those of the cover. A scene of frolicking sea creatures, or *haishou*, enlivens
the bowl of the censer, the high-relief creatures set against a low-relief
pattern of undulating waves, the form of the waves emphasized by incised
ripples. The *haishou* include one fish and ten feline-like animals, the animals
dispersed five to a side, the single fish appearing under one handle. The
bodies of only three animals rise fully above the waves, the waters concealing the others to one degree or another. Their tiger-like bodies varying
little, the playful animals sport a variety of maned and unmaned heads,
from feline heads with blunt snouts, to elephant heads with long, curling
trunks, to sleek, porpoise-like heads with short snouts. A single *haishou*
appears in profile at the center of each long side, its body fully above the
waves, its legs in the 'full gallop' position used in Chinese art since antiquity to convey the impression of swift motion; the other four animals of
each group appear more or less in the corners of their respective sides, each
moving animatedly toward the animal in the center. The animal in the lower
right corner of each side emerges from an indented whirlpool immediately
in front of the central animal, the spiraling waves of the whirlpool bordered
by a ring of whitecaps. Breakers form throughout and cloud heads appear
at intervals along the top. The waters of the bowl, with their amusing *haishou*,
are merely a backdrop for the auspicious dragons and phoenixes that appear
amidst the clouds of the cover, however. One four-clawed *mang* dragon
dominates each long side of the cover, and one phoenix in flight each short
end. A study in opposites, the cover presents a series of complementary
motifs: one dragon with mouth open, the other with mouth closed; one
dragon with claws exposed and the other with claws concealed amidst the

openwork pattern of the scrolling clouds; one phoenix (male) with elaborate tail, heavily feathered neck, and extended claws, the other (female) with bipartite tail, ornamented neck, and retracted claws; and one phoenix shown from above (the male) and the other from below (the female). The coiled closed-mouthed dragon that forms the knob extends one four-clawed foot but conceals the other. A mark with six, thread-relief, *kaishu* (standard-script) characters arranged in three columns appears in a sunken rectangular cartouche in the center of the flat base; the base and interior of the foot-ring are otherwise plain. The darkened interior of the censer is undecorated, though each long side reveals one protuberance corresponding to the whirl-pool on the exterior, the result of indenting the whirlpool by force after casting. The interior of the cover is plain, the interior of the knob visible through the circular opening at its base; a short vertical flange for securing the cover on the bowl encircles the inner edge of the cover's wide flat rim. Traces of rust-brown material on the handles and in the hollows and recesses of the design suggest that the censer and its cover may have been coated at some point to make its brassy surfaces resemble aged bronze.

This censer owes little, if anything, to the Xuande tradition other than its six character mark. Although it pictures several covered vessels[1] and several rectangular ones,[2] *Xuande yiqi tupu* illustrates no rectangular censers with rounded corners resting on a continuous ring foot. The closest parallels to the Clague censer among archaic bronzes are covered, rectangular *xu* vessels, which during the late Western Zhou period served as ritual food containers.[3] Most *xu* vessels have four, short, band-like legs that follow the corners' curvature, but a few boast a short, continuous ring foot of a type that might have inspired the one on this piece.[4] Although *xu* vessels were occasionally imitated in cloisonné enamel during the Qing dynasty,[5] suggesting that the vessel type was known, a relationship between such ancient bronzes and censers of this type remains to be proven. Many Ming-dynasty censers had covers, more than surviving numbers might indicate since many have been lost, but the use of covers increased dramatically during the Qing; openwork covers not only created interesting patterns in the rising smoke but afforded a measure of protection from fire by preventing burning embers from popping out of the censer.

The decorative scheme on this censer evolved from the depictions of dragons and sea creatures (*haishou*) frolicking amidst waves that enliven Ming ceramics and bronzes [12]. In Ming examples, the dragon, whether *feiyu* fish-dragon or standard *long*, is typically set against an undulating sea and surrounded by auspicious sea creatures of some size but, in hierarchical fashion, always smaller than the dragon.[6] In other cases, a horizontally oriented dragon may stride above rolling waves, but as the principal motif, the dragon appears on the vessel itself rather than on the cover.[7] In early Qing examples, as illustrated by this censer, dragons often appear on the cover, amidst the clouds, while sea animals romp in the waters below, the playful creatures having little in common with the serious beasts on Ming ceramics and bronzes. Reflecting the Qing-dynasty interest in cosmological symbolism, Qing decorative arts give new importance to the pairing of complementary opposites, manifested here in the combining of clouds and water, symbolizing heaven and earth; dragons and phoenixes, symbolizing *yang* and *yin*, the male and female forces of the universe; male phoenix (*feng*) and female phoenix (*huang*), symbolizing the duality of life; concealed dragon claws and exposed dragon claws, symbolizing esoteric and exoteric knowledge; open dragon mouth and closed dragon mouth, symbolizing 'ah' and 'om,' the Buddhist mystical syllables that reverberate through the universe, thus animating it.

Introduced to Chinese art from Tibetan Buddhism during the Yuan dynasty, borders comprising squared lotus petals with straight sides, flattened tops, and rounded corners frequently appear on fourteenth-century architectural monuments[8] and blue-and-white porcelains,[9] not to mention on the daises of deities pictured in the frontispieces of fourteenth-century, woodblock-printed Buddhist sutras.[10] The motif graces Buddhist sculptures[11] and sacred texts[12] of the early Ming period, and it often ornaments the borders of imperial porcelains from the late fourteenth and early fifteenth centuries onward.[13] A Wanli-period carved red lacquer bowl, dated to 1589 and now in the Florence and Herbert Irving Collection, has above its foot a panel of rising lotus petals that would seem to be the ancestor of the panel on the Clague censer.[14] Such lotus-petal borders are a standard feature of Sino-Tibetan Buddhist sculpture of the seventeenth and eighteenth centuries.[15]

During his visit to the Clague Collection on 7 June 1992, Yang Boda, Deputy Director Emeritus of the Palace Museum, Beijing, noted that there are numerous Kangxi-period censers of identical shape, decoration, and style in the Qing Palace Collection, confirming this censer's date of manufacture. He further commented that such censers exhibit considerable variation in size and surface color.

It should also be pointed out that the particular combination of dragons and small, playful sea creatures pictured here is a feature of the Kangxi period; Ming-dynasty examples usually surround the dragon with a variety of larger animals of more serious demeanor, while Qianlong examples typically eliminate the sea creatures entirely, sometimes replacing them with additional dragons.[16] In addition, the sea creatures recall Kangxi-period jade animals in style, their smooth surfaces lacking both the detailed texturing of the late Ming and the fine points and sharp angles of the Qianlong era.[17]

22 Circular Censer

with three cabriole legs and two lion-head handles and with eight
auspicious emblems (*bajixiang*) decor

Qing dynasty, Qianlong period (1736-95)
Cast bronze with cold-worked decoration, with induced surface color, and
with a chiseled relief mark in standard-script (*kaishu*) characters reading
Da Ming Xuandenian zhi in a recessed rectangular cartouche on the base
12.4 centimeter diameter
Clague Collection Number 215

STANDING ON THREE CABRIOLE LEGS, this circular, flat-bottomed
censer has a wide bowl with gracefully curved walls, its profile resembling a set of parentheses. Handles in the form of maned lion heads
appear at right and left, well positioned in relation to the legs. Set within
a narrow band, a beaded border encircles the base, while its mate enlivens
the subtly constricted neck. Around its exterior, the bowl sports decoration
of eight auspicious objects linked together by fluttering ribbons: a crackle-
glazed jar, a curtained and fringed umbrella with a jewel at its top, a tiered
and fringed canopy with a circular jewel at its crown, a peony blossom, a
pair of wheels, two fish, an endless knot, and a final object that resembles
a tiered canopy with a jewel at its tip but that is perhaps a conch shell. A
stylized cloud scroll ornaments the bulbous portion of each cabriole leg.
The broad, plain base has at its center a carved mark in six *kaishu* (standard-script) characters arranged in three columns within a recessed
rectangular cartouche. The interior of the censer is undecorated, as are
the backs and undersides of the legs. Resembling a patina, the warm rust-
brown color was likely induced through chemical treatment after casting.

   This vessel derives from a Xuande bronze that *Xuande yiqi tupu*
terms a *gudun lu* (squat-drum-shaped censer) and pictures as a circular,
flat-bottomed container with short bulging walls, three cabriole legs, and
two lion-head handles.[1] Undecorated, the censer illustrated has around its
neck and base a border of small bosses centered in a narrow relief band
[compare 20] that might have inspired the beaded borders on the Clague
censer. Although it does not figure prominently among the border ornaments of Qing bronze vessels, beading typically appears at the tops and
bottoms of the lotus bases of eighteenth-century Sino-Tibetan bronze
sculptures of Buddhist deities,[2] which might have inspired the designer of
this bronze to transform the Xuande bosses into a row of continuous beading.

   As previously noted, many Xuande censers were based on ceramic
forms created in the Song and Yuan dynasties. The ultimate source for
both this censer and its Xuande model is not an archaic bronze but a
narcissus-bulb bowl or flowerpot basin of the type produced at the Jun[3]
and Longquan[4] kilns in the Song, Yuan, and early Ming periods. Although
they lack handles and stand on cloud-scroll feet rather than on cabriole
legs, such elegant accessories for growing plants typically have a low
circular body that rises from a flat bottom supported by three legs and
that often includes a band of bosses below the mouth.

A rather free rendition of the 'Eight Auspicious Emblems,' or *bajixiang*, ornaments the walls of this censer. Introduced to Chinese art from Tibetan Buddhism in the Yuan dynasty, the motif gained a measure of popularity in the decorative arts in the Ming and Qing periods [see discussion, 20]. On this censer, the order of the emblems varies considerably from that established in the Ming, and the conch shell has been replaced by – or perhaps drawn to resemble – a canopy, either through a misunderstanding of the motif or, more likely, through a nonchalant approach to the decoration.

In style, the emblems on this censer find their closest counterparts in the similar emblems on Qianlong porcelains,[5] confirming the censer's eighteenth-century date. In Qianlong fashion, a peony replaces the lotus, which had been used almost exclusively well into the seventeenth century; the jar has a crackled glaze – popular in the Southern Song period and again in the mid-Qing; the umbrella has decorative curtains embellished with cloud scrolls suspended from its tiered crown; and both the umbrella and the canopy have fringed lower edges. Also in Qianlong style, ribbons flutter about each emblem in symmetrical fashion, as if brought to life by a breeze, creating a festive atmosphere and, like rays emanating from a charm, symbolizing the magical powers associated with the emblems.[6]

The bowl, legs, handles, and borders of this censer were integrally cast, but the Xuande mark and the decorative scheme were cold worked after casting as indicated by the chatter marks visible especially in the ribbons. Although the decorative elements appear to stand above the background in slight relief, their surfaces are actually the same height as the background; the illusion of relief derives from the wide, sunken outlines whose beveled outer edges make the objects they surround appear to rise in relief. Long employed in the ceramic tradition, beveled outlines play a role in the decoration of Five Dynasties and Song ceramics, especially in Yue[7] and Yaozhou[8] wares.

23 Circular Ding-shaped Censer
with three columnar legs and two ring handles

Qing dynasty, probably eighteenth century
Cast bronze with cast and cold-worked decoration, induced surface color,
and a chiseled relief mark in standard-script (*kaishu*) characters reading
Da Ming Xuandenian zhi in a recessed rectangular cartouche on the base
7.9 centimeter height
Clague Collection Number 256

STANDING ON THREE COLUMNAR LEGS, this small, unassuming censer has a stepped cylindrical bowl with a shallow, rounded bottom. The bowl's undecorated vertical walls constrict at midpoint to form a narrow, horizontal ledge and then continue their assent upward to the short, vertical lip whose perimeter expands to match the diameter of the bowl's lower portion. A small ledge encircles the interior of the lip, suggesting that the censer might once have had a removeable bronze cover. Appearing at right and left in the recessed channel, handles in the form of simplified lion heads with curly manes anchor the fixed bronze rings that overlap the lower part of the censer. Open on their undersides, the hollow, columnar legs issue from the mouths of maned lion heads that face downward from the lower edge of the bowl. A mark in six *kaishu* (standard-script) characters arranged in three columns of two characters each appears in a recessed rectangular cartouche in the center of the otherwise plain base. The legs are undecorated, as is the interior of the bowl. Chemically induced after casting, the warm chestnut-brown surfaces conceal the brassy color of the metal. In Qianlong style but of uncertain date, a fitted hardwood cover [not shown] with a knob of orange soapstone and a hardwood stand [not shown] with three legs accompany this censer.

Despite its Xuande mark, this censer dates to the Qing dynasty, probably to the eighteenth century; in this case an illustration in the 1526 *Xuande yiqi tupu* confirms that the mark accurately signals descent from Xuande bronzes.[1] Termed a *jingding lu*, or 'wellhead *ding*' censer, the illustrated vessel boasts a stepped cylindrical bowl, an expanding lip, two maned lion-head handle mounts, and three columnar legs. Differing from the Clague piece, its recessed channel, placed higher in proportion to the bowl, constitutes the censer's neck and its horizontal ledge the vessel's shoulder; in addition, its slightly tapering columnar legs descend directly from the bottom of the bowl without animal head mounts, and its lion-head handles – each with a moveable ring – appear on the bowl proper, just below the horizontal shoulder. The similarities underscore the relationship between the two pieces, but the differences clearly indicate that the Clague piece was not copied directly from *Xuande yiqi tupu*. Comments in *Xuande yiqi tupu* indicate that some censers were originally furnished with wooden covers and stands [see discussion, 24].

Although the bowl, legs, and handles of this censer were integrally cast, the handles and leg mounts were extensively cold worked after casting. Both the abbreviated style and the numerous chisel marks indicate that the lion-head handles were given their present form entirely through cold working, having been cast as rounded protuberances, or 'blanks,' ready for the decorator's tools; variations in thickness and other irregularities suggest that the fixed rings at the sides were cast as disks and then carved into rings. The manes and facial details in the legs' lion-head mounts were entirely cold worked.

A paucity of related material hampers precise dating of this censer. It might be noted, however, that the strongly rectilinear form – with its straight sides, angular corners, squared indentation, and short but emphatic lip – finds some parallels in the tall, square-shouldered, porcelain vases produced late in the Kangxi reign with decoration in underglaze cobalt blue, overglaze polychrome enamels,[2] or overglaze gold against a 'powder-blue'[3] or 'mirror-black'[4] ground. The indentation also recalls the squared necks that sometimes occur on late seventeenth- and eighteenth-century porcelain censers from the Dehua kilns.[5] The naturalism of the lion-head leg mounts also points to an eighteenth-century date for this censer, as does the extensive reliance on cold-working techniques for finishing the piece (with even the handles and fixed rings carved after casting).

Tripod vessels rank among the oldest bronze shapes, with clear antecedents in Neolithic pottery. Used mainly for boiling, simmering, and stewing during the Shang and Western Zhou periods,[6] classical *ding* vessels have a circular bowl with a round bottom set atop three legs, the circular mouth usually with two loop handles.[7] Tripod vessels were the most favored of all Chinese bronzes, and they were widely imitated in Ming and Qing decorative arts. Although the ancient bronze tripods were cooking vessels, they were sometimes used as censers on special occasions in later times. The early Ming antiquarian Cao Zhao (flourished 1387-99) had already mentioned in 1388 that archaic bronzes could be used as censers, noting that '[in earliest times] there were no incense burners. ...Ancient vessels used as incense burners today were sacrificial vessels and not [real] incense burners.'[8] Later imitations, such as the present *ding*-shaped censer, were made as substitutes for the ancient vessels which were considered too precious to be used on a regular basis.

24 Cylindrical Zun-shaped Censer

with three cabriole legs and three bands of ribs and with bird and
scrolling floral decor

Qing dynasty, probably eighteenth century
Cast bronze with cast and cold-worked decoration, with induced surface
color, and with a cast thread-relief mark in standard-script (*kaishu*)
characters reading *Da Ming Xuandenian zhi* in a recessed rectangular
cartouche on the base
10.8 centimeter diameter
Provenance: Dr Sidney Smith, Cambridge, England
Clague Collection Number 249

THIS CYLINDRICAL *ZUN*-SHAPED CENSER stands on three evenly spaced cabriole legs, its straight sides tapering slightly at the bottom to soften the transition from vertical walls to flat, horizontal base. Triple-rib bands border the top and bottom of the bowl, while a third band at the midsection divides the surface into two horizontal registers that feature designs engraved in fine lines; a pattern of birds in flight amidst clouds embellishes the upper register while a composite floral scroll ornaments the lower one. A spray of foliage enlivens the bulbous portion of each cabriole leg. The gently rounded lip echoes the plain band at the bottom of the bowl. The unornamented base has at its center a cast mark in six *kaishu* (standard-script) characters arranged in three columns of two characters each within a recessed rectangular cartouche. The interior of the bowl is undecorated, as are the backs and lower portions of the legs. Chemically induced after casting, the dark brown surfaces conceal the brassy color of the metal.

Though spurious, the mark on this censer, like that on the previous one, establishes a link to the Xuande bronze tradition. In fact, *Xuande yiqi tupu* pictures a censer similar to this one, which it terms a *jiuyuan sanji lu*, a reference to the nine rings arranged in three bands.[1] Like the Clague piece, the illustrated censer has three cabriole legs and three sets of triple-rib bands about its cylindrical bowl; differing from the Clague example, it lacks pictorial decoration; its triple bands seem to comprise concave rings rather than relief ribs, and its lowest band of ribs appears a bit higher on the body, thus avoiding interruption by the cabriole legs. More importantly, the notes following the illustration state that the Xuande censer had a mottled surface dappled with cinnabar red and sprinkled with gold and silver 'raindrops and snowflakes.' The comments further indicate that the Xuande censer was furnished with a stand and cover of *zitan* wood, the cover with a *chilong*-shaped knob of white jade.[2]

The name given this censer type in *Xuande yiqi tupu*, that is, *jiuyuan sanji lu* (literally, nine-origins, three-poles censer), employs terms appropriated from the *Yijing*, or Book of Changes, and its commentaries, indicating that by Ming times its ribs were likened to the *Yijing*'s diagrams.[3] (Doubtless playful rather than serious, such an association is consistent with the Ming interest in visual puns and double entendres.) The *liuyao* ☰☰, or quintessential hexagram from the *Yijing*, comprises two trigrams, the male *qian* (representing heaven), which consists of three continuous lines ☰, and the female *kun* (representing earth), which consists of three interrupted lines ☷. The commentary on the *Yijing* notes that although the total number of lines in the *liuyao* is six, the total number of brushstrokes is nine, since the discontinuous lines of *kun* comprise six strokes; as confirmed by the name given the censer type in *Xuande yiqi tupu*, the nine ribs, or *jiuyuan*, correspond to the nine strokes of the *Yijing*'s quintessential hexagram.[4] In addition, the *Yijing* itself states that the various permutations of the *liuyao*'s six lines determine the fate of the *sanji*,[5] or 'three poles,' which refer to 'heaven, earth, and humankind.'[6] The censer's nine ribs thus symbolize the nine strokes of the *Yijing*'s quintessential hexagram, and its three bands represent heaven, earth, and humankind, that is, all existence.

As previously noted [2], cylindrical *zun* 'warm-wine vessels' evolved in the late Warring States period and frequently appear among Han bronzes. Although some are embellished with hunting scenes,[7] others are more restrained, having as decoration only two mask-and-ring handles and three plain, low-relief bands.[8] *Zun* vessels with hunting scenes often stand on legs in the form of crouching bears, but those with relief bands usually rest on cabriole legs. Though they seldom imitated the form of other Bronze Age vessels, Tang craftsmen produced three-legged vessels of cylindrical *zun*-shape in pottery[9] and bronze,[10] usually as cosmetic boxes and incense burners rather than as wine vessels; small horizontal flutes usually ornament the ceramic examples top to bottom, while bronze ones sometimes have horizontal registers of openwork floral decoration. During the Northern Song period, potters at the Ru kilns revived the Han interpretation of the cylindrical *zun*-form for their censers; they took the more restrained Han type as their model, following it with great fidelity.[11] Potters at the Ding kilns also took the restrained Han type as their model; imitating it less faithfully, they produced cylindrical *zun*-shaped censers enlivened with six ribs, typically arranged with three about the midsection, two about the lip, and a single one about the bottom, just above the cabriole legs.[12] Their imagination sparked by ribbed Ding-ware censers, Southern Song potters fashioned cylindrical *zun*-shaped censers in *guan* ware, increasing the number of ribs to nine and arranging them in three bands.[13] The tops of the cabriole legs interrupt the lowest rib in the band around the base in such *guan*-ware censers. With one triple-rib band each around the top, mid-section, and base, the harmonious *guan*-ware censers became the classical interpretation of the shape in the eyes of succeeding generations.

Xuande period designers clearly modeled their *zun*-shaped bronze censers on Southern Song *guan*-ware incense burners, but they raised the lowest band of ribs so that its lines are continuous and they emblazoned the surfaces with gold, silver, and cinnabar red. The Clague censer incorporates elements from both the *guan* ware and Xuande bronze traditions (perhaps through woodblock-printed catalogs); chance contact with a rare Tang bronze example might have inspired the Clague censer's engraved decoration, though such bird and flower motifs are so common in Chinese art that mere coincidence may account for its appearance on both.

Judging by the illustration in *Xuande yiqi tupu*, Xuande censers, like their *guan*-ware models, had a square corner at the bottom of the bowl, rather than the softened transition of the Clague censer. In addition, their legs, like those of *guan*-ware censers, were apparently smaller in proportion to the vessel than those of the present piece. The diameter of the *guan*-ware censer's bowl, however, is greater in relation to its height than that of either the *Xuande yiqi tupu* or the Clague example.

The Clague censer's bowl, legs, and ribs were integrally cast, but its fine-line decoration was engraved after casting. Although many have carved decoration [11, 22] and many others have cast decoration to which fine-line details have been added [13, 21], few Ming and Qing cast bronzes have engraved decoration, perhaps because it is difficult to read, easily overpowered by both the form and the material of the vessel. Still, several large, bronze vases – whose trumpet-mouthed *yanyan* form suggests a date in the late seventeenth or first half of the eighteenth century – possess engraved fine-line decoration, providing a starting point for the attribution of the Clague censer.[14] Though they differ in style, the engraved designs on this censer recall in their complexity the silver-wire inlays on Shisou-manner bronzes of the type conventionally ascribed to the eighteenth century.

25 Circular Ding-shaped Censer
with three legs and with three decorative inscriptions in Arabic script

Qing dynasty, nineteenth century
Cast bronze with cold-worked decoration and with a chiseled mark in
standard-script (*kaishu*) characters reading *Da Ming Xuandenian zao* in a
recessed rectangular cartouche on the base
15.2 centimeter diameter
Clague Collection Number 206

P ERHAPS ONCE PART OF A THREE-PIECE ALTAR SET (*angong*) comprising a censer, vase, and globular covered box,[1] this circular *ding*-shaped censer has a low body set on three solid legs of truncated conical form. The walls rise from the flat base to shape the swollen body, constrict to define the neck, and then flare gently to form the lip. The wide lip comprises two parts, a narrow rim – basically the upper edge of the vessel wall – around the perimeter and a broad, convex ring around the interior, the two separated by a groove. Three inscriptions carved in Arabic script embellish the censer's walls, one centered above each leg; each relief inscription appears against a ring-punched ground in a wide, slightly sunken ogival panel with bracketed ends and with a small barb, top and bottom, at the center. A deeply incised line borders each panel, echoing its barbs, brackets, and contours. The base, legs, and interior are undecorated; a carved mark appears in the center of the base, its six *kaishu* characters arranged in three columns of two characters each within a recessed rectangular cartouche whose ground has been textured to resemble a tabby-weave fabric.

Entirely cold worked, the relief Arabic inscriptions read:

afdalu al-dhikr	The best confessional invocation [is]
la ilaha illa Alahhu	There is no god but God
Muhammad rasul Allah	Muhammad is the apostle of God[2]

Discussing a virtually identical bronze censer in another collection, John Carswell commented on the unusual style of the Arabic lettering, particularly that in the name Muhammad; he also remarked on the swollen forms of the *alif*-like vertical strokes.[3]

The problem of Chinese bronzes with Arabic/Persian inscriptions awaits study and resolution.[4] Conventional wisdom holds that since they seldom turn up in the Near and Middle East, such bronzes were produced for the Chinese domestic market, for use both by foreign Muslims living in China and by the large population of Chinese Muslims. History records that the Hongzhi and Zhengde Emperors took an active interest in Islam and that they not only studied Arabic but they are rumored to have adhered secretly to the Muslim faith.[5] In addition, during the mid- and late Ming many of the palace eunuchs were followers of Islam, having come from the Muslim communities of West China. Taking into account only these historical circumstances, less cautious authors sometimes attribute all Chinese bronzes with Arabic and Persian inscriptions to the sixteenth century, excepting those with Xuande marks, which they occasionally assign to the early fifteenth. Chinese decorative arts with such inscriptions embrace a range of dates, the earliest ones dating to the sixteenth century but the majority to the seventeenth, eighteenth, and nineteenth.

Barring a handful of Yuan-dynasty porcelains with Arabic letters discreetly incorporated into their decorative schemes and presumably made solely for export to the Near and Middle East,[6] the earliest Jingdezhen blue-and-white wares with Arabic/Persian decorative inscriptions date to the early sixteenth-century reign of the Zhengde Emperor;[7] although a few blue-and-white porcelains from the succeeding Jiajing reign also boast such inscriptions,[8] the number of Jingdezhen porcelains with Arabic/Persian inscriptions decreased markedly after the Zhengde era. However, several late seventeenth- and early eighteenth-century Dehua porcelains with carved Arabic letters indicate that such decorative schemes persisted into the Qing dynasty.[9] A Qianlong-marked blue-glass vase in the Brooklyn Museum has a carved Arabic inscription set against a textured ground,[10] and several nineteenth-century cloisonné enamel censers[11] and Dehua porcelains[12] have Arabic-letter inscriptions, indicating that works so ornamented were produced throughout the Qing dynasty in various media. Surviving works clearly show that inscriptions composed of Arabic letters were used as decoration from the sixteenth through the nineteenth centuries; although doubtless correct in some instances, that tenet of traditional knowledge holding that most bronzes and ceramics with inscriptions in Arabic letters were produced in the sixteenth century for use by palace eunuchs must be set aside in favor of more judicious attributions.

Arabic and Persian inscriptions on sixteenth-century blue-and-white porcelains appear within cartouches of various shapes – square, rectangular, circular, ogival – and they are typically set amid floral scrolls called 'Muhammadan scrolls.' Such sixteenth-century decorative inscriptions[13] are usually smaller in proportion to the vessel than those on the Clague censer and they include both religious and secular statements, the latter ranging from moral precepts to prosaic descriptive terms;[14] very few sixteenth-century porcelains feature Koranic inscriptions. Eighteenth- and nineteenth-century examples of glass, ceramics, and cloisonné enamel with decoration of Arabic letters tend to have large inscriptions of a religious nature set in ogival panels; glass and ceramic pieces from the mid- and late Qing often employ such inscriptions to the exclusion of decorative motifs, but cloisonné enamels continue to set them in floral (usually lotus) scrolls. The characteristics of seventeenth-century examples remain a mystery, since few pieces of seventeenth-century date have been identified.

This censer owes its shape to Xuande bronzes, as suggested by the mark on its base reading *Da Ming Xuandenian zao*. Since the wording of the mark is inconsistent with Xuande-period usage, genuine Xuande marks use *zhi* rather than *zao* as the final character,[15] it can be safely assumed that this censer is only loosely associated with the tradition. Sleekly styled, *ding*-shaped censers with small conical legs appear among the illustrations in *Xuande yiqi tupu*, where they are termed *rulu*, that is, 'mammiform censers,' a reference to the shape of the legs;[16] those pictured, however, invariably have inverted lips from which spring two small loop handles. In addition, those illustrated, like those listed in *Xuande dingyi pu*, either are undecorated or are embellished around their upper portions with broad bands of gold with scalloped lower edges, the gold bands termed *xiangyun*, or 'auspicious cloud,' decoration; on the other hand, no vessels whatsoever are pictured or listed with decorative Arabic inscriptions. Although its smart shape signals its descent from Xuande bronzes, the Clague censer's thick rim, strongly everted lip, lack of handles, and decorative Arabic inscriptions indicate that it is a rather distant descendant.

With antecedents in Neolithic pottery, the *ding* cauldron ranks among the oldest of ritual vessel types.[17] However, the Clague censer and its Xuande models owe their stylish form to *guan*-ware censers produced during the Southern Song period[18] rather than to bronzes from high antiquity. Perhaps inspired in turn by the curvaceous *li* vessels of the Western Zhou period,[19] such *guan*-ware censers pioneered the elegantly flattened bodies and short conical legs that were to become the hallmark of the Xuande censer type.

The general shape,[20] the everted lip, and the large Arabic inscriptions set in elongated ogival panels argue for a date in the mid- to late Qing period for the Clague censer; in particular, the similarity of its shape to that of nineteenth-century cloisonné enamel censers, which typically lack handles and which sometimes have a wide lip encircling the mouth,[21] suggests that it was made during the last century of Qing rule. The main reason for attributing the censer to the nineteenth century is its reliance solely upon cold-working techniques in creating the decoration (as indicated by irregularities in the borders and by chatter marks on the sides of the Arabic letters).

Entirely cold worked, the Arabic inscriptions were created by excavating the backgrounds within the decorative panels after the censer had been cast; the reserved letters thus stand in relief in relation to the sunken ground but are actually the same height as the vessel walls. Partially concealed by the ring-punch texturing, deep outlines with beveled outer edges surround each letter, enhancing the relief appearance. First employed in

Tang-dynasty silver, ring-punched grounds had been revived by late Ming times and sometimes appear in works by Hu Wenming [see 12]; such grounds not only provide a foil for the plain letters, making them easier to read, they also conceal the telltale chisel marks imparted in the excavation of the sunken ground. The black composition rubbed into the rings of the punched ground further enhances legibility. In their slightly mannered style the Chinese characters in the carved mark on the base reflect something of the decorative flair of the Arabic letters; in addition, the characters of the mark are also set against a textured ground. Although cast elements were finished through extensive cold working on many late Ming bronzes [see 11, 13], it was probably not until the eighteenth century that bronzes came to be decorated entirely after casting through cold-working techniques[22] [compare 22]. In this case, the stiffness of the Arabic letters and the slight irregularities and imperfections in the borders point to a nineteenth-century date of manufacture.

In the nineteenth century could Arabic inscriptions have been chiseled into an undecorated censer of earlier date? This question is not easily answered, though two points argue against the possibility, at least in this case. As mentioned above, the censer's wide lip compares with the similar ones that sometimes appear on nineteenth-century cloisonné censers with Arabic inscriptions, suggesting that the Clague censer is a late exponent of the Xuande censer type, presumably of the same date as the inscription. More importantly, an identical bronze censer in the collection of Professor Yussif Ibish has the the same Arabic inscriptions in the same unusual script with its swollen vertical strokes.[23] Coincidence of shape, decoration, and style suggest that the two censers were produced by the same workshop at the same time; it seems unlikely indeed that if in the nineteenth century Arabic inscriptions were added to earlier censers, the censers themselves would be identical in shape and style.

26 Two Covered Long-necked Ewers

with long spouts and elaborate handles and with pine and peony decor

Ming to Qing dynasty, seventeenth century
Assembled bodies of raised copper, with cold-worked and appliqué
decoration, and with gilding
26.5 centimeter height
Clague Collection Number 227

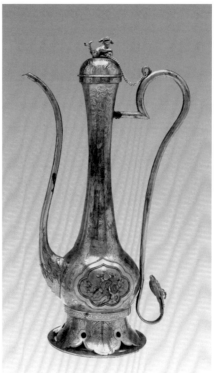

ACH OF THESE TWO VIRTUALLY IDENTICAL gilt-copper ewers sits atop an elaborate, conical foot pierced to form six, descending, scalloped leaves whose rounded tips are affixed to a flat, annular base. Attached to the bottom of the compressed globular body, a short vertical band resembling a footring conceals the join of the tall foot to the body, a join that allows each ewer to rotate up to one hundred eighty degrees on its foot. An attenuated neck rises from the globular body, its slender form flaring gently at the top; a narrow, undecorated, vertical lip encircles the mouth. A high, domed cover with horizontal lip caps each ewer, the knobs in the form of seated lions, each with a ball. A long, tapering, S-curved spout springs from the front of each ewer, its tip reaching as high as the vessel's mouth. A long, tubular handle balances the opposed spout; the handle surges upward, flares outward, and then arches inward near the top of the neck, attaching a short distance below the mouth with a short, horizontal arm. A tiny circular loop at the top of each handle originally anchored the fine chain, now lost, that linked ewer and cover. Complementing the inward curve at the top, the bottom of each handle curves outward and terminates in an ornamental plaque. The ewers are identically decorated, each having two ogival panels of floral decoration, one on each side of the compressed globular body. One panel features a blossoming tree peony growing beside a rock while the other includes an old pine tree clinging to a small hillock, its gnarled trunk with scales and its weathered branches with needles arranged in circular, umbrella-like clusters; a bird glides toward the pine from the left, ready to alight amidst its branches. Set against ring-punched grounds, the decorative elements in the panels rise in relief and incorporate some openwork elements. A wide, undecorated band frames each panel, a narrow line echoing the barbs and contours of its inner edge. A simplified variant of the pine medallion ornaments the plaque at the bottom of the handle, its outer border punched with four abstract cloud scrolls. The engraved floral pattern surrounding each decorative panel has an hibiscus blossom above the panel, the flower shown in profile. Related but flowerless vegetal scrolls embellish the covers and the upper portions of the necks; the midsections of the necks are undecorated. An engraved dragon's head with long whiskers and pointed teeth appears at the base of each spout, the spout issuing from its mouth. A formalized cloud scroll enlivens the vertical band at the bottom of the globular body. Openwork patterns distinguish one leaf from the next on the foot, the leaves having engraved lines that suggest veins and punched dots that texture their surfaces. The undersides of the ewers are plain. Probably for wine, these two ewers have perhaps been a pair from the beginning, rather than simply two identical ewers that led separate lives until matched together in modern times, as indicated by their complementary lion finials: one rests its left foot on its brocaded ball, while the other rests its right foot on the ball.

Often said to be of Middle Eastern form, ewers of this type are firmly rooted in Chinese tradition, though they reflect a degree of influence from Persian metalwork. Their Chinese ancestors are not ritual bronze vessels from high antiquity, but gold, silver, and porcelain ewers made during the Ming dynasty. In relation to Chinese ceramics, the Clague vessels fall midway between Wanli-period blue-and-white ewers with long necks and small bodies[1] and the related but more mannered Kangxi-period ewers,[2] suggesting that they were made in the seventeenth century. Like the Clague vessels, Wanli ewers have a globular body, an elongated neck, an S-curved spout, and an arched handle; their bases are less elaborate, however, and their proportions less attenuated. Kangxi ewers from the late seventeenth century, on the other hand, resemble the Clague vessels in having a tall base, an attenuated neck, and a compressed globular body, but they are often more mannered than the Clague ewers, with an octagonal neck and base framing a circular body and with a handle and spout that are square in section; in addition, on such Kangxi ewers the handles are often painted to resemble plaited rattan and both the spout and the top of the handle issue from the mouths of dragons.

Such bronze and porcelain vessels derive from a type of ewer with body of flattened pear shape that rose to popularity during the first half of the sixteenth century in silver,[3] porcelain,[4] jade,[5] and *guri* lacquer.[6] In addition to their long spouts and arched handles, such sixteenth-century ewers often have a domed cover with a finial in the form of a seated lion;[7] many rest atop a tall, circular foot[8] and some have elongated necks (though not as attenuated as those of the Clague bronzes). Almost all porcelain examples have a loop at the top of the arched handle for linking ewer and cover together with a fine chain, the chain attaching to the cover through the small opening between the lion's legs. An integrally fired ceramic strut virtually always connects the upper end of the spout to the neck on porcelain examples; not needing such structural support, bronze ewers typically forego the cloud-shaped reinforcement. Too fragile for use on porcelains, a decorative panel often appears at the bottom of the handle on sixteenth-century metal ewers, as seen in a silver example in the Carl Kempe Collection, Stockholm;[9] in addition, the spout of the Kempe ewer issues from the mouth of a dragon, as do the spouts of several ceramic examples,[10] as on the Clague pieces. The descending lotus petals in over-glaze gilding that sometimes ornament the tall bases of ceramic examples[11] perhaps inspired the openwork leaves on the bases of the Clague ewers.

Sixteenth-century ewers with bodies of flattened pear shape evolved from the full-bodied, pear-shaped ewers that were popular in Jingdezhen porcelain[12] and Longquan celadon ware[13] during the late fourteenth and early fifteenth century. Although they have short necks and footrings, such pear-shaped ewers have a short, emphatic lip, a long, curving spout (secured by a strut), and an arched handle with both a loop at its crest and an indentation in its spine to complement the vessel's strong curves – the very features that sixteenth-century potters drew upon in fashioning ewers of flattened pear shape and that seventeenth-century metalsmiths elaborated to create the Clague ewers.

Despite the Clague ewers' origins in sixteenth-century Chinese vessels, their attenuated necks and domed covers exhibit the influence of Iranian metalwork. In particular, a large cast-brass ewer in the Victoria and Albert Museum, London, represents a type of sixteenth-century Iranian ewer (aftabe) that perhaps played a role in the development of both the Clague bronze ewers and their Wanli blue-and-white counterparts. Cast in Western Iran about 1560, the large brass ewer has a compressed globular body, long waisted neck, straight vertical lip, and high domed cover with decorative knob.[14] Like the Clague ewers, it has decorative panels surrounded by interlaced scrolls on its circular body but, differing from them, it has small horizontal flutes around its neck and shoulder, a simple, S-curve handle, and a tulip-shaped finial at the end of its spout. Proof that ewers of this type found their way to China awaits discovery, but the similarity of form to Chinese ewers suggests they might have, a realistic possibility given trade relations between China and the Middle East in Ming times, not to mention sixteenth-century Chinese interest in Islam [see 25], and the continuing dialogue between Chinese and Persian art.

Though configured in an S-curve, the handle of the Iranian ewer lacks the decorative flair of the arched handles on the Clague ewers and on sixteenth-century ewers of flattened pear shape. In fact, arched handles come from Chinese tradition, where they had long been a staple of Chinese potters and metalworkers. Tang silversmiths, for example, had equipped ewers with arched, strap-like handles at least as early as the ninth century, often joining the handle to the neck with a short horizontal bar.[15] Potters soon followed suit, probably in the tenth century, producing globular ewers with short cylindrical necks and arched handles, the handles often with a tiny loop at the top of the arch for linking ewer and cover[16] and often with a short horizontal arm connecting handle and neck.[17] A standard feature by the Song, arched handles were incorporated into pear-shaped ewers in the late fourteenth and fifteenth centuries, into flattened pear-shaped ewers in the sixteenth century, into Wanli blue-and-white ewers in the late sixteenth century, and then into the Clague ewers in the seventeenth century.

Differing in shape from the ovoid panels on sixteenth-century ewers, the ogival panels on the Clague ewers have a single barb at the top and two rounded lobes at the bottom, a form that finds precedent in fifteenth-century celadon-glazed ewers from the Longquan kilns.[18] Such celadon ewers often claim peonies as their principal decoration, as do many Ming and Qing ceramics and other decorative arts [see discussion, 27]. By late Ming times the peony was considered a symbol of wealth, due to its numerous petals, so its appearance is regarded as an auspicious wish to the viewer. Because it often attains great age, the pine numbers among the symbols of longevity, its gnarled trunk, weathered branches, and perpetually green needles also standing as emblems of strength in the face of adversity. Reflecting the late Ming interest in both luxury goods and bright colors, the surfaces of the ewers were gilded to simulate pieces fashioned in gold.[19]

These ewers were prepared in sections hammered from sheet copper and joined together with solder; in most cases seams betray the joins. The body and neck of each ewer comprise four separate parts: a round-bottomed bowl, constricting shoulder, attenuated neck, and circular lip. Encircling the widest part of the body, bisecting the decorative panels as it goes, a seam reveals the join of bowl and shoulder. Another seam, partly obscured by the engraved hibiscus scrolls above the ogival panels, indicates the join of neck and shoulder. The seam along the back of the neck resulted from soldering together the longitudinal edges of the copper sheet that was hammered around a form to shape the tubular neck. Hollow tubes, the handle and spout are affixed to the body with solder, the join of handle to body reinforced with pins at the points of attachment; the small loop at the top of the handle and the decorative plaque at its base were affixed with solder. Like the lip, the vertical band encircling the bottom of the body was cut from sheet copper and soldered into place. The foot comprises two pieces soldered together, the flat ring and the collar of leaf-shaped forms; a mechanical join with pins enables the ewer to turn on the foot. Although portions of the decoration within the ogival panels were carved, the high-relief and openwork elements were created separately and soldered into place; the ring-mat backgrounds were punched. The lion-form knobs atop the covers were cast and then attached with pins. The gilding was no doubt achieved through the application of an amalgam of powdered gold and mercury which was then heated to evaporate the mercury, the standard method for affixing a gold coating to metal.

27 Circular Covered Box

with peony and butterfly decor on the cover and with peach, peony, and
bird decor on the box

Qing dynasty, eighteenth century
Assembled body of hammered and turned copper, with cold-worked and
appliqué decoration, with incised decoration, with gilding, and with
induced surface color
7.9 centimeter diameter
Clague Collection Number 255

PROBABLY AN INCENSE CONTAINER, this small, circular, covered box stands on a short footring, its bowl-like container and slightly domed cover of generally matching shape. A slightly sunken, diamond-shaped cartouche with bracketed edges and gilded surfaces occupies much of the broad cover; it features a tree peony growing from a clump of soil nestled in one of the bracketed corners. The peony's stalk divides into two branches immediately above the ground line, each branch having one blossom and one bud, in addition to numerous leaves; a butterfly hovers above the left branch, completing the composition. All of the decorative elements stand in relief against the sunken ground; punched with fine, closely spaced rings in strictly ordered horizontal rows, the ground resembles finely woven fabric in texture. The reddish-orange color of the copper shows through the gilding at the high points of the relief, in the flower buds, the petals at the center of the blossoms, and the wings of the butterfly, for example, perhaps due to wear but possibly due to intentional rubbing after gilding to create subtle but harmonious contrasts in color. The exterior walls of the box, like those surrounding the cartouche on the cover, have been chemically treated to induce the dark, gunmetal gray finish, providing the perfect foil for the gilding within the cartouche. The exterior of the container sports a branch of fruiting peach and another of blossoming peony, the opposed branches separated top and bottom by opposing pairs of birds in flight; the incised and gilded lines of the container's decorative scheme stand out against the dark gray of the vessel wall. Narrow bands of hatching border the edges of box and cover, the gilding in the finely incised lines now much worn. A lip, perhaps the upper edge of a liner held in place by tension and solder, encircles the inner edge of the container to anchor the cover. The lip and the interiors of box and cover are fully gilded but otherwise undecorated. The base and footring are also undecorated, though their surfaces show the same gunmetal gray finish as the surrounding walls.

This box derives from the similar bronze incense boxes [11, 13, and 14] that became fashionable in the late Ming and that trace their lineage through the small jade and lacquer boxes of the early and mid-Ming, to the covered ceramic boxes of the Song, and ultimately to the gold and silver boxes that enjoyed popularity in aristocratic circles during the Tang. Its short footring, low-set proportions, and slightly domed cover set this box apart from late Ming and early Qing examples,[1] however, but link it to Qianlong-period jade ones,[2] placing it firmly in the eighteenth century.

The quadrilaterally symmetrical cartouche with barbs oriented toward the points of the compass represents a cartouche type seldom encountered before the Qing, but frequently encountered in eighteenth-century porcelains from the kilns at Jingdezhen[3] and at Dehua.[4] Although Yuan, Ming, and Qing decorative arts employ them, bracketed cartouches on wares produced before the eighteenth century tend to be wider than they are tall[5] and they sometimes have two rounded lobes at the bottom rather than a single barb[6] [see 26].

History records that the indigenous tree peony (*Paeonia arborea*) was introduced into the imperial gardens in the late sixth or early seventh century, during the short-lived Sui dynasty.[7] With its large, showy blossoms, the tree peony quickly captured the imagination of the Chinese, who began to cultivate it on a wide scale; it numbered among the most popular flowers in the realm by the eighth century and has retained its appeal to the present day. The peony frequently appears in Tang-dynasty Buddhist paintings and in the ornament of Tang gold and silver vessels; numerous secular paintings of blossoming peonies survive from the Song dynasty, typically painted in colors on silk. The peony and the lotus rank among the most popular motifs on Song-dynasty ceramics, particularly in the carved and molded designs on celadon-glazed vessels from the Yaozhou kilns; they also figure prominently in the decorative schemes both of Yuan and early Ming blue-and-white porcelains from Jingdezhen and of early Ming carved red lacquer. Although its popularity as a subject to be depicted in the visual arts endured through the Ming and Qing, the tree peony found special favor during the early Qing period, in the paintings[8] of Yun Shouping (1633-1690), for example, and in Yongzheng and Qianlong period porcelains with designs delicately painted in overglaze *fencai* enamels,[9] particularly those of the so-called Guyuexuan type.

Often called the King of Flowers, or *hua wang*, due to its popularity and to the size of its blossoms, the tree peony is formally known in Chinese as *mudan hua*, which means 'male vermillion flower' and indicates that it is looked upon as the flower associated with the *yang*, or male, principle in the dualistic *yin-yang* system of cosmology.[10] It is, however, also regarded as a symbol of feminine beauty and as an emblem of love and affection. Representing spring, the tree peony figures among the flowers of the four seasons, standing alongside the lotus, chrysanthemum, and plum which, respectively, stand for summer, autumn, and winter; in addition, the peony represents the third month in the Chinese lunar calendar,[11] which generally corresponds to late March and much of April in the Western calendar. Because of its abundant petals, the tree peony is viewed as a symbol of wealth and honor, often called *fugui hua* (literally, honor [and] wealth flower). In fact, during the seventeenth and eighteenth centuries, white-jade amulets were sometimes embellished with a peony blossom on one side and characters reading *yutang fugui* (May you enjoy wealth and honor)[12] on the other.[13]

Although it occasionally appears in the arts of the Ming dynasty, the peach, like the bat [see 19], did not come into its own as a motif in the decorative arts until the Qing. A symbol of longevity,[14] the peach began to serve as a principal decorative motif on porcelains during the Kangxi era, gained prominence during the Yongzheng era, and then soared to popularity during the succeeding Qianlong era.[15] Its appearance here indicates that this small covered box can date no earlier than the eighteenth century.

Craftsmen began to employ chemical and thermal treatments at least as early as the Xuande reign to induce varied surface colors on their bronzes, especially on the so-called Xuande censers [see 15 and 16]. Although descriptions in early catalogs assign them specific names, the surface colors of early Ming bronzes generally fall into the red, orange, yellow, and brown range; the gunmetal gray of this box, by contrast, did not appear until the Qing dynasty, and, even then, apparently not until the eighteenth century. Representing both a different workshop and a different aesthetic, this small box nevertheless finds parallels in its gunmetal gray surfaces in those Shisou-tradition bronzes conventionally assigned to the eighteenth century [compare 17].

The origin of the taste for dark-gray surfaces with gold decoration remains unclear, though it may well lie in those porcelains with so-called 'mirror-black' glaze ornamented with overglaze gilding that enjoyed a note of popularity in the eighteenth century. Applied against a red, green, or white ground to create bold floral patterns during the mid- and late Ming period,[16] overglaze gilding was often used in association with iron-red[17] and powder-blue[18] grounds during the Kangxi era, but in a more painterly fashion. Late in the Kangxi reign, such gilding was sometimes applied over a dense, lustrous, black glaze of a type termed *wujin* (literally, black gold) in China[19] and mirror black in the West.[20] Associated primarily with the Kangxi period, black-glazed porcelains with decoration in overglaze gilding occasionally appear among the wares of the Yongzheng[21] and Qianlong[22] eras, providing an eighteenth-century context for the Clague box.

Of raised copper, this small box was entirely cold worked, from its construction to its embellishment. Used for centering, the pinprick-like depression in the center of the floor and its mate in the center of the base indicate that the box was shaped by turning on a lathe. A similar pinprick depression in the center of its interior reveals that the cover was lathe turned also, the matching depression on the cover's top having disappeared in the creation of the decorative cartouche. A narrow strip cut from a sheet of copper, the footring was soldered into place; a vertical line marks the join of its ends to create a circle. Chatter marks in the vertical walls indicate that the cartouche was carved into the cover. Perhaps struck with a die, the decorative elements were soldered into place within the cartouche, after which the ground was ring punched. Gilding in the cartouche and on the interiors of box and cover was doubtless achieved through the application of an amalgam of powdered gold and mercury; as the box was gently heated, the mercury evaporated, bonding a thin but evenly distributed layer of gold to the copper. The reddish tone of the copper is visible in those areas where the gilding has worn thin, indicating that the surface under the gilding was not darkened. It is possible that the gunmetal gray color was induced on the exteriors of both box and cover after the pieces were shaped but before they were decorated; as the cartouche was excavated into the cover, reddish-orange copper was newly exposed, ready to receive appliqué decorative elements, ring-punch texturing, and mercury gilding.

28 Covered Lobed Cylindrical Ewer
with long spout and elaborate handle and with floral decor

Qing dynasty, probably mid- to late eighteenth century
Assembled body of raised copper, with cold-worked and appliqué
decoration, with induced surface color, and with gilding
18.4 centimeter height
Clague Collection Number 238

GENTLY SEGMENTED INTO SIX LOBES, this ewer has a generally cylindrical body whose walls rise vertically from the flat base and then turn inward at the top to form the narrow shoulder. The neck rises from the center of the relief, gilded, chrysanthemum collar, an elaboration of the type which appeared in the late Ming [see 19]. Its short but emphatic lip echoes the angled ledge at its base. A lightly domed cover with horizontal lip conceals the vessel's mouth, its knob in the form of a cut branch of blossoming plum. The ewer's long, S-curved spout has a wide, ringed base that resembles a bamboo rhizome in form and that gives rise to the two newly sprouted bamboo stalks that ornament the shaft; one of the stalks has a pair of leaves while the other incongruously has a plum blossom. Sectioned to resemble a bamboo stalk, a long, tubular handle balances the opposed spout visually as well as thematically. The ear-shaped handle flares outward and then arches inward at a point even with the top of the cover's dome, attaching just below the shoulder with a short, angled arm; appliqué branches of blossoming chrysanthemum ornament the base of the handle, the stalk of one chrysanthemum overlapping a portion of the vessel wall. Appearing within elongated, slightly sunken, vertical panels and set against ring-punched grounds, low-relief floral sprays embellish four of the ewer's six lobes, the handle and spout claiming the remaining two. Of generally rectangular form, the decorative panels have straight sides, ogival-arched tops, and trefoil-arched bottoms. On one side, the floral sprays include a chrysanthemum and a branch of blossoming plum and on the other, a peony and a second branch of plum; occupying the ogival arch at the top of the panel, a bird or butterfly hovers over each floral spray. Incised peony scrolls enliven the neck and cover, while a band of chevrons encircles the neck. Gilding brightens the neck, cover, and chrysanthemum collar as well as the spout, handle, and decorative panels; a narrow, undulating band of gilding ornaments the lowermost portion of the vessel, though the base itself is undecorated. Chemically treated, the ungilded surfaces boast a dark, gunmetal gray finish.

For hot water[1] or warmed wine, tall ewers with long spouts and fluted sides had appeared as early as the Song dynasty, in both silver and ceramic ware;[2] such early examples typically had a long neck with a flaring lip and a rounded or ovoid body, however. Seldom produced in the Ming, tall, cylindrical ewers with short necks, long spouts, and ornamental handles gained popularity during the Qing, occasionally appearing in paintings and prints.[3] Although Ming and Qing connoisseurs of tea preferred to use small teapots of earth-toned ceramic ware made at the Yixing kilns (near the garden city of Suzhou), less demanding tea drinkers often used larger teapots, even experimenting with metal ones during the Qing dynasty.[4] In fact, during his visit to the Clague Collection, Yang Boda, Deputy Director Emeritus of the Palace Museum, Beijing, termed this vessel a *chahu*, or teapot, noting that such pieces were made for export but by the late eighteenth century had come to be used in China as well.[5]

Adorned with appliqué elements and shaped to resemble parts of a growing bamboo plant, the handle and spout are this ewer's most striking features. Arched handles had appeared by the early Northern Song period [see discussion, 26] as had handles segmented to resemble a stalk of bamboo;[6] Song examples lack the dramatic flare of the present handle, however, not to mention appliqué ornaments. The later taste for vessels with rims, handles, and spouts shaped to resemble stalks of bamboo arose during the Ming dynasty[7] – probably in response to the growing popularity of bamboo both as a subject matter for literati painting and as a material for brushpots, wrist rests, and other accoutrements for the scholar's desk – but did not gain prominence until the Qing [compare 31]. The flowers represented on the ewer, both in the decorative panels and among the appliqué elements, were the most popular in traditional China; all were cultivated in classical gardens and all had been used since Song times for the embellishment of ceramics and other decorative arts. Perhaps most beloved of all, the wild plum (*Prunus mume*) blooms in February, so it naturally stands for both winter and the first month of the lunar calendar (which generally corresponds to late January and much of February in the Western calendar). More importantly, since it blooms in winter, before donning its leaves, it is regarded as a symbol of strength in the face of adversity. In addition, plum blossoms symbolize feminine beauty and the weathered trunk the humble scholar.[8] Hailed the 'King of Flowers,' the tree peony (*Paeonia arborea*) emblemizes wealth and honor, due to its numerous petals, and it represents both spring and the third month of the lunar calendar (basically, late March and much of April). The chrysanthemum (*Chrysanthemum indicum*) symbolizes not only autumn and the ninth month (late September and October) but literary pursuits,[9] since it was the favorite flower of the celebrated nature poet Tao Qian (365-427). Like the plum, bamboo (*Bambusa arundinacea*) is viewed as an emblem of strength in the face of adversity, since it retains its green leaves all year; because it is able to bend without breaking and then immediately to resume its original stance, it is also regarded as a symbol of rectitude, and thus the perfect symbol of the *junzi*, or Confucian gentleman.[10]

Perhaps from the same workshop as the previous incense box [27], this ewer also dates to the eighteenth century, as indicated by its contrasting gold and gunmetal gray surfaces. The presentation of the decorative motifs in vertically oriented, rectangular panels set against plain grounds also reflects its eighteenth-century origins, since that feature is seldom encountered before the Qing dynasty but is occasionally seen in Qianlong-era porcelains with overglaze enamel decoration.[11] Even some Qianlong blue-and-white vessels have their decoration organized into vertical panels, the panels sometimes finished with pointed tops and trefoil-arched bottoms.[12] A characteristic of relatively late bronzes, the abundance of appliqué ornament points to a mid- to late eighteenth-century date.

Entirely cold worked, this raised-copper ewer was prepared in sections hammered from sheet copper, the various pieces held together by solder, rivets, and, in some cases, mere tension; in most cases seams betray the joins. The ewer's walls comprise a single sheet of copper whose ends were soldered together to form a cylinder; the vertical join is visible along the handle side of the vessel's interior. Solder bonds the separately cut, disk-like base to the vessel's walls, as it joins the spout to the body. Relying mainly on tension, a vertical flange projecting downward into the vessel anchors the neck and chrysanthemum collar in place. Rivets attach the handle to metal mounts soldered to the walls to receive it, while solder secures the appliqué ornaments in place on the spout, handle, and cover. Chatter marks in the vertical walls indicate that the decorative panels were carved into the ewer's sides. Standing no higher than the darkened walls surrounding the panels, the low-relief floral sprays may have been carved in place during the excavation of the backgrounds. The ring-mat backgrounds were so densely punched that they resemble tightly woven fabric in texture. The gilding was accomplished through the application of an amalgam of powdered gold and mercury which was then heated to evaporate the mercury, leaving a thin coating of gold; the gunmetal gray finish was induced through chemical means. The exact nature of the chemical treatments and their order of application in relation to the assembly of the vessel remain uncertain.

29 Covered Circular Li-shaped Censer

with three cabriole legs, with two handles in the form of blossoming
branches, and with floral decor

Qing dynasty, probably mid- to late eighteenth century
Assembled body of hammered and turned copper, with cold-worked
and appliqué decoration, and with gilding
19.1 centimeter diameter
Clague Collection Number 232

I
TS COMPRESSED GLOBULAR BODY divided vertically into six lobes, this covered censer stands on three cabriole legs. The short neck rises from the relief, double-chrysanthemum collar that encircles the shoulder, its emphatic vertical lip expanding to receive the reticulated cover. Two appliqué handles, each in the form of a cut tree branch with two serrated leaves, a five-petaled blossom, and a small bud, appear at right and left on the body of the censer. Large in proportion to the vessel, the handles are attached at the shoulder with pins; their blossoms rise to the top of the lip, while their branches project outward to facilitate lifting. A third handle, of virtually identical size and shape, crowns the slightly domed cover, attached with pins to the unpierced disk at the cover's center. Appearing within a slightly sunken quatrefoil panel and set against a ring-punched ground, a low-relief floral motif ornaments each of the censer's six lobes. The flowers represented include the tree peony (*mudan hua*), flowering plum (*mei hua*), orchid (*lan hua*), and chrysanthemum (*ju hua*), with the plum and chrysanthemum each appearing twice; some panels also include a bird or butterfly. A wide, undecorated border frames each panel. The elaborately textured panels contrast with the otherwise undecorated walls which surround them. An incised vegetal scroll encircles the lip while an openwork vegetal scroll graces the cover. The gold has worn away in a few areas – at the top of the lip, for example, and in the high-relief portions of the floral designs – exposing the warm reddish orange tones of the copper beneath.

Censers of this type descend from the *li*-shaped censers popular during the Xuande era. Such early Ming tripod censers share the Clague censer's cabriole legs, constricted neck, and wide, emphatic lip; as pictured in *Xuande yiqi tupu*, however, they differ in having tri-lobed bodies, twisted-vine handles, and undecorated walls.[1] Xuande-period examples apparently lacked covers as well. Through such early Ming bronzes, the Clague censer traces its lineage to Song-dynasty ceramic censers of *li* and *li-ding* form in *guan*[2] and Longquan celadon ware,[3] and thence to the Western Zhou *li* and *li-ding* bronze vessels from which the Song ceramics derive.[4] Even if Xuande-period *li*-shaped censers lacked them, many Ming-dynasty censers had covers, more than surviving numbers might indicate since many have been lost, but the use of covers increased dramatically during the Qing. Openwork covers not only created patterns in the rising smoke but afforded a measure of protection from fire by preventing exploding embers from bursting out of the censer.

The flowers depicted on this censer – peony, flowering plum, orchid, and chrysanthemum – are the same as those on the previous ewer [28], though the orchid is included here. Indigenous to China, the orchid – in particular, the epidendrum and cymbidium varieties – attracted early notice due to its pleasant scent and unusually shaped petals. Confucius is said to have remarked on the orchid's exquisite qualities, with the result that, like the bamboo, it is revered as an emblem of the *junzi*, or Confucian gentleman. Regarded by extension as a symbol of refinement and of the cultivated scholar,[5] the orchid first gained prominence as a subject of Chinese art during the Yuan dynasty, in the paintings of Zheng Sixiao[6] (1241-1318); it remained popular as a subject of Chinese painting through the Ming and Qing dynasties, with such eighteenth-century artists as Zheng Xie (1693-1765) and Dong Xun (1740-1805) virtually restricting themselves to orchids and the occasional clump of bamboo.[7] The orchid entered the repertoire of bronze ornament in the late Ming [see 11] and appeared intermittently throughout the Qing.

The identity of the flowering branches represented by the handles remains uncertain, since the trees whose cut branches are most typically depicted in the decorative arts – plum, peach, pomegranate, and cherry – have smooth-edged leaves rather than serrated ones. The branches may represent those of the yellow-fruited loquat, however, which occasionally appear with serrated leaves on eighteenth-century porcelains with decoration in overglaze enamels.[8]

The quatrefoil panels on this censer are akin in shape to those that sometimes embellish the walls of Qianlong-period porcelain jars,[9] suggesting an eighteenth-century date of manufacture. In addition, the similarity of the petals in the upper ring of this censer's chrysanthemum collar to those in the previous ewer's single-ring collar [28] further suggests a mid- to late eighteenth-century date of origin, as does the extensive reliance on appliqué elements.

Like the three previous examples, this raised-copper censer was entirely cold worked; in most cases seams indicate the join of separately created pieces that are held together by solder, pins, or tension. Circular marks on its interior suggest that the censer's body was turned on a lathe, after which the resulting bowl-like form was modified to create the distinctive *li*-tripod shape. Their slightly uneven length and irregular spacing indicate that the vertical lines separating one lobe from the next were impressed after the bowl had been lathe turned. Solder secures the cabriole legs to the censer's body, while solder or pins hold the (dye-struck?)

chrysanthemum collar in place. A downward-projecting vertical flange anchors the neck assembly to the body, relying mainly on tension for effect. Pins hold the handles in place; now slightly stretched, they permit the joins more play than was originally the case. The openwork designs of the cover were pierced with punches. Chatter marks in the vertical walls indicate that the decorative panels were carved into the censer's sides. Although portions of the decoration within the quatrefoil panels were carved, the high-relief and openwork elements were created separately and soldered into place; the ring-mat backgrounds were punched. The gilding was accomplished through the application of an amalgam of powdered gold and mercury which was then heated to evaporate the mercury, leaving a thin coating of gold.

Technical and stylistic similarities suggest that catalog numbers twenty-six through twenty-nine were most likely created by related workshops. All of the vessels in this group are made of raised copper, partially or completely gilded after cold working, and all except the circular covered box [27] show a similar darkening of the seams where separately prepared elements were soldered together. In addition, the pieces share low-relief floral decoration set against a ring-punched ground in a slightly sunken geometric panel; the floral motifs of the censer [30] and of the pair of tall ewers [26] include stalks and branches soldered into place with small open spaces between their undersides and the ring-punched grounds. Both the censer [29] and the cylindrical ewer [28] have chrysanthemum collars, while the cylindrical ewer [28] and the covered box [27] have gunmetal gray surfaces and ring-mat grounds so finely punched that they resemble tightly woven fabric in texture; the ring-mat grounds of the censer [29] and of the pair of tall ewers [26], on the other hand, are more loosely punched so that they resemble those of Tang silver, the ultimate source for such textured grounds. Each piece in the group is thus linked to another – with the result that they show a marked cohesiveness in style and in technique of manufacture – suggesting that they come from related workshops, or even from the same workshop; small differences in style indicate that they were likely produced over a number of decades.

30 Zun-shaped Vase with butterfly decor

Ming dynasty, late sixteenth to early seventeenth century
Cast bronze with cast bronze decoration gilded and inlaid with
silver and with induced surface color
18.0 centimeter height
Clague Collection Number 273

FOLLOWING THE FORM of the ancient trumpet-mouthed *zun* wine vessel, this tall but well proportioned, circular vase comprises three integrally cast components: a tall, conical base that splays outward, terminating in a ringed foot; a bulbous central knob with gently rounded sides; and an elongated neck with vertically expanding walls that flare near the top to form the trumpet mouth. Butterflies of various types and sizes embellish the three portions of the vase; presented from a variety of vantage points – from above, in profile, and in three-quarter view, for example – the butterflies are mostly shown in flight with wings spread. The butterflies rise in low relief against a plain background. Most of the butterflies are inlaid with sheet silver, the silver held in place by integrally cast, thread-relief outlines; those not inlaid with silver show sufficient remains of gold to indicate that they were originally completely gilded. A plain, narrow band, top and bottom, frames the decoration on the central knob, while two pairs of bowstring lines – one at the bottom of the neck and the other at the top of the base – set off the knob itself, underscoring the vessel's tripartite division. The lip and ring foot were originally gilded, as were the spaces from the outer bowstring lines to the inner edges of the narrow bands at the top and bottom of the knob, further emphasizing the vessel's divisions on the one hand, but establishing a unifying rhythm on the other. The interior of the vase is undecorated, as is the underside. The warm, dark brown surface tone was induced through chemical treatments.

This handsome vessel was most likely made as a flower vase. In the same manner that they used archaic bronzes as incense burners on special occasions, connoisseurs from Song times onward occasionally used ancient ritual vessels as vases for cut flowers and as pots for growing plants. Late Ming treatises, for example, recommend archaic bronzes, especially the *gu* and *zun*, as the most suitable vases for winter, and Song and early Ming ceramic vases as best for summer, noting that well patinated old bronzes that have been buried for a long time will keep flowers fresh and bright.[1] Paintings of the period, especially those depicting scholars at their leisure, often include archaic bronzes, some of which occasionally function as flower vases and incense burners. Collectors realized that too frequent use of their treasured antiquities would ruin them, so they surrounded themselves with newly made bronzes as well; some, like the present vase, followed ancient forms but used contemporary decorative motifs.

This vase derives from the late Shang *zun*, a stately vessel that in antiquity was used for offerings of warmed wine.[2] Although the *zun* resembles the *gu* beaker in shape, the *zun*'s greater diameter – and thus its somewhat more squat proportions – distinguish it from the elegantly attenuated *gu*. Eclipsed by the *gu*'s popularity, the trumpet-mouthed *zun* was seldom crafted in either bronze or ceramic ware during the Song, but with the growing interest in antique forms, it attracted a following in the late Ming and Qing periods. Several ceramic vases of *zun* shape were recovered from the early seventeenth-century tomb of the Wanli Emperor, some from the Jingdezhen kilns with enamel decoration,[3] and some from the Dehua kilns, seemingly undecorated.[4] In fact, the nearest parallels to the Clague vase in shape are porcelain *zun* with lightly incised floral decoration, made at the Dehua kilns in the late sixteenth or early seventeenth century.[5] Closely akin to the Dehua *zun*-shaped vase recovered from the Wanli Emperor's tomb, such vases have the same basic shape and proportions as the Clague vase; they even have the paired bowstring lines above and below the central knob, exactly as in the Clague vase. The similarity strongly suggests that the Clague vase was made at about the same time.

An occasional theme of both poetry and painting, the butterfly has ancient cultural associations in China. The Warring States-period philosopher Zhuangzi (traditionally, 369-286 BC) – whose writings, along with those of Laozi (traditionally, 604-531 BC), constitute the foundation of the Daoist tradition – mentioned butterflies in several parables. In the most famous one, he relates that he once dreamt he was a butterfly; when he awoke, he paused to wonder how he could determine objectively whether he is a man who dreamt he was a butterfly or whether he is now a butterfly dreaming he is a man.[6] An old Chinese tale, said to be from Zhuangzi, tells of a young student who, chasing a beautiful butterfly, unwittingly stumbled into the private garden of a magistrate. Seeing the official's daughter in the garden, the student was so stricken by her beauty that he vowed to work industriously, and to win her as his bride; in devoting himself to hard work, he not only gained the young woman's hand in marriage but rose to a position of high rank.[7] Its affinity for flowers makes the butterfly a natural symbol for summer. Because of Zhuangzi's dream, the butterfly also represents joy, due to the joy the butterfly experienced in fluttering from flower to flower, and symbolizes philosophical musings; in addition, as in the tale about the student finding a bride, the butterfly emblemizes conjugal felicity.

The association of butterflies with flowers not only underscores the function of this vessel as a vase but recalls a well known story, possibly true, involving the Northern Song Emperor Huizong (1082-1135; reigned 1100-25). An accomplished painter and calligrapher, the Emperor once selected as the theme for a painting competition a line from an old poem that might be translated 'The scent of trampled flowers follows the hoofs of the returning horse.' After reviewing the many submissions, the Emperor adjudged the winning painting to be one depicting butterflies trailing after a horse, capturing the sense of the poem.[8]

The Clague vase is extremely rare not only in featuring butterflies as its principal decorative motif but in presenting them so naturalistically and in such profusion. Although they frequently appear in paintings from the Song onward, butterflies only occasionally appear in the decorative arts during most of the Ming, always in association with flowering plants.[9] It is possible that in the decorative arts butterflies first appear as primary subject matter, independent of flowering plants, on bronzes of the late Ming period such as this vase. Butterflies sometimes stand as the principal ornament on early Qing porcelains, where they appear in smaller numbers and in more formal arrangements. Decorated in overglaze polychrome enamels, a celebrated Kangxi-period *meiping* in the Palace Museum, Beijing, features butterflies against a patterned ground of so-called cracked-ice type,[10] for example, while many small bowls from the Yongzheng-period have butterfly roundels painted in overglaze enamels.[11] By the eighteenth century, several painters, including Shen Quan (1682-after 1760) and Ma Quan[12] (active 1700-50), had become known for their depictions of butterflies. Although they figure more prominently in the decorative arts of the Qing, butterflies did become important as a decorative motif in the late Ming, in such examples as the Clague vase.

Though comparative material is limited, the Dehua porcelain *zun*-shaped vases mentioned above reliably establish a late sixteenth to early seventeenth-century date for this vase. A recent publication attributes a small inlaid bronze vase with related decoration to the first half of the seventeenth century on the similarity of its technique of manufacture to that of Hu Wenming bronzes with inlaid decoration.[13] Perhaps for incense tools, the pear-shaped vase has two registers of butterfly decor, the low-relief butterflies either gilded or inlaid with sheet silver, exactly as in the Clague vase. In addition, the vase's lip, footring, and dividing central band are gilded, as are the corresponding elements of the Clague vase. The traditional idea that bronzes inlaid with sheet gold or silver are 'early' (that is, late Ming) whereas those inlaid exclusively with wire are 'later' (that is, Qing) supports the attribution proposed here; even though inadmissible as evidence at this time, the hypothesis offered by traditional knowledge should be noted in the event that future research one day substantiates it as fact.

This bronze vase was cast as an integral unit. Those few areas that have lost their inlay reveal that at least some of the low-relief surfaces were cold worked after casting to prepare them to receive the sheet-silver inlays. Since most of the inlays are still intact, the extent of the cold work remains uncertain; chisel marks along the insides of the thread-relief borders around the inlays suggest that most of the surfaces destined to receive inlays were at least minimally cold worked. The vase's dark brown hue was apparently achieved through chemical treatments after the completion of the cold work but before the inlays were fitted into place and the gilding applied. The almost complete disappearance of the gilding may have resulted only from wear but it might also have to do with the application of the gold to a chemically altered surface. The gilding was no doubt achieved through the mercury-amalgam process that was standard until replaced by electroplating in the twentieth century.

31 Tall Baluster Vase

with bamboo-stalk rims, with three looped bamboo-stalk legs, with two
bamboo-stalk handles, and three lion-head handles with suspended rings

Qing dynasty, Kangxi period (1662-1722)
Cast bronze with applied elements, with induced surface color, and with
a cast relief mark in standard-script (*kaishu*) characters reading *Da Ming
Xuandenian zhi* in a recessed rectangular cartouche on the base
46.0 centimeter height
Clague Collection Number 211

C ALLED A BALUSTER VASE IN ENGLISH and a *fengwei zun*, or phoenix-tailed *zun*, in Chinese, this large, trumpet-mouthed vessel may have served as a receptacle for flowers or merely as a stately ornament. The tall vase stands on three semicircular feet in the form of looped stalks of bamboo that descend from an ornamental ring, also segmented to look like bamboo, that encircles the lower edge of the base. The truncated conical base rises in three stages, from a short, vertical ring at the bottom through two concave registers that, together, resemble a section of bamboo stalk. Perched atop the base, the wide, bulbous body is of compressed globular form; its flat shoulders lead inward to a low-relief band that receives the soaring neck. Its walls rising almost vertically, the elongated neck culminates in a dramatically flaring mouth; a relief ring segmented to resemble a bamboo cane borders the lip, echoing the ornamental ring at the bottom of the vessel. Akin to the bowstring lines similarly placed on smaller vessels of the same type, two relief bands on the shaft of the neck continue the bamboo theme, as do the two appliqué S-curved handles above. Three high-relief lion heads ornament the shoulder, placed one above each leg; each crisply cast lion head grasps a moveable scalloped ring in its mouth. The flat floor of the vessel – which corresponds to the midpoint of the base's upper concave register – has on its underside a cast mark of six relief characters in a slightly sunken rectangular ground. The surface displays a warm brown exterior hue, artificially created.

Like the previous *zun*-shaped vase decorated with butterflies [30], this tall vase derives from the late Shang *zun* wine vessel. Though separated in date by a century or less, the pieces illuminate the aesthetic sensibilities of two very different eras. More faithful to the ancient *zun* in its proportions, the previous vase reflects the conservative Ming taste for self-contained vessels; the present vase reflects the more daring Qing taste for vessels with dramatic profiles and appliqué ornaments. Among Qing ceramics, the closest relatives to the present vessel are Kangxi-period baluster vases with decoration in underglaze cobalt blue[1] or overglaze polychrome enamels.[2] Though not identical in shape, such Jingdezhen porcelains sufficiently resemble the Clague vase to establish a Kangxi date for the latter.

Apart from its classic, early Qing shape, this vessel's most striking feature is its ornament in the form of sections of bamboo stalk. Bamboo-shaped borders first appeared in Ming lacquer;[3] used only infrequently during the Ming, such borders gained a broader following during the Qing, though they apparently never attained widespread popularity. A related bronze vase in the Field Museum of Natural History, Chicago, also has bamboo-shaped rims and handles, but its low-relief decoration of bamboo and its dramatically attenuated form have earned it an attribution to the Qianlong period.[4] Perhaps closest in style to the Clague vase is a covered rectangular censer recently auctioned at Christies New York; attributed to the 'seventeenth/eighteenth century' in the catalog, the bronze censer has rims and handles in the shape of bamboo stalks and three legs in the form of curved bamboo canes, just as on the Clague vase.[5]

Although bamboo and wood had been used in China since remote antiquity for functional articles as well as musical instruments, their appropriation as materials for the decorative arts came only in the Ming.[6] The literati's attraction to bamboo as a material was no doubt sparked by their interest in bamboo as a subject for painting and as a symbol of the Confucian gentleman. With its Confucian overtones, its relationship to painting, and its warm monochrome color, bamboo was a logical material for the host of new scholars' accoutrements that appeared in the Ming, from brushpots to wristrests and even to small sculptures.[7] Such infatuation with bamboo led to its incorporation into the decorative arts as borders, handles, spouts [28], and even as subject matter [14, 18].

The well modeled lion-head handles on the shoulder resemble those on the Clague collection's circular censer with decoration of eight auspicious emblems [22]. Differing from the usually thin, plain, circular rings on Song, Yuan, and Ming vessels, the somewhat thicker rings on Qing bronzes often have their edges scalloped and their surfaces textured to make them resemble coiled dragons, phoenixes, or clouds; the rings on the Clague vase, for example, include stylized dragons from whose mouths issue cloud scrolls. In addition, since they are anchored with pins, the rings on Qing vessels are often able only to swing back and forth, rather than to rotate freely like the fully moveable rings on earlier bronzes.

As indicated above, the similarity in shape to Kangxi-period porcelain baluster vases establishes the late seventeenth or early eighteenth century date of this vessel. The addition of legs to a vessel type that traditionally stands on a circular foot reflects the early Qing penchant for experimentation, as potters and metalsmiths competed to expand the range of vessel shapes and decoration. In addition, the heads of the stylized dragons on the rings suspended from the lion-head handles find parallels in the borders of Kangxi-period jade plaques.

Although it claims this vase to have been made during the early Ming reign of the Emperor Xuanzong, the six-character mark reading *Da Ming Xuandenian zhi* on the base is spurious, as indicated by its weak calligraphic style. More importantly, the character *de* (second graph in the name Xuande) includes the horizontal stroke at its center that is invariably absent from genuine Xuande marks in any medium – the stroke that appears between the 'four' and 'heart' elements in the dictionary form of the character.[8] Also, neither vessels of this shape nor decoration of this type was made in any medium during the early fifteenth century.

This vessel was assembled from three separately cast sections: base, compressed globular body, and elongated neck with trumpet mouth. Either cast together with the base, or fused there after casting, the vessel floor appears in the upper part of the base, even with the midpoint of the upper concave ring. Now concealed from view, the top of the base projects into the globular body; its upper edge finished in saw-tooth fashion, the projecting flange was hammered flat to join the two sections together, the join perhaps sealed and bolstered with solder. A short flange joins the neck to the body, the join reinforced with both rivets and solder. The bamboo border encircling the foot was integrally cast with the base, as the bamboo border around the lip and the double bamboo rings encircling the shaft were integrally cast with the neck. The lion-head handles seem to have been cast together with the body, but the semicircular bamboo-form legs appear to have been separately cast and soldered into place. The bamboo-form handles were independently cast and riveted into place, as the moveable rings were separately cast and fitted into the mouths of the lions. The warm surface hue resulted either from chemical treatments after assembly or from the application of a brown coating.

32 Two Foliate Gu-shaped Vases

on attached bronze stands, the vases with *chilong* decor

Qing dynasty, Kangxi period (1662-1722)
Cast bronze with attached cast-bronze stands, the decoration cast and
cold worked, the *chi* dragons gilded
27.3 centimeter height
Clague Collection Number 261

IDENTICALLY SHAPED AND DECORATED, these two foliated and elegantly attenuated *gu*-form vases rest on affixed bronze stands cast in the form of small wooden pedestals. In the form of a low hexagonal table, each stand has a flat top with a broad circular platform to receive the vase. A short in-curving leg with indented spine and spreading foot descends from each of the stand's six corners; short aprons with bracketed lower edges join the tops of the legs. In traditional fashion, each *gu*-shaped vase comprises three sections: a truncated conical base, a bulbous central knob, and an elongated neck terminating in a trumpet mouth. Each base consists of two registers: the flaring lower one and the cylindrical upper one. Each register exhibits a relief pattern of descending chrysanthemum petals with rounded tips; the petals in the upper register are centered on the indentations between the petals of the lower register. The small, bulbous central knob sports two playful low-relief *chi* dragons picked out in gilding. Echoing the base, the upper portion of each vessel rises in two stages, from a short cylindrical shaft to the flaring trumpet mouth that climaxes in a cusped rim. A relief panel of rising chrysanthemum petals with rounded tips encircles the lower portion of the neck, corresponding to the chrysanthemum collar that embellishes the upper register of the base. Slightly taller and thinner, the chrysanthemum petals above the central knob are thus also slightly more numerous than their cousins below. The foliations in the upper portion of the neck correspond to the cusps at the mouth. Smaller and twice as numerous as the foliations, the petals in the neck's lower register are positioned such that every other one is centered on a foliation while the alternating ones are centered on the indentations between foliations. Relief lines on the interior of the neck correspond to the indentations. Their bodies depicted from above, the gilded, low-relief *chi* dragons on the central knob maintain slightly different stances, the body of one arching upward, the body of the other curving downward. Shown in profile, the head of the *chilong* with upward-arching body has a trunk-like snout; shown from above, the head of the other *chilong* has a single horn atop its blunt-nosed triangular face. The surfaces of the trumpet mouth, flaring base, and table-top portion of the stand are smooth, but those of the central knob, chrysanthemum panels, and legs and aprons of the stand are textured; the texturing of the central knob recalls ring punching while that of the other elements resembles loosely woven fabric. The low-relief brackets on the aprons were enlivened with diagonal hatching. Artificially created, the warm brown surface hues conceal the brassy metal beneath.

Called *hua gu*, or flower *gu*, these two identical vessels might have served as ornamental vases but they could have functioned as flower vases only with the aid of liners, since their bottoms are pierced to accommodate the pins that anchor the stands. The vases follow the form of the Shang-dynasty *gu* beaker, a slender vessel with flaring mouth that in antiquity was used for offerings of warmed wine.[1] Ancient *gu* beakers had a very slender shaft, thus distinguishing them from their close relative, the *zun* wine vessel [compare 30, 31]. Popular in celadon-glazed stoneware during the Southern Song,[2] *gu*-shaped vessels were seldom fashioned during the Yuan and Ming dynasties. The same interest in antiquity that led to the creation of *zun*-shaped vessels in the late Ming and Qing periods sparked a resurgence in the popularity of the *gu* during the Kangxi[3] and Qianlong eras.[4]

Although they varied slightly in their decorative schemes, Bronze Age *gu* and *zun* vessels typically featured the *taotie* mask as their principal ornament; neither sported *chi* dragons. Regarded as a young, or immature, dragon, the *chilong* had been popular since Warring States and Han times [see discussion, 13]. Occasionally represented in the decorative arts of the Song, Yuan and Ming periods, the *chilong* found special favor in the late Ming and Qing, numbering among the most prominent motifs, especially in carved jades. Usually shown creeping as if stalking prey, the playful *chi* dragons are typically depicted in pairs or in the company of adult dragons (thus forming families). *Chi* dragons always have long coiled tails, often bifurcated or even trifurcated; they sometimes have furry manes and they frequently have flames emanating from their joints, symbolizing their super-natural status.

Presented as diagonally symmetrical pairs during the Ming [see 13], *chi* dragons are usually presented as pairs of complementary opposites during the Qing, in keeping with the Qing taste for *yin-yang* symbolism [compare 21]. In the present vases, for example, each pair of *chi* dragons has one with upward-arching body and the other with downward-curving body, one with bifurcated tail and the other with undivided tail, one with head shown from above and the other with head shown in profile, one with a trunk-like snout and the other with a blunt nose, and one with a horn and the other without.

If the interest in complementary opposites supports the general attribution to the Qing dynasty, the style of the *chi* dragons underlies the specific attribution to the Kangxi period. Shown in profile, the sleekly styled, smooth skinned head of the snouted *chilong* is closely related in style and general appearance to the heads of several sea creatures on the Kangxi-period covered rectangular censer in the Clague Collection [21], for example, and to those of the *kui* dragons that border Kangxi-period white jade plaques and amulets.[5] The interest in texturing otherwise undecorated surfaces – such as the low-relief chrysanthemum panels above and below the central knob on these vases – is a Kangxi characteristic, as is the use of varied but subtle texture patterns. Late Ming bronzes rely on bolder texture patterns – square *leiwen* spirals, ring punching, or diapering drawn from the lacquer tradition – which they restrict to the ground against which decorative motifs are set. Qianlong and later bronzes typically ornament the surfaces or leave them plain, but seldom use texture patterns as ornament.

Another Qing characteristic is the substitution of cast bronze stands for the small wooden pedestals with which the vases might otherwise have been outfitted, the bronze stands conceived as integral, though separately cast, parts of the finished works. Often paired with treasured antiquities, small stands, or pedestals, have a long history in China; their early evolution remains unclear, but some miniature bronze vessels had been mounted on bronze stands at least as early as the Northern Wei period,[6] their four-legged, square stands virtually identical in form to the bases of contemporaneous gilt bronze Buddhist sculptures. The archaeological recovery of miniature pieces of wooden furniture from Southern Song tombs confirms that fine craftsmanship was being applied to the production of small-scale wooden objects by the late twelfth century;[7] whether or not the same workshops might also have crafted wooden stands for antiquities remains unknown, but the topic warrants investigation. The table-like bases on some Yuan bronzes [see 5] and ceramics[8] suggest that such stands were in frequent use by Yuan times. The *Xuande yiqi tupu* records that many Xuande bronze censers were furnished with hardwood stands and covers [see discussions, 23, 24], while Ming paintings and illustrations in Ming woodblock-printed books reveal that stands were in common use by Ming times for vases and censers[9] and for so-called scholar's rocks, which the literati collected and often displayed in their studies.[10]

Probably introduced in the seventeenth century and inspired by the Qing fascination with pyrotechnical displays of virtuosity, trompe l'oeil stands imitating wooden ones had gained popularity by the early eighteenth century, as implied by a Yongzheng-marked porcelain bowl with integrally fired stand in the Palace Museum, Beijing, the bowl with a light blue glaze imitating Jun ware and the stand with a dark purple brown glaze imitating *zitan* wood.[11] In one group of Xuande-type bronze censers, each *li*-shaped censer is paired with an unattached bronze stand.[12] Although they typically bear (spurious) Xuande marks, the censers and stands are clearly later; in some cases, the styles of the stands suggest that the pieces might date to the first half of the seventeenth century.[13] Unattached bronze stands might provide the bridge between wooden and affixed trompe l'oeil stands.

These vessels were each cast in two parts: the vase proper with its flaring base, central knob, and trumpet mouth and the table-like stand with its circular platform. The vases proper lack floors; instead, each relies on the stand to cover the opening on its underside, thus indicating that vase and stand were conceived as a unit from the beginning. Soldered in place, a horizontal bar traverses the interior of each base; the bar anchors the long pin that secures the stand to the vase. The dark surface hue resulted from the application of a brown coating and perhaps also from chemical treatments. The coating makes it difficult to ascertain whether the surface textures were imparted through casting or through cold working, but casting seems likely. The gilding was doubtless achieved through the mercury-amalgam process.

33 Small Globular Vase
with long neck and with plum, peony, and garden rock decor

Qing dynasty, eighteenth century
Cast bronze with cast and cold-worked decoration
12.8 centimeter height
Clague Collection Number 252

STANDING ON A SPLAYED CIRCULAR FOOTRING, this small, unassuming vase has an almost spherical body topped by an elongated cylindrical neck with lightly flaring mouth. The decorative scheme features a branch of blossoming plum intertwined with a flowering tree peony, the tree peony growing beside a rock to suggest a garden setting. Presented against a ring-punched ground, the decorative motifs spread over the entire vessel, without the constraint of formal borders, except the narrow, unembellished lip that echoes the plain footring. The underside of the vase is undecorated, as is the interior. A medium brown coating, visible especially in the hollows of the leaves and flowers, softens the brassy tone of the metal.

Perhaps a flower vase, this elegant vessel finds its ancestors among the similarly shaped ones produced in celadon-glazed stoneware during the Song dynasty by the Yaozhou and *guan* kilns, among others.[1] Inspired by the *baoping* vessels, the so-called ambrosia bottles that were popular in silver,[2] bronze,[3] and ceramic ware[4] during the Sui and Tang dynasties, such organically shaped vases were eclipsed by the pear-shaped *yuhuchun ping* bottles that appeared in the fourteenth century and commanded favor during the late Yuan and early Ming periods in silver,[5] porcelain,[6] and stoneware.[7] Spherical bodied vases enjoyed a revival in the eighteenth century in both monochrome-glazed porcelain and bronze, however, along with a number of other Song shapes.

As decoration, this vase presents the two flowers more popular than any others in traditional China, the tree peony (*mudan hua*) and the wild flowering plum (*mei hua*). Blooming in the third month of the Chinese lunar calendar, the tree peony symbolizes spring; due to its numerous petals, it also represents an auspicious wish to the viewer for wealth [see discussion, 27]. Because the wild plum blooms during the first month of the Chinese year, it stands for winter, and, by extension, for the promise of spring to follow; seeing virtue in its ability to bloom while snow covers its branches, Confucians claim the plum as a symbol of strength in the face of adversity. Others see the delicate blossoms as an emblem of feminine beauty and the rough bark as an emblem of the humble scholar [see discussion, 28].

Depicted in painting and the decorative arts since Tang and Song times, the peony and the plum figure prominently in the decorative arts of the Ming and Qing. In Ming ceramics, flowers of various types are seldom intertwined, though they are often paired with bamboo and occasionally with a pine and rock; when different flowers are presented together, each type usually stands alone, silhouetted against its own backdrop.[8] Even in the sometimes congested decoration of carved red lacquer, a single flower type usually predominates on any given piece; in those cases where several varieties appear together, the flowers are typically segregated by type rather than commingled.[9] Eighteenth-century bronzes and ceramics, by contrast, not only present flowers of varied types together to suggest a garden, but often intertwine them.[10]

The lack of formal borders also points to an eighteenth-century date for this vase, as does the use of a single decorative motif that spreads over the entire vessel surface, from bottom to top. Occasionally omitted, elaborate borders generally played an important role in the ornament of the decorative arts during the Ming;[11] by contrast, borders were often eliminated in the eighteenth century, especially in those pieces with less conservative decor.[12] In addition, during the Ming, formal borders were sometimes used to emphasize a change in vessel profile, underscoring the shift from shoulder to neck, for example, by a change in decorative motif. A desire for surface unity led eighteenth-century craftsmen to adapt their motifs to changes in vessel profile so that a single motif could envelop the entire surface.[13] The very light texturing of the background with half circles, lightly struck with a half-circle punch, recalls the similar, subtle texturing of the ground on the central band of the Kangxi-period *gu*-shaped vases [32], suggesting a date during the first half of the eighteenth century for this vase.

Although the decorative motifs were probably integrally cast with the vase itself, the form and articulation of detail were accomplished through cold working. The ring-mat ground was mechanically punched and the relief decoration finished with a hammer and chisel, which accounts for the relief elements' impeccably straight, vertical sides and for the chatter marks along their edges. Partially concealed by the ring-punch texturing and by the brown coating, intaglio outlines with beveled outer edges surround each decorative element, enhancing the appearance of relief. The ring punching not only imparts a handsome texture to the background, it provides a foil for the decorative elements, making them easier to read; it also conceals the telltale chisel marks imparted in cold working.

34 Large Ovoid Vase with gold splashes

Qing dynasty, Kangxi period (1662-1722)
Cast bronze with applied gold splashes, with brown coating, and a chiseled
relief mark in standard-script (*kaishu*) characters reading *Da Qing
Kangxinian zhi* in a recessed rectangular cartouche on the inset bronze base
29.2 centimeter height
Provenance: Dr Sidney Smith, Cambridge, England
Clague Collection Number 251

THE THICK WALLS OF THIS HEAVY, ovoid vase rise almost vertically, then curve inward at the top to form broad, angled shoulders; after constricting to shape the neck, they terminate in the rounded edges of the gently flaring lip. Carefully arranged gold splashes in three sizes – large, medium, and small – ornament the otherwise plain surfaces of the exterior. Placed just far enough into the underside of the vessel to allow a short footring and then affixed with solder, the separately prepared flat base has at its center a carved reign mark of six relief characters in a slightly sunken rectangular ground; gold splashes identical to those on the exterior walls surround the mark. All interior and exterior surfaces display a warm brown hue, artificially created, that conceals the brassy color of the bronze.

Because so many bronzes with gold-splashed decoration bear spurious Xuande marks [see 35], this Kangxi-marked vase is important in establishing the characteristics of the Kangxi style. Carved in bold standard-script (kaishu) calligraphy, the well written mark on this vase corresponds in style to those on genuine Kangxi ceramics and gives every indication of authenticity.

Said to imitate Tang sancai, or three-color, lead-glazed ware,[1] this stately vase resembles in shape the so-called wannian guan, or myriad-year jars,[2] that were exceedingly popular in porcelain, stoneware, and lead-glazed earthenware during the Tang.[3] Taller than its model, this vase nevertheless incorporates the Tang ovoid jar's flat base, broad shoulders, short neck, organically flowing profile, and lightly flaring lip with rounded edge.

Although bronze horse trappings and ceremonial weapons were sometimes inset with turquoise during the Shang dynasty and although bronze vessels were frequently inlaid with gold, silver, malachite, and turquoise during the Warring States and succeeding periods, abstract splashes of gold were apparently first used as decoration only during the Xuande reign of the early Ming. As Xuande-period craftsmen expanded the range of decoration and surface color on their bronzes, they introduced splashes of gold dispersed over the surface, the best ones said to have gold the color of the peaches of immortality [see discussion, 15 and 16].

Though its exact origins remain unknown, this radically new style of decoration might well have been inspired by the iron-brown splashes that were occasionally applied to qingbai ware[4] and to Longquan celadon ware[5] during the late Song and Yuan periods; since they drew heavily on Song aristocratic ceramics for their shapes, Xuande bronzes could easily have borrowed decorative elements from Song ceramics as well.[6] Used for painting and calligraphy, fine paper enlivened with flecks of gold and silver was just beginning its ascent to popularity in the early fifteenth century and might also have played a role in the creation of such abstract decoration, either directly inspiring those who designed the bronzes or indirectly molding taste to appreciate objects sprinkled with gold and silver.[7]

The varied sizes of its gold splashes distinguish the Clague vase from its Xuande models. Although the paucity of genuine Xuande bronzes renders a precise description of their appearance impossible, illustrations in the 1526 edition of *Xuande yiqi tupu* show those with gold-splashed decoration, called *shenjin* style, with their gold evenly distributed over the vessel surface in a pattern of small dots and flecks.[8] In addition, *Xuande yiqi tupu* and other early sources term the gold and silver splashes *dian*, or dots, and compare them to raindrops and snowflakes,[9] further indicating that the splashes must have been small and presumably evenly dispersed. With their varied sizes and patterned arrangement, the gold splashes on the Clague vase differ from those on Xuande bronzes but resemble designs on a rare variety of Tang *sancai* ware that has as its only ornament splashes of colored glaze, often blue, set against an otherwise plain white ground.[10]

Rarely remarked upon by scholars and critics, early Qing experiments with archaism extended to the use of Tang ceramics as models. The Kangxi period saw the introduction of a variegated green, yellow, aubergine, and white glaze,[11] often called egg-and-spinach glaze in English, that is believed to have been inspired by Tang *sancai*, for example, whereas Yongzheng period witnessed the production of vessels in such Tang shapes as double-fish vases[12] [see discussion, 56] and dragon-handled amphorae.[13] Probably considered rustic or even crude during the Ming, Tang ceramics held at least some appeal as sources of inspiration during the Kangxi and Yongzheng eras, as potters and bronze casters strove to expand their repertoires to meet the demands of an increasingly sophisticated, and sometimes jaded, clientele.

This vase was integrally cast, except for its flat base described above. The mark in the center of the base was cold worked with hammer and chisel, as indicated by the slightly irregular edges of the cartouche and by the chatter marks on the straight vertical walls of the characters. The gold splashes were doubtless applied through the standard mercury-amalgam method, though the process may well have involved several stages.[14]

35 Covered Circular Gui-shaped Censer

with two elephant-head handles and with gold splashes

Qing dynasty, probably early nineteenth century
Cast bronze with applied gold splashes, with rust-brown coating, and with
a chiseled relief mark in standard-script (*kaishu*) characters reading *Da
Ming Xuandenian zhi* in a recessed square cartouche on the base, the cover
hammered, turned, and cold worked
15.2 centimeter width across handles
Clague Collection Number 222

ORNAMENTED WITH A PAIR OF HANDLES in the form of elephant heads, this covered censer comprises a circular bowl resting on a footring of medium height. The bowl has a slightly constricted midsection and a gently flaring lip; a raised band encircles the bowl just below its midsection, emphasizing its bombe form. A wide, slightly concave lip borders the cover, while an openwork pattern of interlocking T's embellishes its subtly domed central portion. A flange on the underside secures the cover in place when set atop the censer. Gold splashes in small, medium, and large sizes enliven the bowl and its cover, footring, and base. A carved reign mark of six relief characters in a slightly sunken rectangular cartouche appears in the center of the base. A tea-brown coating on the exterior surfaces of both censer and cover conceals the brassy color of the bronze.

Claiming a Xuande date for the censer, the six-character mark reading *Da Ming Xuandenian zhi* on the base is spurious, as indicated by the use of the dictionary form of the character *de* (second ideograph in Xuande) with the horizontal stroke at its center that is invariably absent from genuine Xuande marks in all media [see discussion, 31]. The style of the calligraphy derives from Kangxi marks rather than from Xuande marks, as a comparison of the last two characters, *nian zhi*, with the same characters in the genuine Kangxi mark on the following vase [36] reveals. In fact, the present mark's alternation between thick strokes and ones so thin they appear spindly points to a nineteenth-century date of manufacture.

With its circular foot, bowl-shaped container, and animal-head handles, this censer descends ultimately from late Shang and early Western Zhou ritual bronze *gui* vessels, which in antiquity were used for offerings of boiled grain. The relief band about the midsection finds no *locus classicus* among Bronze Age vessels, however, suggesting the possibility of influence from less ancient models as well; in fact, one variety of bowl crafted in silver[1] and ceramic ware,[2] and presumably also in bronze, during the Tang dynasty displays a virtually identical profile, the rounded ridge on this censer corresponding to a similar ridge on the ceramic bowls and to a crest on the silver ones.[3] Like the previous vase [34], this censer finds inspiration for its shape, and perhaps for its splashed decoration, in the arts of the Tang.

Despite its Xuande mark, this censer seems to reflect little relationship to the Xuande bronze tradition. *Xuande yiqi tupu* does not illustrate any censers of this shape, for example, nor does *Xuande dingyi pu* describe any that resemble it. In addition, the Tang-style shape argues against an early Ming connection, suggesting instead that the form was newly invented in the Qing,[4] probably without reference to the Xuande tradition it claims to follow. If there is indeed a connection to Xuande bronzes, it surely lies in the gold-splashed decoration, a style of ornament introduced in the Xuande reign and forever associated with it in the minds of succeeding generations. Illustrations in *Xuande yiqi tupu* suggest that Xuande bronzes with gold-splashed decoration displayed small flecks of gold,[5] however, rather than the large splashes that are characteristic of Qing bronzes. A typical feature of Yuan, Ming, and Qing vessels [see discussion, 17], the elephant-head handles may also indicate a tie to the Xuande tradition, since an illustration in *Xuande yiqi tupu* reveals that at least a few Xuande bronzes had such handles.[6]

The elephant heads' simple style and cursory finish, evident in the unembellished tops of their heads and in the unarticulated spaces within their ears, point to a nineteenth-century date of manufacture for this censer, a date consistent with the mark's calligraphic style. It remains unclear, however, whether this censer represents an original nineteenth-century design or merely a copy of a Kangxi original (as suggested by its Tang-style form and Kangxi-style calligraphy).

The hardwood covers with which some censers were outfitted [see discussion, 24] could be used only when the censers were cool, their fires completely dead; such covers served practical as well as aesthetic functions, protecting the censer from dust, which might taint the fragrance of the incense, and completing the censer's form when not in use by covering its yawning mouth. Openwork metal covers, in contrast, were used while burning incense; also serving both aesthetic and practical functions, they imparted patterns to the rising smoke and prevented exploding embers from popping out of the censer, thus reducing the chance of fire. Planned to complement the decor of the censer, reticulated designs vary considerably from cover to cover: some, such as the present example, feature formal geometric patterns; others incorporate floral scrolls [29]; and yet others include dragons and phoenixes amidst clouds [21].

Of ancient origin, covers for incense burners date at least as early as the Han dynasty. Han bronze and ceramic *boshanlu* censers have mountain-shaped covers with tiny openings often partially hidden from view;[7] reflecting no interest in openwork patterns *per se*, the tiny apertures were concealed behind the subsidiary peaks that flank the main mountain mass with the hope that the emerging smoke would hover about the cover like mist enshrouding a soaring peak. Buddhist censers of the Tang dynasty typically have domed covers with circular openings, the openings and their arrangement clearly a carefully considered element of the design. The most prized secular censers of the day – spherical ones of gold, silver,[8] and bronze[9] – often have openwork floral designs. A ninth or tenth-century Xing porcelain circular box in the Carl Kempe Collection, Stockholm, has an openwork cover with a swastika in the center surrounded by a floral scroll.[10] An auspicious Buddhist emblem and an abbreviation of the character *wan*, or 'ten thousand,' the reticulated swastika on the Kempe box is the distant ancestor of the formalized patterns on the cover of this censer, while the openwork floral scroll is the remote forebear of the designs on the cover of the Clague Collection's gilt copper censer [29]. The pattern of interlocked T's on the present cover recalls similar geometric patterns on Warring States-period textiles and bronze mirrors.[11]

This censer was integrally cast with its footring and medial ridge; riveted into place, the elephant-head handles were also cast, though their eyes were cold worked. The cover too was cast, but its openwork patterns were cold worked, as indicated by the telltale chisel marks and by the slightly irregular spacing of the design elements. Carved with hammer and chisel, the reign mark on the base was also entirely cold worked. The gold splashes are unusually thick, suggesting that they may have been applied through a method other than the mercury-amalgam method; in some cases, their appearance suggests that molten gold might have been dabbed on the surface in carefully configured patterns. The tea-colored hue of the bronze appears to have been achieved through the application of a rust-brown coating.

36 Square Hu Vase
with two stylized-dragon handles and with lotus decor

Qing dynasty, Kangxi period (1662-1722)
Cast bronze with cold-worked decoration, rust-colored coating over golden
flecks, and with a chiseled relief mark in standard-script (*kaishu*) characters
reading *Kangxinian zhi* in a recessed square cartouche on the base
15.0 centimeter height
Clague Collection Number 229

SQUARE IN SECTION, THIS LONG-NECKED VASE has a low-set rectangular body atop a short splayed foot. The walls constrict dramatically at the angled shoulder to form the vertical neck, which terminates in a lightly flared lip. The mouth's size matches that of the foot, while the lip's flare balances the curvature of both shoulder and foot. Two opposed loop handles, each with a projecting spur at the bottom, appear at the top of neck. Representing cloud scrolls, or possibly stylized dragons, the flattened handles have smooth inner edges but scalloped outer ones. Bordered top and bottom by a pair of bowstring lines, a single band of incised decoration embellishes that portion of the neck framed by the handles. Set against a punched ground, the decoration features lotus blossoms with scrolling foliage. A carved reign mark of four relief characters in a slightly recessed square cartouche appears in the center of the flat base. Evenly and generously distributed, small gold flecks cover the exterior surfaces of the vase and handles, including the untextured areas of the lotus scroll but excluding the base and interior of the foot. A reddish-brown coating on the exterior surfaces conceals the brassy color of the bronze and lessens the impact of the gold flecks, giving them the subtle character of so-called shattered-ice cracks within a fine Song celadon glaze.

This vase numbers among the small group of bronzes with Kangxi marks; like the Clague Collection's gold-splashed ovoid vase [34], it is thus important in establishing the characteristics of the Kangxi style. Well carved in powerful *kaishu*, or standard-script, characters, the mark corresponds in style to those on Kangxi ceramics and gives every indication of authenticity. In style, the characters are slightly more fluid than those of marks associated with earlier reigns, suggesting a slightly more cursive model. In addition, many horizontal strokes are relatively thick, as in the character *nian* (era) in the upper left corner, and most of them are set on a slight diagonal, rising from the lower left to the upper right. Also characteristic is the pointed lower tip of the long vertical stroke in the character *nian*. In many Kangxi marks the outer, vertical stroke in the 'knife' element of the character *zhi* (made) curves inward slightly at the top. (The 'knife' element comprises the two parallel vertical strokes in the character's upper right quadrant.) These features are evident both in this mark and in the one on the gold-splashed ovoid vase [34]; many are also apparent in the spurious Xuande mark on the gold-splashed circular censer with elephant-head handles [35], indicating that the spurious mark is based on a Kangxi mark rather than on a Xuande original.

The shape of this vase derives ultimately from the long-necked, bottle-like variant of the *hu* that was popular in both bronze[1] and ceramic ware[2] during the Han dynasty. Although this interpretation of the *hu* disappeared after the fall of Han, it found renewed popularity during the Southern Song, as illustrated by a variety of examples in ceramic ware[3] and bronze [3]. Han-dynasty examples are typically of circular section, but Southern Song ceramic examples include both circular and faceted ones, the faceted ones usually octagonal in section. In the Clague vase, the interpretation of the shape may have been influenced by a rare variety of faceted blue-and-white porcelain vase that was produced during the Xuande period.[4] Except for those made in direct imitation of ancient bronzes, square and polygonal vessels were relatively uncommon during the Ming and Qing; they did, however, enjoy limited popularity during the Kangxi era,[5] as potters and bronze casters explored new shapes and decorative schemes, providing a context for this vase.

Regarded as an emblem of purity and perfection because of its association with the Buddhist church, the lotus also symbolizes summer, standing alongside the peony, chrysanthemum, and plum as one of the flowers of the four seasons [see 19]. Popular in the secular decorative arts since Tang and Song times, the lotus was often depicted on ceramics of the Kangxi period.[6] Described in outline fashion, the lotus blossoms on this vase are close in style to those in Kangxi-period representations of the *bajixiang*, or 'Eight Auspicious Emblems'[7] [see discussion, 20].

The shape and decoration of this vase are fully consistent with its Kangxi date. The background of the floral register, punched with a pointed implement rather than with a ring punch, also reflects the Kangxi taste for finely textured grounds [see 32, 33]. In addition, with their scalloped edges and scrolling cloud form, the handles recall the the moveable rings on the Clague Collection baluster vase with bamboo decor [31].

The foot and base were integrally cast with the vessel itself. Lacking rivet heads and traces of metal at their points of attachment that would indicate they were affixed with solder (or molten bronze), the handles may have been integrally cast with the vase or they may have been cast-on, that is, separately cast in advance and set into the main mold, so that in casting the vessel molten metal surrounded the handles' anchor plates.[8] The floral decoration and reign mark were created entirely through cold working. The thick coating that imparts the rich rust-brown color prevents detailed study of the vessel surface; the method by which the gold flecks were applied thus also remains unknown.

37 Baluster-shaped Temple Vase
with two ring handles and with *taotie* decor

Qing dynasty, Yongzheng period (1723-35)
Cast bronze with cast and cold-worked decoration, a brown coating,
a chiseled relief inscription in standard script reading *Jing zhi* in a recessed
rectangular cartouche on the lip, and a cast relief mark in standard script
reading *Da Qing Yongzhengnian zhi* in a recessed cartouche inside the foot
54.0 centimeter height
Clague Catalog Collection Number 265

T HIS LARGE AND IMPRESSIVE VASE consists of a tall, splayed foot, an ovoid body with rounded shoulders, and a flaring neck with vertical lip. The vertical footring is undecorated, but the splayed foot has two ornamental registers with low-relief decoration, the lower one with four descending lappets, with a stylized cicada at the center of each lappet, and the upper one with two pairs of stylized, strapwork *kui* dragons set against a *leiwen* ground. Two raised bowstring lines bordering a narrow undecorated band distinguish the body from the foot. The body displays three ornamental registers, the registers separated by plain bands bordered by parallel relief lines. Highly formalized and bilaterally symmetrical, a low-relief pattern comprising two pairs of confronting *kui* dragons placed against *leiwen* enlivens the middle register, a single square *leiwen* spiral set on a corner marking the join of the two dragons of each pair. Each subsidiary register has two pairs of *kui* dragons against a *leiwen* ground.

Like those of the Kangxi reign, marked bronzes of the much shorter Yongzheng era are extremely rare, making this handsome vase an important document in charting the evolution of bronze style during the eighteenth century. A recently published *ding*-shaped censer has a mark dated to the first year of the Yongzheng reign (1723);[1] as might be expected, its calligraphic style derives from that of the preceding Kangxi period though it is distinguishable from it. The six-character mark on the present vase, by contrast, shows the fully developed Yongzheng style, which is based on characters in woodblock-printed books rather than on the calligraphy of brush-written texts. The mark is identical in style to those on imperial porcelains of the day, confirming the authenticity of the vessel.

The two characters on the lip reading *Jing zhi* (Respectfully made) indicate that the vase was a presentation piece, probably for a temple. This vase and a probable mate would likely have been used with a large *ding*-shaped censer[2] as a three-piece altar set or, with the addition of two candlesticks, as a five-piece set [38]. Large temple vases probably appeared during the late Song period and were established by the Yuan dynasty, as illustrated by the noted pair of blue-and-white porcelain vases in the Percival David Foundation, London,[3] dated by inscription to 1351 and presented with an incense burner by Zhang Wenjin 'as a prayer for the protection of the whole family and for the peace and prosperity of his descendants.'[4] The Clague vase was no doubt given in the same spirit.

Although its tripartite division might suggest that it derives solely from Shang-dynasty ritual bronze *zun* vessels, the Clague vase actually traces its lineage through a series of related blue-and-white vases to vessels of the David Collection type.[5] At the same time, the Clague vase represents Yongzheng antiquarianism at work in bringing the shape and proportions of the standard temple vase into conformity with those of Bronze Age *zun*; it combines elements from standard temple vases with ones from late Shang bronze *zun* and with ones from Kangxi-period baluster vases.[6] The vessel thus harmonizes not only with the ancient bronze-style decor with which it is ornamented but with *ding*-shaped censers of the type with which it was probably used. Eighteenth-century ceramic counterparts to the Clague vase are rare, but a late Kangxi cobalt-blue glazed vessel in the Museum of Fine Arts, Boston, has an ovoid body with a related ring on its inclined shoulder, providing a context for the Clague vase.[7] In contrast, a blue-and-white presentation vase dated to 1740 and formerly in the Laurent Heliot Collection, Paris, illustrates the more mannered interpretation characteristic of the Qianlong period.[8]

The size, symmetrical decor, and balanced shape with clearly defined units imbue this vase with a monumentality unknown in bronzes of the Kangxi era. Like the calligraphy of its mark, the vase reflects a self-confident new style, at once powerful and mature, restrained and appealing. The style reflects a keen interest in antiquity, yet it avoids the slavish imitation that is the bane of many archaistic bronzes; thus, it borrows *taotie* masks, *kui* dragons, triangular lappets, and *leiwen* grounds from ancient bronzes, but combines them in a new and fanciful way with strapwork dragons that have more to do with Kangxi white jade amulets[9] than with antiquity. Meticulously wrought, the intricate *leiwen* patterns represent a turn away from the subtly textured grounds of the Kangxi era, reflecting the influence not only of late Shang bronzes but of contemporaneous carved red lacquer, the latter a trend that would become even more pronounced during the Qianlong era [see 39]. The very dark coating applied to the *leiwen* ground may also reflect influence of the lacquer tradition, since eighteenth-century carved red lacquers sometimes feature their relief ornaments against a diapered black lacquer ground.[10]

This heavy vase is so perfectly finished that it is difficult to ascertain whether it was integrally cast as a single unit or whether it was cast in two or three sections. The rings and their supporting escutcheons were separately cast and affixed. The principal decorative motifs were likely cast in relief but articulation of detail was cold worked. The six-character reign mark was integrally cast, but the two characters on the lip were cold worked. The base was separately prepared and inset.

38 Five-piece Altar Set

comprising one circular ding-shaped censer with two flaring handles and three cabriole legs and with dragon and cloud decor, a pair of pricket candlesticks with dragon and cloud decor, a pair of pear-shaped vases with ring handles and with dragon and cloud decor

Qing dynasty, Qianlong period, mid-eighteenth century
Cast bronze with cast and cold-worked decoration, with brown coating,
and with a cast thread-relief mark in standard-script (*kaishu*) characters
reading *Da Qing Qianlongnian zhi* in a recessed rectangular cartouche on
the base of the censer
32.2 centimeter height for the censer, 38.1 centimeter height for the
candlesticks, 26.7 centimeter height for the vases
Clague Collection Number 223

T HE ONLY KNOWN COMPLETE Qianlong-period five-piece bronze altar set outside of China, and probably made for use in one of the Qing imperial palaces, this exquisitely finished altar set includes a *ding*-shaped censer, two pricket candlesticks, and two pear-shaped flower vases. Of compressed globular form, the censer rests on three plain cabriole legs that issue from the mouths of maned leonine heads. A pair of opposed s-shaped handles rises from the shoulders. The decoration on the body of the censer consists of three, five-clawed dragons, each pursuing a flaming pearl. Centered over the front leg, the horned, whiskered, and maned principal dragon is coiled about a pearl. The subsidiary dragons face the principal one, their bodies trailing around the censer's sides and their tails decorating its back. Wisps of flame emanating from their joints symbolize the dragons' extraordinary powers, while enveloping clouds indicate the celestial setting. A ring of stylized lotus petals borders the top of the shoulder; two pairs of confronting dragons enliven the neck. A medium-brown coating conceals the brassy color of the bronze on the censer as well as on the candlesticks and vases. Dragons pursuing pearls constitute the candlesticks' principal decorative motif, appearing on the column, drip tray, and bell-shaped base. Like the censer and candlesticks, the vases have dragons pursuing pearls as their principal ornament.

Introduced by the Buddhist church, five-piece altar sets (*wugong*) comprising a censer (*xianglu*), candlesticks (*zhutai*), and vases (*huaping*) probably first appeared in the Southern Song period,[1] with illustrations in woodblock-printed books confirming that they were definitely in use by the Yuan.[2] Although their use was limited to religious altars, such sets were quickly appropriated by other Chinese religious institutions, so that they appear in Confucian and Daoist temples as well as in shrines honoring various local and city gods, in halls dedicated to the spirits of ancestors, and on altars in the tombs of high-ranking officials. Five-piece altar sets were invariably arranged in a line across the altar, with the censer in the center, the vases on the ends, and the candlesticks between the censer and vases, as indicated by illustrations in early woodblock-printed books[3] and by archaeological investigations.[4]

In antiquity, *ding* tripods and other three-legged vessels were apparently intended to be placed with their handles at right and left and with two legs in front and a single one in back, as indicated by the orientation of their inscriptions;[5] illustrations in woodblock-printed books show that the convention had become misunderstood by Song times. Censers with a compressed globular body and cabriole legs issuing from the mouths of animals derive from ritual bronze *ding* vessels of the Western Zhou period. Of loop type, the handles of most Shang and early Western Zhou *ding* vessels spring directly from the vessel lip, but by the tenth century BC, *ding* vessels were sometimes fitted with lids, necessitating a shift of the handles from the lip to the upper vessel wall. The earliest of such vessels have L-shaped handles that rise vertically,[6] but from the early Eastern Zhou onward the vertical elements often incorporate a slight curve.[7] So-called heaven-soaring handles, large, S-curved handles like those on the Clague censer, apparently first appeared during the Song. Interpretations of the *ding*-shaped censer were cast during the centuries from Song to Qing, but illustrations in woodblock-printed books indicate that from the Yuan dynasty onward ones of compressed globular form with heaven-soaring handles were preferred for use on altars.[8] The ancestry of the present censer can be traced through related bronze examples produced during earlier Qing reigns,[9] to similar ones made during the Ming,[10] to fourteenth-century blue-and-white porcelain ones[11] based on bronze models.

Archaeological excavations at Song sites have yielded pricket candle-sticks with bell-shaped bases and dished drip trays, though such Song pieces usually lack the tall columns that are characteristic of Yuan, Ming, and Qing examples.[12] Ancestors of the present pieces, candlesticks with tall columns number among the items recovered from the remains of the Chinese merchant ship that sank off the coast of Sinan, Republic of Korea, in 1323.[13] Illustrations in woodblock-printed books confirm that pricket candlesticks were definitely in use by Yuan times, some with bell-shaped bases,[14] some with tripod stands.[15] Pricket candlesticks were produced in blue-and-white porcelain during the Ming dynasty[16] and in cloisonné enamel,[17] carved red lacquer, and blue-and-white porcelain[18] during the Qing, the Qing examples with the same shape as the Clague ones.

Song and Yuan book illustrations show that globular vases with long necks [3] – sometimes with tubular appendages at the mouth in the manner of a miniature *touhu* vessel [4, 9] – were frequently used in early times,[19] though baluster vases[20] [37] and pear-shaped ones predominated in the Ming and Qing. Distantly descended from Bronze Age *hu* wine jars, these vases represent the Qing incarnation of the pear-shaped vase that became popular in the early Ming [7]. Handles of scalloped C-form, termed cloud-scroll or *ruyi*-head handles, were an innovation of the Qianlong era.[21]

Regarded already in late Zhou and Han cosmology as one of the four directional animals, the green dragon represents the east, alongside the red phoenix of the south, the white tiger of the west, and the intertwined black snake and tortoise of the north [44]. Dragons are usually considered symbols of the *yang*, or male, forces of the universe, the *yin*, or female, forces represented by the phoenix. During Ming and Qing, the five-clawed dragon (*long*) served as the emperor's insignia, so that many works destined for the palace bear the emblem.

The pairing of dragon and pearl seems to represent a combination of elements from two separate traditions, the dragon from Chinese mythology and the pearl from Buddhist iconography. The pearl derives from the Buddhist *cintāmaṇi*, or wish-granting jewel (Chinese, *ruyi baozhu*), that is held by a number of Buddhist deities, including the Bodhisattvas Ruyilun Kuanyin (Cintāmaṇi-cakra Avalokiteśvara) and Dizang (Kṣitigarbha). The *cintāmaṇi* is thus not a pearl in the strict sense of the term, but a talismanic jewel that symbolizes transcendent wisdom and can grant every wish. The flames surrounding the jewel symbolize its magical powers. Expanding upon Buddhist tradition, Chinese lore maintains that the magical jewel is obtained not only from the relics of a Buddha, but from the dragon-king of the sea or from the head of the mythical hybrid creature known as a *makara*.[22] The motif of dragon and jewel thus associates the dragon with knowledge and supernatural powers; as an imperial emblem, it associates those attributes with the emperor.

Dragons of various types ornament Neolithic painted pottery and Bronze Age ritual vessels. The distant ancestor of the slender, scaled, serpentine creature with long neck and tail that we recognize as the Chinese dragon first appeared during the late Zhou or Han period.[23] Linked with water, especially with rain for the nation's crops, the dragon is usually presented amid clouds and is often shown striding above cresting waves. The earliest pairing of dragon and pearl is difficult to pinpoint, but the association perhaps began in the Tang, as suggested by the placement of the dragon in relation to the hemispherical knob on the backs of some Tang-dynasty bronze mirrors; the popularity of the motif soared in the Yuan period, perhaps along with the then newly introduced *bajixiang* and *babao* motifs, respectively, the Eight Auspicious Emblems and the Eight Treasures [see discussion, 20]. Favored as a subject for painting on paper and silk during the Tang and Song dynasties, the dragon has been among the most prominent motifs in the decorative arts since the Song, the imperial five-clawed dragon, often shown with the flaming pearl, predominating on pieces made for the palace in the Ming and Qing. Carved stone architectural elements within the Forbidden City bear the same motif.

Ding-shaped censers in bronze and ceramic ware were embellished with dragons by the Song and Yuan periods.[24] The presentation of the principal dragon with its face shown frontally and its coiled body shown in profile signals the Qianlong date of this altar set,[25] as do the dragon's rectangular face, square jaw, and humanlike nose; such features appear in most Qianlong-era representations of dragons.[26] Both the style of the dragons and the relatively small number of clouds (compared to those on later Qianlong bronzes)[27] indicate that this altar set was made early in the reign, probably before 1750, a dating that accords with the calligraphic style of the reign mark.

The integrally cast mark on the base of the censer reading *Da Qing Qianlongnian zhi* indicates that this altar set was made during the Qianlong reign. Its characters modeled on those in woodblock-printed books, the thread-relief mark is like those on Yongzheng bronzes [see 37], though the lack of a thick, ornamental flourish at the right end of the horizontal strokes distinguishes its characters from ones in both Yongzheng marks and printed books. The connection to Yongzheng marks suggests a date of manufacture early in the reign, before the mature Qianlong style had evolved. Marks on large bronzes produced later in the reign typically have characters boldly written with thick strokes [see 39]; in addition, such marks often appear prominently placed on the vessel lip and they often use *zao* (created) as the final character rather than *zhi* (made).[28]

The five bronzes in this set were cast, though all have attached parts and show extensive evidence of cold working.[29] The decorative motifs were selectively worked with hammer and chisel after casting to define form and to articulate detail, giving them the crispness associated with the carved red lacquers on which they are modeled.

39 Circular Covered Box with dragon and phoenix decor

Qing dynasty, Qianlong period, second half eighteenth century
Assembled body of hammered and turned bronze with cold-worked
decoration and with a chiseled relief mark in standard-script (*kaishu*)
characters reading *Qianlongnian zao* in a recessed square cartouche on
the base, the interior of the box and cover lined with pewter
20.3 centimeter diameter
Clague Collection Number 210

O F FLATTENED HEMISPHERICAL FORM, this covered circular box
has a wide, bowl-shaped container resting on a broad, vertical
footring; the tall cover has straight sides and a top that is nearly
flat, the top and sides joined by the rounded shoulders. Set against a
ground lightly textured to resemble woven fabric, a series of low-relief
dragon and phoenix motifs graces the box and its cover. Surrounded by
wispy clouds, a five-clawed, horned dragon and a phoenix with segmented
tail appear in the cover's central medallion. Occupying the lower half of
the composition, the S-curved dragon strides toward the viewer's right,
its legs extended and its head turned to face the flaming pearl set atop a
stylized lotus blossom at the center of the medallion. Its wings extended
in flight, its long tail fluttering behind, the phoenix occupies the upper half
of the composition; though it flies toward the viewer's left, the phoenix
turns its head to face the flaming pearl at the medallion's heart. A band of
simplified *leiwen* resembling interlocked T's borders the medallion. Three
confronting dragon and phoenix motifs embellish the cover's sides, while
another three enliven the walls of the bowl; a stylized peony blossom and
a stylized lotus with flaming pearl appear between the heads of each confronting pair, while enveloping clouds set the celestial context. Identical
bands of interlocked-T *leiwen* encircle the lips of box and cover; a similar
but more emphatic *leiwen* band ornaments the footring. The interiors of
both box and cover are plain, though both are lined with pewter.

The four-character mark reading *Qianlongnian zao* on the base indicates that this box was made during the Qianlong reign. The use of *zao*
(created) as the final character further indicates that the box was made
during the second half of the eighteenth century, a dating that agrees
with the bold calligraphic style of the mark [38]. Though they seldom merit
praise as fine calligraphy, the characters in marks of fully developed Qianlong
style are typically powerful, their power deriving not only from their relatively large scale and their tendency to intrude into each other's space,
but from their thick yet modulated strokes, the vertical and diagonal ones
often with pointed ends, and their diagonally oriented horizontal strokes.

This circular covered box is an almost literal copy of a contemporaneous box in carved red lacquer.[1] Lacking Bronze Age prototypes, such
boxes trace their ancestry to the smaller gold and silver boxes that were
popular in aristocratic circles during the Tang [see discussion, 12]. Imitated
in Ding porcelain and in a variety of celadon-glazed stonewares during
the Song, such small containers inspired larger boxes with domed covers
during the Yuan, both in *qingbai* porcelain[2] and in carved red and black

lacquer.³ Covered circular boxes were produced in lacquer throughout the Ming and Qing, their popularity prompting imitations in bronze, porcelain,⁴ and cloisonné enamel⁵ from the late Ming onward. The decoration often spreads across the entire cover in Yuan and early Ming carved lacquer boxes, but by the mid-sixteenth century the principal decorative motif usually appears within a central medallion.

Popular as subjects of the decorative arts since the Tang, dragons and phoenixes were usually presented separately until the Yuan,⁶ after which they were occasionally presented together. Symbolizing the interdependence of complementary opposites, *yang* and *yin*, male and female, emperor and empress, the motif of paired dragon and phoenix found favor during the Wanli era, often embellishing imperial porcelains of the day,⁷ and soared to popularity during the Qing, frequently appearing on materials destined for the palace [compare 21].

The decoration reflects typical Qianlong style, evident in the overall complexity of the design and especially in the cusped lower edge of the phoenix heads. Diligently copied, the insistent *leiwen* bands are a characteristic feature of Qianlong carved lacquer boxes, as are the cloud heads, which are simplified renditions of those on carved Ming lacquers. The lightly textured ground is less a reference to the subtly textured grounds of Kangxi bronzes [see 32, 33] than to the sometimes lightly stippled yellow grounds of Qianlong carved lacquers.

Perhaps this covered box's most remarkable feature is that it was not cast but completely cold worked. The cover comprises two pieces of metal separately crafted and fused together: the flat top, which extends about two centimeters beyond the *leiwen* band bordering the central medallion, and the vertical sides with their rounded shoulders and *leiwen* embellished lip. Encircling the central medallion like a halo, a line indicating the join of top and sides is visible in some parts of the design. A vertical seam marks the join of the two ends of the metal piece that constitutes the cover's walls and shoulders. In essence a mirror image of the cover, the bowl comprises a flat base plate, corresponding to the cover's flat top, and a curving cavetto, corresponding to the cover's walls and shoulders; a vertical seam indicates the join of the cavetto's two ends. Fused into place with molten metal, the separately prepared footring conceals the join of cavetto and base plate. Soldered around the interior of the box, just inside the mouth, a short flange projects upward to receive the cover, the solder bolstered with four evenly spaced rivets whose heads are visible on the exterior of the box, just below the *leiwen* ornamented lip. The pewter lining conceals the joins from view on the interior and perhaps also acts as a binder, reinforcing the joins and helping to keep all parts together. The reign mark on the base was chiseled and the decoration was entirely cold worked with a hammer and a variety of implements, as indicated by the marks along the sides of the low-relief elements.[8] In addition to enhancing the legibility of the decorative motifs, the lightly textured grounds conceal the chisel marks and other evidence of cold working. In sum, this covered box imitates not only the style of carved lacquer but something of its techniques of decoration as well; as a result, the box captures the crispness of carved lacquer designs.

40 Double Pear-shaped Vase
with strapwork-dragon decor

Qing dynasty, Qianlong period, probably last quarter eighteenth century
Cast bronze with cast and cold-worked decoration, applied gold splashes,
with localized applications of grayish-brown coating, and with an incised
intaglio mark in standard-script (*kaishu*) characters reading *Qianlongnian
zhi* on the countersunk base of the larger vase
8.9 centimeter height
Clague Collection Number 201

THIS UNUSUAL DOUBLE VASE is made up of two small pear-shaped vases, a larger one and a smaller one joined at midsection. Each ovoid vase has a lightly swollen body and a constricted neck. A band of low-relief cicada-shaped lappets encircles the shoulder of each vase; set within the cicada panel on the front and back of each vase is a small, animal-mask escutcheon from which descends a fixed ring decorated with bosses. Dominating these symmetrically placed and regularly occurring elements is an overlay of archaistic, strapwork dragons arranged asymmetrically. Splashes of gilding contrast with brown-coated areas, the applied coating betrayed by tiny brushstrokes. The vessel, its bases, and decoration appear to have been integrally cast, though various ornamental details were imparted through cold working.

Reading *Qianlongnian zhi*, the four-character mark indicates that this double vase was made during the Qianlong reign. Lacking the finesse of cast and carved marks [contrast 38 and 39], this incised mark appears clumsily written on first inspection, but it corresponds to ones incised on works of cloisonné enamel[1] and Peking glass[2] from the Qianlong era.

From one of the Qing palaces,[3] this vase probably served an ornamental rather than practical function, though it might have held water for use at a desk. It reflects the Qianlong taste for paired objects,[4] for archaistic designs, and for ever more unusual styles. The newly invented vase shape was most likely inspired by small (but longer necked) vases of so-called 'hanging gall' (*danping*) form that were made in *guan* ware during the Southern Song and Yuan periods[5] and that were treasured during the Qing, as indicated by examples in the imperial collection.[6] The archaistic, disembodied dragons, however, derive ultimately from the dragon interlaces that frequently appear on bronze vessels of the Eastern Zhou period.[7] Strapwork dragons had been used as borders on white jade plaques of the Kangxi period[8] and, set against a *leiwen* ground, as the principal decorative motif on Yongzheng bronzes [37]; new here is the arrangement in an asymmetrical design that breaks with the traditional Chinese preference for symmetry.

The double vase's insistent asymmetry suggests a date of manufacture late in the Qianlong era, when artists dared experiment with mannered forms in creating works for the palace. Two similar double vases in enamel bear inscribed dates of 1786, supporting the dating proposed here.[9] A double vase almost identical to the Clague vessel was formerly in the collection of W. W. Winkworth, London.[10]

41 Circular Lobed Hand Warmer

with bail handle and with rock and floral decor

Qing dynasty, eighteenth century
Raised copper with cold-worked decoration
19.1 centimeter diameter
Clague Collection Number 233

RESTING ON A SHORT, VERTICAL FOOT, this hammered copper hand warmer has a compressed spherical body segmented into eight lobes, each lobe identically ornamented with a chrysanthemum, a peony, and a sprig of bamboo. The medallion at the center of the openwork cover depicts two boys dancing on a rocky outcropping. An openwork lotus scroll with spiky leaves and stylized blossoms surrounds the medallion.

Hand warmers were used in the studio, the scholar's hands particularly susceptible to cold since they had to remain ungloved for writing and painting.[1] In his *Zhangwu zhi* of 1637, Wen Zhenheng notes that ancient bronze *pen* basins and *fu* and *gui* food vessels could be used as hand warmers (*shoulu*), as could three-legged, drum-shaped Xuande bronzes with animal-head handles[2] [22], suggesting that hand warmers and censers shared similar origins and that some of the bronzes labeled censers today may have served as both incenser burners and hand warmers. Reinforcing the association is a group of Kangxi ceramic incense burners fashioned in the shape of bronze hand warmers.[3]

The earliest bronzes distinguishable specifically as hand warmers bear the mark of Hu Wenming[4] [11 and 12]. Though a few are circular, most of the small number of known Hu Wenming examples are low and square-bodied with rounded corners.[5] Qing-dynasty warmers are both square and circular, the circular ones sometimes suggesting baskets in shape.[6]

The style of this hand warmer indicates a mid-eighteenth-century date. The inclusion of plants of several types within the same decorative panel is an eighteenth-century trait,[7] and the depiction of peonies next to chrysanthemums is like the decoration on Qianlong enameled porcelains.[8] A *leiwen* band at the foot and the tight decorative scheme recall those on Qianlong lacquers and bronzes [39], and the cover's lotus scroll with its spiky leaves resembles floral arabesques painted on Qianlong porcelains.[9]

Though it bears neither mark nor signature, this hand warmer can be attributed on the basis of style to Pan Xiangfeng.[10] Known only from a four-character mark reading *Pan Xiangfeng zhi* (Made by Pan Xiangfeng) on a recently published hand warmer,[11] Pan Xiangfeng remains a virtually unknown artist. His warmer has the same shape, profile, and proportions as the Clague warmer, including the rare and distinctive vertical foot.[12] With its large, boldly written, closely spaced characters, the mark on the recently published piece recalls those on mature Qianlong bronzes [39] and cloisonné enamels.[13] Such relationships, along with the warmers' stylistic features, suggest that Pan Xiangfeng was active in the Qianlong period.

42 Circular Hu Vessel
with three ring handles and with *taotie* decor

Qing dynasty, late eighteenth-nineteenth century
Cast bronze with cast and cold-worked decoration, damascened
overlays of silver and gold, and brown coating and induced patina
43.5 centimeter height
Clague Collection Number 241

INSPIRED BY ANTIQUE INLAID WINE VESSELS, this jar derives from Warring States *hu* vessels, as indicated by its low-set, pear-shaped body and flaring neck of medium length,[1] rather than from the short-necked, spherical-bodied ones of the Han.[2] The use of three ring-handles, rather than two, quickly distinguishes this jar from late Bronze Age vessels, however, as does the relief decoration of *taotie* masks, *kui* dragons, and descending lappets, features associated more with Shang and Western Zhou bronzes than with those of Warring States and Han.

Colorful and luxurious, inlaid bronzes found a ready market from the Song onward, appreciated for their unmistakable link to that utopian age known as the Three Dynasties (Xia, Shang, and Zhou) during which King Wen, King Wu, the Duke of Zhou, Laozi, Confucius, and other cultural heroes lived. In general, inlaid bronzes made during the Song, Yuan, and early Ming follow the manner of Warring States and Han inlaid bronzes, creating their designs with their gold and silver inlays; set directly into the vessel wall, the gold and silver elements are flush with its surface.[3] Although some late Ming and Qing bronzes retain this approach,[4] many of these later inlaid bronzes are cast in low relief, using inlays of gold and silver merely to ornament the relief elements.[5] Probably introduced in the late Ming,[6] damascening became popular in the Qing, supplanting traditional inlay in which the gold and silver elements, whether wires or small sheets, are set into prepared recesses with undercut edges [44]; in damascening, sometimes called false inlay, the surface areas to be embellished with gold or silver are scored with a fine network of hatched lines so that thin pieces of gold and silver adhere to the roughened surface when hammered into place.[7]

The embellishment of the relief designs with gold and silver indicates a date no earlier than the late Ming for this vessel, and the reliance upon damascening, rather than inlay, points to a date in the late eighteenth or nineteenth century. With long, curved snouts and with mouths agape, the *kui* dragons argue for a late Qianlong or post-Qianlong date,[8] as do the patternized *taotie* masks, whose open, nearly toothless mouths recall yawns more than ferocious snarls. The results of a thermoluminescence (TL) test performed on a sample of casting core removed from under the foot-ring of this jar are consistent with a late Qing attribution.[9]

Integrally cast, the relief decoration shows traces of cold finishing. The base was added after casting; the ring-handles appear to have been separately cast and fused into place. All gold and silver elements, including the lip's silver-wire *leiwen* border, were applied through damascening.[10]

43 Water Vessel in the form of a recumbent lion

Yuan to Ming dynasty, fourteenth – fifteenth century
Cast bronze vessel with cast decoration
5.1 centimeter height x 10.2 centimeter length
Clague Collection Number 236

T HIS WATER CONTAINER for the scholar's desk was cast in the form of a recumbent lion. Lying on its stomach, the lion lifts its head from its exceptionally long-clawed paws and turns to its right, so that the composition forms a C-curve. The lion's eyes are open and its lips parted, exposing its teeth, which imparts a ferocious demeanor. The tightly curled mane frames the lion's face. Smoothly modeled knobs along the back indicate the spine, while subtly modeled vertical ridges suggest ribs. The long tail lies close to the body, its curls echoing those of the mane. Perhaps originally fitted with a cover, the circular opening in the back permitted the vessel's hollow interior to be filled with water. The lion's left rear leg was entirely omitted. The base is flat and plain.

Preferably a detached pavilion within a garden, at least a separate room within a house, the studio was a retreat in which the scholar could study, paint, write poetry, examine antiquities, and entertain friends. Scholars took great pride in their studios and appointed them in an elegant manner that expressed their learning and taste.[1] Apart from ink, inkstone, brush, and paper, the so-called *wenfang sibao*, or 'four treasures of the scholar's studio' that were actually used for writing and painting, numerous other implements were crafted for the desk: brushpots, wristrests, paper-weights [45-47], brush washers, water droppers [44] and brushrests [48, 49]. Since water was required not only for preparing ink but for rinsing the brush, a variety of small vessels evolved for keeping a supply at hand, of which this lion-shaped container is one.

Fashioned in jade, bronze, and porcelain, animal-shaped vessels were especially popular as water containers during the Song, Yuan, and early Ming. The very long claws,[2] ferocious demeanor, smooth body surfaces, plain base, and limited number of spinal knobs[3] distinguish this lion as a work of the Yuan or early Ming period. With its very regular curls, the mane resembles those of lion-head handles on Xuande bronze censers.[4] Small sculptures rather than vessels, recumbent dogs and lions crafted in jade in the Tang and Song usually have more strongly articulated ribs and spines,[5] whereas ones from the mid- and late Ming tend to have more insistently patterned surfaces (with tufts of fur on either side of the spine, for example). In addition, mid- and late Ming examples are typically less ferocious and more contrived, shown following a leader [14], playing with a brocaded ball, or grasping a blossoming branch or a stalk of *lingzhi* fungus in their mouths [compare 13]. The lack of cold work on this integrally cast vessel also points to its early date and associates it with Yuan and early Ming bronze vessels.[6]

44 Water Dropper

in the form of a tortoise with a snake on its back, the tortoise grasping
a two-handled oval cup in its mouth

Ming dynasty, late sixteenth – first half seventeenth century
Cast bronze with decoration inlaid in gold and silver
5.1 centimeter height x 12.7 centimeter length
Clague Collection Number 259

OR THE SCHOLAR'S DESK, the tortoise holds an 'eared cup', a shallow, elliptical cup with flange-like handles on its long sides, in its mouth. Inlaid silver wires indicate the tortoise's eyes, wrinkles, knees, and toes and define the hexagon design of the shell, each hexagon with a pattern of inlaid dots at its center. Lying along the top of the tortoise's back, the snake curves around the circular well that opens into the interior cavity. An inlaid silver wire indicates the snake's spine and inlaid silver dots suggest its patterned skin. An opening at the back of the tortoise may have anchored a separately prepared tail.

The water dropper allowed the scholar to regulate the tonality of the ink by adding water to the inkstone drop by drop. In this case, the water was dispensed onto the inkstone from the cup, to which it was transferred via the small hole at the front of the tortoise's mouth. The step inside the well on the tortoise's back suggests that the larger opening may have been fitted with a stopper.

Inkstones and solid ink cakes had appeared by the Han,[1] and water droppers of bronze, jade, and ceramic ware were in use by the Six Dynasties, if not earlier. This water dropper was inspired by a type of water dropper popular during the Six Dynasties that took the form of a *bixie* chimera grasping an eared cup.[2] In 1637, Wen Zhenheng wrote that his contemporaries used a variety of antique water droppers, some of them animal-shaped vessels made for other purposes but modified in the late Ming to make them suitable for use as water droppers.[3]

The eared wine cup first appeared during the Warring States period.[4] Made of bronze, jade, gold, silver, painted lacquer, or ceramic ware, it was apparently a regular feature of Han life. Its popularity began to wane with the fall of Han, but examples exist from the Six Dynasties.

An emblem of longevity, the tortoise appears on Neolithic painted pottery and on archaic ritual bronzes. By the Han dynasty, it was intertwined with the snake to represent both north and winter.[5] Since black is the color associated with north, and thus with intertwined tortoise and snake, the pair is sometimes known as Xuanwu, the Dark Warrior. The Zhou-dynasty *Liji*, or Book of Rites, states that along with the dragon, phoenix, and *qilin*, the tortoise is one of the *siling*, or four intelligent creatures,[6] which, according to Chinese mythology, appear together only during the reigns of extraordinarily virtuous emperors.

The integral casting, straightforward archaism, and inlays of wires and of bands into relatively deep channels with undercut edges signal the late Ming date of this water dropper.[7]

THE ROBERT H. CLAGUE COLLECTION   199

45, 46, 47 Paper Weights

in the form of recumbent mythical animals

Ming dynasty, late sixteenth – first half seventeenth century
Cast bronze with cold-worked surface details
2.2 centimeter height x 7.6 centimeter length; 6.4 centimeter height x 6.4
centimeter length; 3.8 centimeter height x 5.1 centimeter length
Clague Collection Numbers 216, 228, 217

U SED AS PAPER WEIGHTS, these small sculptures represent mythical animals, as indicated by the wisps of flame emanating from their joints and by their horns and bifurcated tails. Lying quietly with their bodies in a C-curve, the animals gaze at the viewer, their eyes wide open. His head raised, exposing his scaled neck and chest, number 47 scratches his left ear with a rear paw. A short mane frames the back of his head while a single horn crowns its top; tufts of fur embellish the spinal ridge and deeply articulated spirals mark the joints. The underside of the feline body is flat and plain. Number 45 rests his disproportionately large head between the extended front paws, his bulging eyes fixed in a glare, his slightly open mouth revealing long teeth. Springing from a single point in the center of the forehead, two horns distinguish this creature from a lion. Repeating half circles, representing scales, texture the surface; similar scales cover the underside of the body, incised lines marking the pads and claws on the bottoms of the paws. Although its small body and slender legs with cloven hooves resemble those of a sheep or goat, the mythical animal represented by number 46 has what appears to be a horse's head, which it holds high. Standing before the coiffed mane at the back of the head, a horn rises from amidst the forelock; a conventional mane, parted to fall to both right and left, covers the back of the neck, its striations echoing those of the tail. Overlapping fish scales cover both the body (excepting the head) and the flat underside of the piece.

Although bronze scroll weights (*yachi*) of elongated rectangular form had been introduced by the Song,[1] the date of the first appearance of animal-shaped paper weights remains unknown. First published in 1341, *Guyu tu* (Illustrated Compendium of Ancient Jades) notes that the famed painter and calligrapher Zhao Mengfu (1254-1322) once bought an ancient jade *bixie*, which he used as a paper weight,[2] however, indicating that such were in use by the Yuan. Wen Zhenheng commented in his *Zhangwu zhi* of 1637 that ancient jade sculptures make the most elegant paper weights (*zhenzhi*) but that 'bluish green toads, crouching tigers and *chi* dragons, sleeping dogs, inlaid *bixie*, recumbent horses, and tortoise-dragons of bronze also could be used.'[3] In general, the three animals in the Clague Collection answer to Wen Zhenheng's description of bronze paper weights; though their exact identification remains uncertain, numbers 45 and 47 may represent *bixie* chimeras[4] [compare 12], and number 46 a *qilin* or *longma*.[5]

The identification of Chinese mythical beasts is notoriously difficult, as is their dating. Solid cast and relatively heavy, these three recumbent animals share a number of stylistic features and thus probably date to the same period: alert countenances, textured surfaces, schematized bodies, and cursorily rendered feet. Such characteristics stand apart from those of bronze animals cast during the early Ming [see 43], which usually have curly manes and tails, textured surfaces contrasted with smooth, plain ones,[6] and at least a passing reference to naturalistic description evidenced by the careful delineation of ribs, toes, and other anatomical features. A range of dates from Yuan to late Ming has been proposed for animals of this type, though in discussing them, writers have tended to discuss everything but the reasons for their dating. Both the elements of style just mentioned and the technique of decoration, which, like late Ming bronze vessels, relies heavily on cold work, point to the late Ming as the most likely date of manufacture. The striations in the manes of all three were imparted through cold working, as were the scaled surfaces of numbers 45 and 46. Because the raised paw hinders access to the proper left side of the animal's head, the artisan was unable to finish the tuft of the mane under the left ear of number 47; the rough appearance of the tuft reveals that although cast in relief, such elements were intended to be finished through cold working. The surface of number 45 has an applied brown coating and that of number 46 has traces of black lacquer or other black substance in the intaglio lines.

48, 49 Brush Rests

in the form of five mountain peaks rising from rolling waves; in the form of two interlocked *chi* dragons

Ming dynasty, late sixteenth – first half seventeenth century
Cast bronze with cast and cold-worked surface details
16.5 centimeter height x 21.0 centimeter width; 6.4 centimeter
height x 17.1 centimeter width
Clague Collection Number 264, 260

THE BRUSHREST SUPPORTED AN INKED BRUSH when set aside for a moment, allowing the scholar to alternate between brushes of different sizes or textures. Fashioned in the form of five peaks, this brushrest [48] represents one of the most popular types. More elaborate than most, waves at the bottom lap the bases of the three central mountains and the columns of the gateway below the central peak. Emerging from the waves, a dragon enters the gateway. Rocky outcroppings rise in front of the faceted main peaks; clouds envelop the tips of the three central peaks, the clouds supporting a disk with the character *ri* (sun) on the peak to the right of the central one, and a disk with the character *yue* (moon) on the one to the left. The interior of the brushrest is hollow.

With the Chinese love of rocks and the important role that mountains play in Chinese thought and painting, it is appropriate that brushrests were made in the shape of mountains.[1] In his *Zhangwu zhi* of 1637, Wen Zhenheng commented that in antiquity people used small rocks as brushrests (*bige*).[2] He further noted that jade, bronze, and porcelain are suitable materials for brushrests, stating that mountain-shaped ones in jade and Ding porcelain are especially desirable, as are bronze rests in the form of mountains or *chi* dragons; in speaking of Ding ones, he specifically mentioned three- and five-peak forms.[3]

With its five peaks, this brushrest symbolizes China's Five Sacred Mountains.[4] The dragon (*long*) and gateway (*men*) appear as part of a visual pun, to be read together as 'Longmen,' indicating that the waves represent the waters of the Yellow River at the falls of Longmen in Henan, not far from Mt Song,[5] the central peak of the Five Sacred Mountains. The dragon symbolizes success in the civil service examinations, for use by a scholar, official, or successful examination candidate [see 56, 57].

Ming mountain-form brushrests descend from the Song ones mentioned by Wen Zhenheng, which, in turn, were inspired both by the fine rocks used as brush supports and by the ceramic rockeries produced in earthenware during the Tang.[6] In the Ming, five-peaked brushrests were frequently made in porcelain[7] and bronze[8] during the Zhengde period, their popularity continuing through the end of the dynasty. Late Ming mountain-shaped brushrests are typically more complex than the earlier ones, often incorporating waves at the base and sometimes dragons striding in the clouds above.[9] The complexity of the design, the height of the relief, and the strong interest in visual puns,[10] all point to a late sixteenth- to early seventeenth-century date for this mountain brushrest.[11]

The dragon brushrest [49] was fashioned in the form of two intertwined *chi* dragons whose sinuously curved bodies create an openwork design of horizontal c-form. Elegantly attenuated, the bilaterally symmetrical dragons have tubular bodies with arched spines, the spines articulated with a ridge; turning their heads over their backs to confront each other, they step on their own bodies. Each *chilong* has a long s-curved beard, a coiled snout, and two short pointed horns; each raises its proper right front leg as if striding, the leg echoing the s-curve of the dragon's firmly planted left front leg and balancing the strong curve of its undivided tail. Each *chilong* has large paws with three well defined toes, the claws clearly indicated.

In his discussion of elegant appointments for the scholar's studio, Wen Zhenheng comments that among the most desirable brushrests are bronze ones in the form of either a single *chi* dragon or of intertwined double ones.[12] Although he offers no description, Wen's intertwined *chilong* brushrests probably correspond to this one in the Clague Collection.

Evocative of the late Zhou and Han periods, the *chilong* had long been popular as decoration on materials destined for the scholar's studio [see 13]. Already in the Yuan dynasty, some porcelain water droppers for the desk were furnished with openwork handles in the form of a *chi* dragon with an arched spine.[13] By the late Ming, such dragons often appeared as high-relief ornament on *touhu* vessels [9] and on a variety of bronze and porcelain vases.[14] In fact, the dragons that make up this brushrest might best be considered translations of high-relief ornamental *chi* dragons into fully three-dimensional ones.

The similarity in style to ornamental dragons on late Ming vessels establishes the late sixteenth to early seventeenth-century date of this brushrest. The bilateral symmetry is also a late Ming trait, early Qing examples presenting pairs of *chilong* as complementary opposites [see 32] rather than as mirror images of each other [see 13]. Qianlong brushrests embrace a markedly different style, depicting the dragons as mother and cub rather than as twins; the long snouts and large, three-toed paws, so characteristic of late Ming *chilong*, disappear from such Qianlong pieces, the legs and paws, in some cases, much reduced.[15] At least two other late Ming brushrests in the form of intertwined *chi* dragons are known, both virtually identical to the one in the Clague Collection.[16]

50 Ancestral Figure
representing a woman seated on a bench

Ming dynasty, Jiajing period, dated to 1532
Cast bronze with cold-worked surface details, with traces of black
lacquer(?) in the hair and details, and with a chiseled intaglio inscription
in standard-script (*kaishu*) characters on the back
23.2 centimeter height
Clague Collection Number 205

AN IDEALIZED REPRESENTATION rather than an actual portrait, this sculpture represents a woman seated on a bench in a formal pose, her head held high, her shoulders squared, her back straight, her legs pendant. Her tunic has a floral band across the knees and a floral border about its edges; her jacket has a floral border along its upper edge and badges of rank, so-called Mandarin squares, on its front and back. The badges depict clouds, or possibly highly stylized flowers, against a punched ground, rather than the animals or birds that traditionally indicate civil and military rank. Arranged in an elegant coiffure and held in place by a diadem, the woman's long hair clings tightly to her head, forming a point at the center of her forehead and exposing her ears with their jeweled earrings. The back of the sculpture is plain except for the rank badge, the decorated collar, and several hair ornaments. A rust-brown skin conceals the color of the bronze; traces of black lacquer appear in the hair and drapery ornament.

Human figures rank among the most perplexing of later bronzes in terms of dating and of identity of individuals portrayed. Because the inscription incised on the back and sides of its bench mentions both a date and a place of manufacture, this modest ancestral figure assumes a documentary importance far beyond its artistic merits.[1]

With hands concealed in the sleeves and shoes peeking from under the robe, the pose represented is one associated with formal portraits of women at least since Song times, in paintings, sculptures, and woodblock-printed illustrations.[2] This sculpture's elongated but fleshy face and its bulging forehead are akin to those of a monumental bronze head of a woman that has been attributed to the Yuan dynasty but that might date to the early Ming.[3] Although chairs were available, people of means frequently sit on benches without backs in woodblock-printed illustrations of the Yuan and early and mid-Ming periods, even in formal settings.[4]

Except for the head, this sculpture was integrally cast. Visible in the hollow interior, a tenon anchors the head to the body, but it is not evident whether head and body were fused together after casting or whether the head was cast-on.[5] The facial features and strands of hair were cast, but the decoration on the garment was entirely cold worked. Although not used extensively in the decoration of bronze vessels until the second half of the sixteenth century, cold working was employed in ornamenting sculptures during the first half of the century, as proven by this sculpture.

51 Figurine

representing a standing deity on an attached bronze
stand, the deity wearing an official's hat and robes and carrying
a calabash gourd on his back

Ming dynasty, sixteenth – first half seventeenth century
Cast bronze with cast and cold-worked surface details
33.5 centimeter height
Clague Collection Number 271

STANDING ON A SQUARE, bronze socle with openwork panels, this figure wears an official's hat with long tails that trail over the shoulders, and a plain, knee-length robe secured at the waist with a belt enlivened with circular and rectangular markings that represent jade plaques; boots protect his feet. The bearded gentleman cups his hands in front of his chest, the position of the hands suggesting that he might once have held an object, now lost, or that he is displaying a ritual gesture, akin to a Buddhist *mudra*. Held in place by a cord, the calabash gourd appearing between his shoulder blades indicates that he is a deity rather than a mere human. Lacking a base, the gourd is open all the way through.

The absence of specific attributes makes identification difficult, but the hat, boots, and tunic suggest that this might represent Guandi, God of War and patron deity of literature, revered by the literati because he was supposedly able to recite the entire *Chunqiu Zuozhuan* (Zuo Commentary on the Spring and Autumn Annals). Known by various names, he was an historical personnage, born Yu Changsheng (162-219); a sworn brother of Liu Bei (162-223), he was a mighty warrior celebrated for his loyalty. China's most renowned military hero, he was ennobled as duke in 1120, raised to the rank of prince in 1128, and named a *di*, or deity, in 1594.[1] As God of War, Guandi typically wears full body armor and shows a serious, almost minatory demeanor;[2] as patron of literature, he wears boots and military tunic, but exhibits a gentle, benevolent expression.[3]

The masculine features, slight contrapposto, and elegantly simple but windswept robe are akin to those of carved ivory figures attributed to the late Ming, suggesting a sixteenth- to early seventeenth-century date for this sculpture.[4]

52 Figurine

representing a standing Daoist immortal on an attached bronze rockery stand, the immortal wearing informal robes and holding a rolled scroll

Ming dynasty, sixteenth – first half seventeenth century
Cast bronze with cast and cold-worked surface details
45.7 centimeter height
Clague Collection Number 269

THIS SCULPTURE REPRESENTS A LAUGHING IMMORTAL standing on a rocky base. The figure wears a long, simple robe that falls to the ankles but that is only loosely closed, exposing his emaciated chest. His ears are unusually fleshy, their tops curling over on themselves. Clad in thin-soled, soft shoes, the figure's feet protrude from under the robe; a kerchief-style hat partially covers his domed, bald head, its long tails trailing over his shoulders. He holds a furled scroll in his raised right hand; the hand and the scroll are replacements. His lowered left hand is concealed in the long sleeve. Suggesting a mountainous setting, the modeled bronze base has a lower section in the form of a rockery and a flat-topped upper section which supports the figure.[1]

The identity of this figure remains unknown, but the rocky base, disheveled robes, emaciated chest, peculiar ears, and furled scroll confirm that it is a Daoist immortal, the scroll doubtless symbolizing the esoteric knowledge possessed of immortals but beyond the comprehension of mere humans. The circular perforations around the mouth and above and in front of the ears were for the attachment of a beard, probably of human hair. (Traces of black hair remain in some of the perforations.) The use of actual hair for such beards was intended to imbue the figure with life, the hair assuming spiritual and symbolic functions more than aesthetic ones. Although they sometimes appear on Qing-dynasty Dehua, or blanc-de-Chine, molded porcelain figurines, such beards have a long history, stretching back at least to Tang times, when they were occasionally affixed to pottery tomb figurines.[2] Carved ivory sculptures were sometimes supplied with such beards in the Yuan and Ming,[3] as were wood and bronze ones.[4]

The fluid lines, masculine features, and emaciated chest suggest a late Ming date for this sculpture, as do the alert face, animated gestures, and billowing robe (which suggests movement). A related but smaller figure in the Palace Museum, Beijing, has been attributed to the late Ming period (sixteenth-to-seventeenth century) by the Museum's curators.[5]

53 Figurine

representing a standing, armor-clad Daoist deity

Ming to Qing dynasty, seventeenth century
Cast bronze with cast and cold-worked surface details and with a
chiseled intaglio inscription in standard-script (*kaishu*) characters
on a plaque worn at the figure's waist
25.4 centimeter height
Clague Collection Number 268

T HIS POWERFUL SCULPTURE depicts a standing, stern-faced military figure clad in chain mail armor. His face set in a grimace, his lips parted to reveal teeth and fangs, the figure stares out at the viewer with bulging eyes under heavy eyebrows, the fangs attesting to his celestial rank. He wears a short robe over his knee-length armor, which is edged with fur along the bottom; a wealth of scarves and sashes, some festively tied in bows, further attests to his celestial rank. His feet planted in a firm stance, the figure extends his left hand but holds his right one tensely at his side. A slant-topped, cylindrical cap ornamented with a blossom conceals his hair, except for two horn-like wisps that appear above the ears. Tall, *ruyi*-toed boots shield his feet, the tenons on their heels once anchoring the figure to a bronze base, now lost and replaced by a wooden one carved in the form of scrolling clouds. Inscribed with eight intaglio characters, a round-topped rectangular plaque appears at the figure's waist, neatly tied with a tasseled cord to a narrow jade disk that is itself suspended from a silk sash draped over his shoulder.[1]

In standard-script (*kaishu*) characters, the inscription translates:

Exiting [and] entering [by the] golden gate,
Not restrained [by the] heavens above.[2]

The inscription apparently does not identify the figure but suggests that he is a deity, able to travel wherever he wishes without restraint. The reference to the heavens has generated speculation that the figure may have been made as part of a set of Daoist astronomical deities;[3] while not impossible, such specific identification awaits further research.[4]

Military figures clad in chain mail armor appear in the visual arts from the Tang through the Qing, in painting,[5] sculpture,[6] and woodblock prints.[7] Although they change slowly, depictions of armor evolve over time from the simple to the more complex. With its tongue-like flap of fabric between the legs, its windblown scarves and drapery edges, its numerous but seemingly extraneous decorative elements, and its extensive cold working, this sculpture bears some similarity to a cast bronze sculpture in the Field Museum of Natural History, Chicago, that is dated by inscription to 1624 and that represents Bishamen, one of the Sitianwang, or Four Heavenly Kings, perhaps in his Daoist aspect as Moli Shou.[8]

54 Candlestick

in the form of a dancing woman on an attached bronze stand,
the woman wearing long-sleeved robes

Ming dynasty, sixteenth – first half seventeenth century
Cast bronze with cast and cold-worked surface details and gilding
42.6 centimeter height
Clague Collection Number 272

ET ON A SMALL STOOL-SHAPED BASE with four cloud-scroll legs, this candlestick was cast in the form of a court dancer with right arm raised and left one lowered, the openings at the ends of the sleeves intended to support candles. The woman wears a long-sleeved tunic that is tucked into her floor-length skirt, the skirt secured at the waist with a cincture. The scarf and sash at the chest are also tucked into the top of the skirt; draped from the belt, a second scarf appears at the back of the image in a U-shaped configuration, its ends trailing down the side of the skirt to the feet, where they are animated by the graceful movement of the dance. Swept into an elaborately styled bun atop her head, the woman's long hair is held in place by a diadem and hairpins. Her pointed shoes protrude from under the hem of her skirt, but her hands are entirely concealed within the long sleeves. Although it covers most of the front of the image, the thin layer of gilding appears on the back in narrow horizontal bands that contrast with the alternating plain surfaces. It is possible that this candlestick was made as one of a pair, its mate now lost or separated.

Ewers[1] and candlesticks[2] in the form of dancing human figures enjoyed a measure of popularity during the Ming in both bronze and porcelain; candlesticks depicting long-sleeved dancers apparently first appeared in Yuan or early Ming times, as shown by a pair recently published with an attribution to the fourteenth or fifteenth century.[3] The tunic, scarves, and high-waisted skirt indicate that this figure is modeled on a Tang court lady, as do the tall coiffure and full, oval face, the characteristics well known to the people of the day from Tang and Tang-style paintings that survived into the Ming.[4] Often associated with customs imported from Central Asia via the fabled Silk Route, and often associated with the Tang when they were assuredly popular, dances involving performers wearing costumes with exceptionally long sleeves had been a feature of Chinese culture at least since Han times.[5]

The dancer's planar forehead, square shoulders, and robust proportions argue for a date in the late Ming for this candlestick; Qing images of women, by contrast, reveal a taste for frail beauties with elongated bodies and disproportionately large heads set on narrow, sloping shoulders,[6] while early and mid-Ming ones typically have slightly fleshier faces with bulging foreheads[7] [see 50]. The contrasting of gilded and ungilded surfaces is also a late Ming characteristic,[8] perhaps related to the similar phenomenon in Hu Wenming bronzes [see 11, 12].

55 Figurine representing a seated White-robed Guanyin

Qing dynasty, second half seventeenth century
Cast bronze with cast and cold-worked surface details, with inlaid silver
wire, with traces of black lacquer(?) coating, and with a mark inlaid in
silver wire in clerical-script (*lishu*) characters reading *Shisou* on the back
12.7 centimeter height
Clague Collection Number 262

THIS SERENE IMAGE REPRESENTS the White-robed Guanyin seated in a modified lotus position.[1] Especially popular in China from the Song onward, the White-robed Guanyin (Baiyi Guanyin) is one of the thirty-three manifestations of Guanyin Pusa (Sanskrit, Bodhisattva Avalokiteśvara).[2] Although they are males in the Indian tradition, bodhisattvas, and Guanyin in particular, tend to be shown as females in China beginning at least as early as the Song dynasty. Only the *ūrnā*, or raised dot at the center of the forehead, distinguishes this figure as a deity;[3] the combination of robe, coiffure, relaxed pose, and facial appearance identifies the image as the White-robed Guanyin, an identification based on type rather than on specific attributes.

The image became the most characteristic single emblem of Buddhist piety among the intelligentsia of China and Japan. Popular among Zen (Chinese, Chan) Buddhists, White-robed Guanyin imagery was one part of the movement to present deities in approachable, humanized form.[4] Although the transformation of Guanyin into a feminine deity was largely a Chinese phenomenon, there is a basis in Indian scripture for the presentation of the White-robed Guanyin as feminine, as John Rosenfield and Elizabeth ten Grotenhuis have noted: 'Called in Sanskrit the Pāndaravāsinī (literally, white-clothed; in the feminine gender), she appears in the Taizō mandala in the sector allotted to Avalokiteśvara (in the lower left corner) in conventional Indian guise: seated in the lotus position, wearing a *dhoti*, scarf, and lavish crown, and by no means feminine in form. For reasons that are not yet entirely clear, she seems to have caught the imagination of monks and laymen, and emerged as the object of an independent cult.'[5]

Often shown seated on a rock in a bamboo grove,[6] the White-robed Guanyin remained popular well into the Qing dynasty, late Ming and Qing versions sometimes showing her holding a child.[7] Literati artists of the late Ming occasionally depicted the White-robed Guanyin in secular paintings,[8] and scholars of the late Ming and Qing often kept a sculpture depicting a *luohan* or a White-robed Guanyin on the desk, less as a votive image than as a reminder of the spiritual realm.[9]

The two-character mark on the back reads *Shisou*, and refers to the elusive artist whose name often appears on bronzes inlaid with silver wire [see 16-18]; attributions to his hand remain unverifiable. The elegantly simple but expressive style relates this sculpture to Dehua porcelain images of the White-robed Guanyin that have been attributed to the second half of the seventeenth century, suggesting an early Qing date for this piece.[10]

56 Double Vase in the form of two leaping carp

Qing dynasty, Kangxi period (1662-1722)
Cast bronze with cast and cold-worked surface details,
and with brown coating
39.5 centimeter height
Clague Collection Number 212

T HIS DOUBLE VASE WAS CAST in the form of two leaping carp, the arc at the base a reference to the rolling waves from which they emerge. Pressed belly to belly, the fish appear in profile, one larger, one smaller. The fish have smooth-skinned faces with large circular eyes and long whiskers that extend the line of the upper lip. An arched band separates the heads from the bodies, which display large, overlapping scales. Both the short ventral fins and the long dorsal ones are striated, as are the tails. A low-relief grid pattern, reminiscent of those on some antique bronze vessels, ornaments the flat, countersunk base. Visible especially in the hollows, a grayish brown coating partially covers the surface. Thick walled and very heavy, this vase was integrally cast, though the striations on the fins and tails show traces of cold finishing.[1]

The fish is one of the most enduring motifs in Chinese art, appearing on Neolithic painted pots and Shang bronzes. A symbol of rank and power in early times, it later came to symbolize abundance both because fish are plentiful and because the words for 'fish' and 'abundance' are homonyms in Mandarin Chinese, both pronounced *yu*. As the fish can swim in any direction, it also signifies freedom from restraint. The pairing of fish and water is a rebus, or visual pun, for *yushui hexie*, 'May you be as compatible as fish and water,' a reference to marital harmony and, by extension, to fecundity.[2] One of the *bajixiang*, or Eight Auspicious Emblems [20 and 22], the double fish motif appeared frequently in Chinese decorative arts after its introduction in the Yuan.[3] Although leaping carp also represent young scholars [see 57], this pair more likely refers to marital and familial relationships, the hierarchically arranged fish symbolizing husband and wife or mother and child.[4] Such vases were popular as wedding gifts during the Qing.

An innovation of the late Tang, vases in the form of two leaping fish appeared in a variety of ceramic wares in the ninth century and remained popular into the Northern Song.[5] The vessel type seldom appears in the Yuan and Ming, but it recurred in the Kangxi era when potters and metalsmiths not only revived a number of Tang forms [34] but began to experiment with paired objects [40].

As representatives of the Kangxi style, these carp compare favorably with contemporaneous ones in glazed porcelain[6] and their smooth heads correspond to those of Kangxi-era *haishou* [21]. Reflecting the archaism of the day, carp vases from the Yongzheng period exhibit fidelity to their Tang models;[7] Qianlong carp vessels favor the dramatic, typically showing the carp with a dragon's head [57].

57 Censer

in the form of a leaping carp transforming itself into a dragon

Qing dynasty, Qianlong period (1736-95)
Cast bronze with cast and cold-worked surface details and with brown
coating, the eyes inset with black polished glass or stone
20.3 centimeter height
Clague Collection Number 253

WITH THE BODY OF A FISH and the head of a dragon, the carp changes into a dragon as it leaps vertically from the water. Although the head and upper body face upward, the tail and caudal portion lie flat, forming the base. Its mouth open, revealing teeth, fangs, and a pointed tongue, the removeable head is that of a dragon, with snout, horns, mane, whiskers, bearded lower jaw, and frontally placed bulging eyes; with its scales and striated ventral and caudal fins, the body is that of a fish, except for the row of dragon spikes that has replaced the dorsal fin. Inset with polished glass or stone, the jet-black eyes imbue the creature with life. Incense would have been burnt in the hollow body, the smoke emerging from the mouth, conveying the impression of a fire-breathing dragon. The lightly scalloped interface of head and body suggests the gills. A rust-brown coating conceals the brassy hue of the bronze.

Apart from symbolizing abundance, freedom from restraint, marital harmony, and fecundity [see 56], the carp has long represented literary success, an emblem of the young scholar or examination candidate. The association of carp with scholars and literary success derives from popular tradition, which holds that the carp in the Yellow River swim upstream every spring, during the third lunar month, and that those that succeed in leaping the falls at Longmen are transformed into dragons.[1] Confucians seized the leaping carp as the perfect symbol for success in the exams; as carp are transformed into dragons, so are young scholars transformed into learned men and, ultimately, into high officials. The leaping carp, especially the dragon-headed carp, is thus a rebus for *liyu tiao longmen*, 'The carp has leaped through the dragon gate,' a saying popular in Ming and Qing times as an allusion to literary success [compare 48].

Fish-shaped vessels were popular as gifts during the Qing. Those with traditional carp heads [56] could be used for newlyweds or scholars, but those with dragon heads were intended for scholars (or for families with sons aspiring to officialdom). Rare in porcelain, fish-shaped vessels with dragon heads frequently appear in bronze and jade.[2]

An innovation of the Qianlong era, the combination of dragon head and fish body signals this censer's eighteenth-century date. Earlier fish vases depict the fish with its natural head, while earlier references to literary success typically show the carp already fully transformed into a dragon, the dragon sometimes presented in combination with a gateway to underscore the rebus, *longmen* [see 48].

58 Censer in the form of a seated *Qilin*

Ming dynasty, first half seventeenth century
Cast bronze with cast and cold-worked surface details and traces of gilding
25.1 centimeter height
Clague Collection Number 207

THIS RARE AND UNUSUAL CENSER was cast in the form of a *qilin* seated on its haunches, its gaping, fang-lined mouth opened toward the sky. The hollow, plump beast has four legs that terminate in cloven hooves. The *qilin* paws the air with his proper right front hoof, extending its left front leg diagonally as a brace. Scales line the chest and abdomen and a mane encircles the short neck; a bushy tail flows behind. Under braided eyebrows, the beast's bulging eyes stare fiercely upward; a single, faceted horn grows from the crown of the head, its tip curving forward. Naturalistically rendered as fur, tongues of flame issue from the joints, signaling the *qilin*'s supernatural status. The flat base is unornamented.[1]

Sometimes termed a unicorn in English, the *qilin* is one of the *siling* mentioned in the Zhou-dynasty *Liji* (Book of Rites) along with the dragon, phoenix, and tortoise.[2] A creature of good omen, the *qilin* symbolizes longevity, grandeur, felicity, illustrious offspring, and wise administration. Descriptions vary widely, but the *qilin* is usually said to resemble a large stag. Other descriptions state that the *qilin* has two horns, that it has the body of a horse, and that it is covered with scales like a fish[3] [46]. The *qilin*'s voice is melodious, like the sound of bells.

Xuande yiqi tupu reveals that bronze censers in the form of lions, cranes, *jiaoduan*, and other auspicious animals were popular in the early fifteenth century, the censers based on Tang and Yuan models.[4] In fact, lion and *qilin*-shaped censers were popular throughout the Ming and Qing, in bronze, porcelain, and jade.[5] The Clague Collection *qilin* is both rare and elegant in the context of such censers, since most feature an even more rotund and stylized beast standing on four stubby legs; most such censers were cast in two parts, the hinged or removeable head serving as a cover.[6]

In such details as braided eyebrows and hatched scale edges, this *qilin* resembles a censer dated by inscription to the second year of Tianqi (1622), recently offered at auction by Sothebys Hong Kong, establishing an early seventeenth-century date for the Clague censer.[7] The piece is similar to a small carved-bamboo sculpture in the Asian Art Museum of San Francisco depicting a *qilin* that has been dated to the first half of the seventeenth century on the basis of its similarity to images in the *Ten Bamboo Studio Album of Stationery* (*Shizhuzhai jian pu*), first printed in 1644.[8]

This censer was integrally cast, except for its tail.[9] Chatter marks indicate that the beautifully striated mane and tail were cold worked, as were the edges of the ears and scales. It has been suggested that bronzes with thin, spotty traces of gilding of the type on this *qilin* may have had gold leaf applied, which was then melted onto the surface.[10]

Notes

Notes

Introduction

1. 'Bronze' is used as a generic term in this study to refer to a variety of copper-based metals, from copper itself to brass (an alloy of copper and zinc) to traditional bronze (an alloy of copper and tin). Since a variety of copper-based metals was used in the later 'bronze' tradition and since scientific identification of all the alloys represented in the Clague Collection was not possible, the use of 'bronze' as a generic term seems more objective than attempts at specific identifications of varied metals by sight that might later prove incorrect and thus, in the interim, misleading. On the positive side, the creation of similar, even identical, shapes and decorative styles in different metals justifies the use of 'bronze' as a generic term. In fact, it should be pointed out that some workshops – that of Hu Wenming, for example – used a variety of metals, but fashioned them into objects of related style. In those instances where the metal is clearly copper [12, 41], the material is so identified.

2. Later Chinese bronzes were cast through the lost-wax, or *cire-perdu*, process. In creating such vessels, a solid core, or inner mold, was made of clay, the core corresponding in size and shape to the vessel's interior hollow. After drying and firing, the core was fully coated with wax, in which all of the vessel's decorative surface details were meticulously worked. Layer after layer of fine clay was then applied over the wax, forming the outer casting mold. The finished mold was heated to prepare it to receive the molten metal which would occupy the spaces vacated by the melted (or 'lost') wax. After cooling, the mold was removed, revealing the vessel. Apparently introduced in the late Zhou, the lost-wax process existed side-by-side with the piece-mold technique, gradually replacing it by the Six Dynasties, so that virtually all post-Han bronzes, whether Buddhist images or secular vessels, were cast by the lost-wax process.

3. Archaic Chinese bronzes were cast through the piece-mold technique, a difficult and complicated process that, if mastered, yields superior results. In creating piece-mold-cast vessels, a solid model of the vessel was first fashioned in clay; all of the exterior surface details were then carefully worked on the surface of the model, after which it was dried and fired. The outer casting mold was prepared in sections by pressing moist clay against the solid model; after the mold sections had been removed from the model, the impressions on their inner

surfaces could be further defined and sharpened and minor flaws could be corrected (an advantage not possible with lost-wax casting). After all of the mold pieces had been prepared, dried, and fired, they were fitted together around a solid core, or inner mold, and molten bronze poured into the space between. For information on piece-mold casting, see Noel Barnard, *Bronze Casting and Bronze Alloys in Ancient China*, Canberra: The Australian National University and Tokyo: Monumenta Serica, 1961; W. Thomas Chase with the assistance of Jung May Lee, *Ancient Chinese Bronze Art: Casting the Precious Sacral Vessel*, New York: China Institute in America, 1991; Rutherford John Gettens, *The Freer Chinese Bronzes*, volume 2: *Technical Studies*, Washington DC: Smithsonian Institution, Freer Gallery of Art, Oriental Studies Number 7, 1969.

4. Iron was used at least from the fifth century BC onward, side by side with bronze, but for different purposes.

5. Buddhism arose in northern India and spread across Asia, reaching China at least by the mid-first century AD; growing slowly at first, the Buddhist church expanded rapidly after the fall of Han.

6. Such philosophical speculation gave rise to the quintessentially Chinese philosophies of Confucianism, Daoism, and Legalism, among others; those speculations had less to do with metaphysics than with the proper role of human beings in nature on the one hand (Daoism) and in society on the other (Confucianism, Legalism).

7. For information on rise of Buddhism and the growth of the Buddhist church in China, see Arthur F. Wright, *Buddhism in Chinese History*, Stanford CA: Stanford University Press and London: Oxford University Press, 1959; E. Zürcher, *The Buddhist Conquest of China: The Spread and Adaptation of Buddhism in Early Medieval China*, Leiden: E.J. Brill, 1959, 2 volumes; Kenneth K.S. Ch'en, *Buddhism in China: A Historical Survey*, Princeton NJ: Princeton University Press, 1964; Kenneth K.S. Ch'en, *The Chinese Transformation of Buddhism*, Princeton NJ: Princeton University Press, 1973.

8. For information on the Silk Route and the luxury goods it brought, see Ryoichi Hayashi, *The Silk Route and the Shōsō-in*, volume 6 in *The Heibonsha Survey of Japanese Art*, New York and Tokyo: Weatherhill/Heibonsha, 1966 and 1975 (translated by Robert Ricketts); Jessica Rawson, *Chinese Ornament: The Lotus and the Dragon*, London: British Museum Publications, 1984; Edward H. Schafer, *The Golden Peaches of Samarkand: A Study of Tang Exotics*, Berkeley: University of California Press, 1963.

9. See Robert Poor, 'Notes on the Sung Dynasty Archaeological Catalogs,' *Archives of the Chinese Art Society of America* (now, *Archives of Asian Art*) (New York), volume 19, 1965, 33-44.

10. Archaism began to play a role in Chinese painting in the late Northern Song, as attested by the landscape handscroll by Wang Ximeng (1096-

1119) that revives the Tang blue-and-green manner; it gained strength during the Southern Song in the blue-and-green landscapes of the brothers Zhao Boju (died about 1162) and Zhao Bosu (1124-1182) and asserted itself as a mainstream phenomenon during the Yuan in the works of Qian Xuan (about 1235-after 1301) and Zhao Mengfu (1254-1322), who explored not only Tang blue-and-green landscapes but the ink landscapes of such Five Dynasties masters as Dong Yuan (died 962) and Juran (active 960-980).

1

1. For *hu* vessels with strapwork decoration, see Higuchi Takayasu, *Shō Shū no dōki* (Shang and Zhou Bronzes), *Nezu bijutsukan zōhin shirizu* 2 (Nezu Museum Collection Series 2), Tokyo: Nezu bijutsukan, 1986, not paginated, number 20; Nezu Museum, compiler, *Nezu bijutsukan meihin mokuroku* (Treasures of the Nezu Museum), Tokyo: Nezu bijutsukan, 1974, 155, number 589; Hayashi Minao, *In Shū seidōki sōran: In Shū jidai seidōki no kenkyū* (Conspectus of Yin and Zhou Bronzes: Studies on Yin and Zhou Bronzes), Tokyo: Yoshikawa kōbunkan, 1984, plate volume, 301-07.

2. See W. Thomas Chase, with the assistance of Jung May Lee, *Ancient Chinese Bronze Art: Casting the Precious Sacral Vessel*, New York: China Institute in America, 1991, 57, number 20; Max Loehr, *Ritual Vessels of Bronze Age China*, New York: Asia Society, 1968, 132-33, number 58.

3. See Max Loehr, assisted by Louisa G. Fitzgerald Huber, *Ancient Chinese Jades from the Grenville L. Winthrop Collection in the Fogg Art Museum, Harvard University*, Cambridge MA: Fogg Art Museum, Harvard University, 1975, 249-50, number 372-74; 255-56, number 382-83.

4. See Dawn Ho Delbanco, *Art from Ritual: Ancient Chinese Bronze Vessels from the Arthur M. Sackler Collections*, Cambridge MA: Fogg Art Museum, Harvard University, and Washington DC: Arthur M. Sackler Foundation, 1983, 127, number 51; 133, number 54; and 142, number 59.

5. Max Loehr, 'The Emergence and Decline of the Eastern Chou Decor of Plastic Curls,' in Loehr, *Ancient Chinese Jades*, 21-28.

6. See Chase, *Ancient Chinese Bronze Art*, 61, number 24; 62, number 25; 63, number 26; and 65, number 28.

7. See Higuchi, *Shō Shū no dōki*, not paginated, number 21; Nezu Museum, *Nezu bijutsukan meihin mokuroku*, 155, number 59.

8. See, for example, William Watson, 'On Some Categories of Archaism in Chinese Bronze,' *Ars Orientalis* (Washington DC), volume 9, 1973, 3-13; Zhou Zheng, 'Xuanhe shanzun kao' (Research on the Xuanhe-period Shan Zun), *Wenwu* (Beijing), 1983, number 11, 74-75 and 67.

9. See Hasebe Gakuji, *Sō* (Song), volume 12 in *Sekai tōji zenshū* (Ceramic Art of the World), Tokyo: Shogakukan, 1977, 80, number 71; 207, numbers 205-06.

10. In her letter of 12 February 1990 to Robert H. Clague, Chen Peifang, Curator of Bronzes at the Shanghai Museum, stated that on the basis of photographs, she believes this *hu* to be from the Song dynasty, citing this combination of characteristics as evidence.

11. Although bronzes were avidly collected and cataloged during the Song, scholarly study of their inscriptions and dating was still in its infancy. With the understanding that twentieth-century archaeology and scientific analysis have given us, we are generally in a better position to distinguish old vessels from new ones and to assign dates and places of manufacture than were people of the Song (and Yuan, Ming, and Qing).

2

1. See Robert D. Mowry, *Handbook of the Mr and Mrs John D. Rockefeller Third Collection*, New York: Asia Society, 1980, 52, number 17.1; Wen Fong editor, *The Great Bronze Age of China: An Exhibition from the People's Republic of China*, New York: Metropolitan Museum of Art and Alfred A. Knopf, 1980, 298, number 95.

2. See Yang Boda editor, *Zhongguo meishu quanji* (The Great Treasury of Chinese Art), volume 3, part 10, *Gongyi meishu bian: Jin yin boli falang qi* (Crafts: Articles of Gold, Silver, Glass, and Enamel), Beijing, Wenwu chubanshe, 1987, 28, number 58.

3. See Yutaka Mino, with the assistance of Katherine R. Tsiang, *Freedom of Clay and Brush through Seven Centuries in Northern China: Tz'u-chou Type Wares AD 960-1600*, Indianapolis: Indianapolis Museum of Art, and Bloomington: Indiana University Press, 1980, 73, number 24; 75, number 25.

4. See Hasebe, *Sō*, 46, number 38; 47, number 39; Elinor L. Pearlstein and James T. Ulak, *Asian Art in The Art Institute of Chicago*, Chicago: Art Institute of Chicago, 1993, 60.

5. For more information on these phenomena, see Chu-tsing Li and James C.Y. Watt editors, *The Chinese Scholar's Studio: Artistic Life in the Late Ming Period*, New York: Thames and Hudson in association with the Asia Society, 1987.

6. Robert D. Mowry, 'Catalogue,' in Li and Watt, *The Chinese Scholar's Studio*, 177, number 62; 189-90, numbers 82-83.

7. See Mowry, *Handbook*, 52, number 1979.107; Loehr, *Ritual Vessels*, 175, number 8 (termed a *lien*); James C.Y. Watt, *Chinese Jades from Han to Ch'ing*, New York: Asia Society in association with John Weatherhill, 1980, 155, number 127.

8. Wang Zhenduo, 'Zhang Heng houfeng diyung yi di fuyuan yanjiu (xu)' (The Restoration of the Zhang Heng *houfeng didung yi* continued), *Wenwu* (Beijing), 1963, number 4, 1-20; Guo Yong, 'Shanxisheng Youyu-xian chutu di Xi Han tongqi'

(The Western Han Bronzes Unearthed at Youyu County, Shansi Province), *Wenwu*, 1963, number 11, 4-22; Watt, *Chinese Jades*, 154, number 127.

9. An unpublished Eastern Zhou tea-kettle-shaped bronze *he* vessel in the Grenville L. Winthrop Collection at the Harvard University Art Museums, Cambridge, rests on three legs in the form of nude standing men (accession number 1943.52.92). Another unpublished Eastern Zhou vessel in the Harvard University Art Museums, a circular *jian* basin in the Arnold Knapp Collection, stands on three legs in the form of clothed standing men (accession number 1956.78).

10. See Ministry of Culture and Information (Republic of Korea), Bureau of Cultural Properties compiler, *Sinan haejŏyumul: Charyo p'yŏn*, 1 (Relics from the Sea Floor at Sinan: Material Remains Section, volume 1), Seoul: Tonghwa ch'ulp'an sa, 1983, 109-10, numbers 13a-b.

11. A large Tang-period Buddhist pagoda at Xiudingsi Temple, near Anyang, Henan province, for example, boasts architectural ornament of a type that might have inspired not only the decoration on this censer but the numerous diaper patterns that typically appear on Song and Yuan bronzes [see 4 and 5] and their descendants on Ming bronzes [see 9, 11, 13]. Constructed of brick, the Tang pagoda has an all-over veneer of decorative earthenware tiles on its exterior walls. The tiles vary in shape, but those on the main faces are square or lozenge-shaped; set on their corners, the tiles have braided, rope-like borders, and many have floral embellishments at their centers. See Sun Dajang and Yu Weiguo, *Jianzhu yishu bian: Zongjiao jianzhu* (Architecture: Religious Architecture), volume 4, part 4 in *Zhongguo meishu quanji* (The Great Treasury of Chinese Art), Beijing: Zhongguo jianzhu gongye chubanshe, 1988, 28-29, numbers 29-30; Jane Portal, 'A Tang Dynasty Tile in the British Museum,' *Orientations* (Hong Kong), volume 21, number 3, March 1990, 67-71; Paula Swart and Barry Till, 'The Xiudingsi Pagoda: A Buddhist Architectural Masterpiece Unveiled,' *Orientations* (Hong Kong), volume 21, number 5, May 1990, 64-76.

12. See Machida International Print Museum, compiler, *Chūgoku kodai hanga ten: Chūgoku hanga 2000 nen ten, dai san bu* (Exhibition of Ancient Chinese Woodblock Prints: Third Section of an Exhibition of 2000 Years of Chinese Printing), Tokyo-to, Machida-shi: Machida shiritsu kokusai hanga bijutsukan, 1988, 84-85, number 8, scrolls 1-7.

13. See Tsien Tsuen-hsuin, *Paper and Printing*, volume 5, part 1 in Joseph Needham editor, *Science and Civilisation in China*, Cambridge: Cambridge University Press, 1985, 254, figure 1167; Machida International Print Museum, *Chūgoku kodai hanga ten*, 1988, 26, illustration at top of page.

14. Although such ceramic tiles must have been a common feature in the courtyards of important temples and palaces of the Tang dynasty, they have not been preserved in great quantity; more precisely, they have not been published in quantity in recent books and journals. For a Korean example of Unified Silla (668-935) date that mirrors the Tang style, see Rene-Yvon Lefebvre d'Argencé editor, *5000 Years of Korean Art*, San Francisco: Asian Art Museum of San Francisco, 1979, 91, number 101; Kim Chewon and Lena Kim Lee, *Arts of Korea*, Tokyo, New York, and San Francisco: Kodansha International, 1974, 222, figure 192.

15. A related subject of inquiry should be the possible influence of woodblock-printed design elements on the diapered grounds of early Ming carved cinnabar lacquer. The frontispiece to scroll 4 of the *circa* 1160 *Lotus Sutra* mentioned above, for example, includes design elements representing paved terraces, rolling waves, and scrolling clouds that would seem to prefigure those in both Yuan-period secular printed books and early Ming carved lacquer. Proof of a relationship between printed books and carved lacquer would answer questions that have been addressed in several earlier studies; see, for example, Sir Harry Garner, 'Diaper Backgrounds on Chinese Carved Lacquer,' *Ars Orientalis* (Washington DC), volume 6, 1966, 165-89.

16. Zhang Guangyuan (Chang, Kuang-yüan), 'Dingxingqi di fangwei yu mingwen weizhi di guanxi' (The Orientation of *Ding* Vessels in Relation to the Position of Inscriptions), *Gugong jikan* (The National Palace Museum Quarterly) (Taipei), volume 10, number 4, Summer 1976, 67-87 (English-language summary 41-50).

17. Unpublished; Harvard University Art Museums loan number LTL59.1984.

3

1. See John Alexander Pope, Rutherford John Gettens, James Cahill, and Noel Barnard, *The Freer Chinese Bronzes*, volume 1: *Catalogue*, Washington DC: Smithsonian Institution, Freer Gallery of Art, Oriental Studies 7, 1967, 597, number 118.

2. See Okazaki Takashi, *Chūgoku kodai* (Ancient China), volume 10 in *Sekai Tōji Zenshū* (Ceramic Art of the World), Tokyo: Shogakukan, 1982, 212, number 197.

3. See Clarence W. Kelley, *Chinese Gold and Silver from the Tang Dynasty (AD 618-97) in American Collections*, Dayton OH: Dayton Art Institute, 1984, 81-83 and frontispiece, numbers 49-50; Jason C. Kuo editor, *Born of Earth and Fire: Chinese Ceramics from the Scheinman Collection*, College Park MD: Department of Art History and Archaeology, University of Maryland at College Park, and Baltimore: Baltimore Museum of Art, 1992, 78, number 57.

4. See Hasebe, *Sō*, 89, number 81.

5. See Hasebe, *Sō*, 78, number 69; 206, numbers 202-03.

6. See Kuo, *Born of Earth and Fire*, 87, number 68.

7. See Hasebe, *Sō*, 76-77, numbers 67-68.

8. See Robert J. Maeda, 'The "Water" Theme in Chinese Painting,' *Artibus Asiae* (Ascona, Switzerland), volume 33, number 4, 1971, 247-90.

9. See Kuo, *Born of Earth and Fire*, 87, number 68; Hasebe, *Sō*, 245, number 288.

10. See Rose Kerr, *Later Chinese Bronzes*, (Victoria and Albert Museum Far Eastern Series), London: Bamboo Publishing in association with the Victoria and Albert Museum, 1990, 42-43, figures 31-32; 58-5, figures 46-47; Rose Kerr, 'Metalwork and Song Design: A Bronze Vase Inscribed in 1173,' *Oriental Art* (London), new series number 32, Summer 1986, 164-68, figures 1-5.

11. See also Kerr, *Later Chinese Bronzes*, 47, figure 35.

12. See Hasebe, *Sō*, 67, numbers 55-56.

13. See Watt, *Chinese Jades*, 134-35, number 111.

14. See Mowry, *Handbook*, 78, number 1979.176; Suzanne G. Valenstein, *Ming Porcelains: A Retrospective*, New York: China Institute in America, 1971, 44, number 16; 48, number 20; Percival David Foundation of Chinese Art compiler, *Imperial Taste: Chinese Ceramics from the Percival David Foundation*, San Francisco: Chronicle Books, Los Angeles: Los Angeles County Museum of Art, and London: Percival David Foundation of Chinese Art, 1989, 63, number 33; Fujioka Ryoichi, and Hasebe Gakuji, Min (Ming), volume 14 in *Sekai Tōji Zenshū* (Ceramic Art of the World), Tokyo: Shogakukan, 1976, 179, number 185; Shanghai Museum compiler, *Shanghai bowuguan cang ci xuanji* (The Shanghai Museum: Ceramics), Beijing: Wenwu chubanshe, 1979, number 76.

4

1. Circular vases with cylindrical appendages on the neck – of the shape indicated in note 2 below – are frequently pictured as flower vases in Yuan and early Ming woodblock-printed illustrated books, though it is impossible to ascertain whether such vases are made of bronze or ceramic ware. In illustrated secular dramas they often appear in pairs on Buddhist altars flanking a *ding*-shaped censer. Such vases were doubtless used in both religious and secular contexts. See Shanghai Museum facsimile edition of a 1478 woodblock-reprint of *Xinbian quanxiang shuochang zuben Hua Guan Suo chushen zhuan deng si zhong* (Newly Compiled, Fully Illustrated Biography of Guan Suo in Four Parts), not paginated, illustrations on front and back of first page and on front and back of last page, volume 1, in *Ming Chenghua shuochang cihua congkan: Shiliu zhong fu baitu ji chuanqi yi zhong*, Shanghai: Shanghaishiwenwu baoguan weiyuanhui and Shanghai bowuguan, 1973.

2. See Rene-Yvon Lefebvre d'Argencé editor, *Treasures from the Shanghai Museum: 6000 Years of Chinese Art*, San Francisco: Asian Art Museum of San Francisco, 1983, 101, number 82.

3. See Loehr, *Ritual Vessels*, 51, number 17; 83,

number 33; for additional *hu* vessels with appendages, see Hayashi, *In Shū seidōki sōran*, plate volume, 297-305.

4. See Loehr, *Ritual Vessels*, 133-35, numbers 58-59; Fong, *The Great Bronze Age*, 237, number 62.

5. See Loehr, *Ritual Vessels*, 155-163, numbers 69-73; Fong, *The Great Bronze Age*, 277, number 69; 282, number 73; 292, number 91; 299, number 96.

6. See Fogg Art Museum compiler, *Grenville L. Winthrop: Retrospective for a Collector*, Cambridge MA: Fogg Art Museum, Harvard University, 1969, 39, number 39.

7. See Mikami Tsugio, *Ryō Kin Gen* (Liao, Jin and Yuan), volume 13 in *Sekai tōji zenshū* (Ceramic Art of the World), Tokyo: Shogakukan, 1981, 73, number 57; 79, number 61; 210-11, numbers 199, 204.

8. See Percival David Foundation, *Imperial Taste*, 49, number 23.

9. See Percival David Foundation, *Imperial Taste*, 51, number 24; 54-58, numbers 27-29; Suzanne G. Valenstein, *A Handbook of Chinese Ceramics*, New York: Metropolitan Museum of Art, revised and enlarged edition, 1989, 122, number 134; 135, number 131.

10. See Kerr, *Later Chinese Bronzes*, 42-43, figures 31-32; 58-59, figures 46-47; Kerr, 'Metalwork and Song Design,' 164-68, figures 1-5.

11. See Loehr, *Ritual Vessels*, 63, number 23; 67-69, numbers 25-26; 75, number 29; 81, number 32.

12. A thermoluminescence (TL) test performed at the Research Laboratory for Archaeology and the History of Art, Oxford University, on a sample of casting core removed from one of the cylindrical appendages on this vase confirmed its antiquity. The test certificate, dated 26 October 1990 and bearing the signature of Doreen Stoneham, indicates that the sample (number 566k6) was last fired between three hundred and five hundred years ago.

13. See Rose Kerr, 'The Evolution of Bronze Style in the Jin, Yuan and Early Ming Dynasties,' *Oriental Art* (London), new series number 28, Summer 1982, 15, figure 9.

14. See Kerr, 'The Evolution of Bronze Style,' 150, figure 10.

15. See Kerr, 'Metalwork and Song Design,' 171, figure 10.

16. See Ministry of Culture and Information, *Sinan haejŏ yumul*, 112, number 142; 117, number 146.

17. See Ministry of Culture and Information, *Sinan haejŏ yumul*, 117, number 146.

5

1. See Machida International Print Museum, *Chūgoku kodai hanga ten*, 110, number 13.

2. See Kerr, *Later Chinese Bronzes*, 29, figure 16.

3. See Kerr, 'The Evolution of Bronze Style,' 150, figure 10.

4. See Editorial Committee of the Joint Board of Directors of the National Palace Museum and National Central Museum, *Three Hundred Master-*

pieces of *Chinese Painting in the Palace Museum*, Taizhong, Taiwan: National Palace Museum, 1959, volume 4, number 175.

5. See Robert J. Herold, 'A Family of Post-Han Ritual Bronze Vessels,' *Artibus Asiae* (Ascona, Switzerland), volume 37, number 4, 1975, 264, figure 13b (vessel in center); 266, 16c.

6. See Mikami, *Ryō Kin Gen*, 127, number 102; 186, number 168 (piece in upper right corner of illustration); 205, number 180; 207, number 188 (two pieces at left of illustration); Ministry of Culture and Information, *Sinan haejō yumul*, 4, number 33; 86-87, numbers 13-18.

7. See Ministry of Culture and Information, *Sinan haejō yumul*, 167, number 223.

8. See Wai-kam Ho, Sherman E. Lee, Laurence Sickman, and Marc F. Wilson, *Eight Dynasties of Chinese Painting: The Collections of the Nelson Gallery-Atkins Museum, Kansas City, and The Cleveland Museum of Art*, Cleveland: Cleveland Museum of Art, 1980, 113, number 92.

9. See Shanghai Museum facsimile edition of a 1478 woodblock-reprint of *Xinbian quanxiang shuochang zuben Hua Guan Suo chushen zhuan deng si zhong* (Newly Compiled, Fully Illustrated Biography of Guan Suo in Four Parts), not paginated, illustration on front and back of first page, volume 1 in *Ming Chenghua shuochang cihua congkan: Shiliu zhong fu baitu ji chuanqi yi zhong*, Shanghai: Shanghaishiwenwu baoguan weiyuanhui and Shanghai bowuguan, 1973.

10. See Rosemary Scott, 'China,' in Jonathan Bourne and others, *Lacquer: An International History and Collector's Guide*, Marlborough, Wiltshire, England: Crowood Press in association with Phoebe Phillips Editions, 1984, 31, illustration at top of page. For a related miniature table excavated from the tomb (dated 1189) of Yan Deyuan, see J.M. Addis, *Chinese Ceramics from Datable Tombs and Some Other Dated Material: A Handbook*, London and New York: Sotheby Parke Bernet, 1978, 29, number 19c.

11. See Mikami, *Ryō Kin Gen*, 215, numbers 220, 222.

6

1. See Hasebe, *Sō*, 211, number 218; Mikami, *Ryō Kin Gen*, 206, number 185; Fujioka and Hasebe, *Min*, 13, number 6; Kerr, *Later Chinese Bronzes*, 41, figure 27.

2. See Delbanco, *Art from Ritual*, 93, number 34; Loehr, *Ritual Vessels*, 121, number 52. (Contrast Loehr, *Ritual Vessels*, 119, number 51, for the appearance of a dragon in a similar context.)

3. A feline head, with diamond-shaped marking on its brow, that graces a *zun* in the collection of the University Museum, University of Pennsylvania, Philadelphia, is especially close in appearance to the feline mask on the Clague vase. See Loehr, *Ritual Vessels*, 119, number 51.

4. See Delbanco, *Art from Ritual*, 41-49, numbers 8-12.

5. See Loehr, *Ritual Vessels*, 119-121, numbers 51-52.

6. Compare Delbanco, *Art from Ritual*, 41, number 8.

7. See Percival David Foundation, *Imperial Taste*, 46, number 21.

8. See Kuo, *Born of Earth and Fire*, 87, number 68.

9. See Kerr, 'Metalwork and Song Design,' 172, figure 12.

10. See Kerr, *Later Chinese Bronzes*, 25, figure 14 (left).

7

1. For a variety of *hu* vessels of types that could have served as models for the Clague vase, see Hayashi, *In Shū seidōki sōran*, plate volume, 297-307.

2. See Chase, *Ancient Chinese Bronze Art*, 57, number 20; Loehr, *Ritual Vessels*, 133-35, numbers 58-59.

3. See Maeda, 'The "Water" Theme in Chinese Painting,' 247-90.

4. See Machida International Print Museum, *Chūgoku kodai hanga ten*, 85, number 8, scrolls 4 and 6.

5. See Kerr, 'Metalwork and Song Design,' 172, figure 12.

6. See Kerr, *Later Chinese Bronzes*, 42-43, figures 31-32; 58-59, figures 46-47; Kerr, 'Metalwork and Song Design,' 164-68, figures 1-5.

7. See Kuo, *Born of Earth and Fire*, 87, number 68; Hasebe, *Sō*, 245, number 288.

8. For a contrast between Yuan and early Ming designs, see, respectively, Mikami, *Ryō Kin Gen*, 67, number 53; 73, number 57; 79, number 61; Fujioka and Hasebe, *Min*, 24, number 16; 36, number 27; 37, numbers 28-29.

9. See Daisy Lion-Goldschmidt, *Ming Porcelain*, New York: Rizzoli, 1978, 38, diagram (translated by Katherine Watson).

10. See Sichuan Cultural Properties Commission, 'Chengdu Baima-si liuhao Ming mu qingli jianbao' (Report on the Excavation of Ming Tomb Number 6 at White-horse Temple, Chengdu), *Wenwu* (Beijing), 1956, number 10, 43, figure 3 (pieces *in situ* on the altar table); 45, figure 12 (bronze pieces photographed separately); Kerr, 'The Evolution of Bronze Style,' 156, figures 20-21.

11. Shanghai Museum facsimile edition of a 1478 woodblock-reprint of *Xinbian quanxiang shuochang zuben Hua Guan Suo chushen zhuan deng si zhong*, not paginated, illustrations on front and back of first page and on front and back of last page.

12. Sichuan Cultural Properties Commission, 'Chengdu Baima-si liuhao Ming mu,' 49.

8

1. For examples of the *jue*, see Hayashi, *In Shū seidōki sōran*, plate volume, 164-88.

2. For examples of the *jiao*, see Hayashi, *In Shū seidōki sōran*, plate volume, 189-92.

3. See Loehr, *Ritual Vessels*, 97, number 40; number 41; 117, number 50; Delbanco, *Art from Ritual*, 89, number 32.

4. Rose Kerr has noted that his biography in the *Ming Shi* (Official Ming History) indicates that Liu

230   CHINA'S RENAISSANCE IN BRONZE

Wei was from Ciqi in Zhejiang province, that he received his *jinshi*, or doctorate, in 1439, and that he served in Guangdong province during his last offical career posting. Kerr, *Later Chinese Bronzes*, 106, note 43.

5. See Ministry of Culture and Information, *Sinan haejŏ yumul*, 130, number 164; 183, number 247.

6. Urban Council, Hong Kong, and the Jingdezhen Museum of Ceramic History compiler, *Imperial Porcelain of the Yongle and Xuande Periods Excavated from the Site of the Ming Imperial Factory at Jingdezhen*, Hong Kong: Urban Council, 1989, 116, number 17.

7. See Lion-Goldschmidt, *Ming Porcelain*, 79, plate 39; 156, plate 137.

8. See Yang Boda, *Zhongguo meishu quanji: Jin yin boli falang qi*, 89, number 170.

9. See Yang Boda, *Zhongguo meishu quanji: Jin yin boli falang qi*, 90, number 172.

10. See Yang Boda editor, *Zhongguo meishu quanji* (The Great Treasury of Chinese Art), volume 3, part 9, *Gongyi meishu bian: Yuqi* (Crafts: Jade), Beijing, Wenwu chubanshe, 1986, 163, number 286.

11. See Kerr, *Later Chinese Bronzes*, 31-32, figures 17-18.

12. Mowry, 'Catalogue,' in Li and Watt, *The Chinese Scholar's Studio*, 166-67, number 37.

9

1. For information on the arrow game and its vessels, see Robert Poor, 'Evolution of a Secular Vessel Type,' *Oriental Art* (London), new series volume 14, number 2, Summer 1968, 98-106; G. Montell, 'T'ou-hu: The Ancient Chinese Pitch-pot Game,' *Ethos*, volume 5, 1940. Much of this entry has been adapted from a catalog entry that the author wrote on a related *touhu* vessel in the collection of the Shanghai Museum, published in Mowry, 'Catalogue,' in Li and Watt, *The Chinese Scholar's Studio*, 178, number 63.

2. James Legge translator, *The Ch'un Ts'ew with The Tso Chuen*, volume 5 in The Chinese Classics, reprint by Hong Kong: Hong Kong University Press, 1960, 638-41, especially 639.

3. Ch'u Chai and Winberg Chai editors, *Li Chi: Book of Rites*, New Hyde Park NY: University Books, 1967, volume 2, 397-401 (translated by James Legge).

4. See Poor, 'Evolution of a Secular Vessel Type,' 99, figure 1; 100, figure 3.

5. See Thomas Lawton, *Chinese Figure Painting*, Washington DC: Smithsonian Institution, Freer, Gallery of Art, 1973, 34-37, number 3; Bradley Smith and Wan-go Weng, *China: A History in Art*, NY: Doubleday, not dated but about 1972, 212-13.

6. See Hayashi, *The Silk Road and the Shōsō-in*, 160, figure 188.

7. See Pope and others, *The Freer Chinese Bronzes*, volume 1, 597, number 118.

8. See Okazaki, *Chūgoku kodai*, 212, number 197.

9. See d'Argencé, *Treasures from the Shanghai Museum*, 101, number 82.

10. The creation and breaking of formal borders is a characteristic apparent in media other than bronze in the late Ming and early Qing periods; for an example in bamboo, see Li and Watt, *The Chinese Scholar's Studio*, 115, number 55.

11. See Kerr, *Later Chinese Bronzes*, 42, number 29.

12. Kerr, *Later Chinese Bronzes*, 3; John Ayers, 'Blanc-de-Chine: Some Reflections,' *Transactions of the Oriental Ceramic Society* (London), 1986-87, 23.

10

1. Will. H. Edmunds, *Pointers and Clues to the Subjects of Chinese and Japanese Art*, London: Sampson Low, Marston and Company, not dated but about 1934, 131 (Hü Yeo and Ch'ao Fu); Herbert A. Giles, *A Chinese Biographical Dictionary*, London: Bernard Quaritch, and Shanghai and Yokohama: Kelly and Walsh, 1898, 84-85 (Ch'ao Fu); 311-12 (Hsü You). The author is indebted to Donald Jenkins, Curator of Asian Art at the Portland Art Museum, Portland OR, for identifying the subject matter depicted on this vase.

2. See Loehr, *Ritual Vessels*, 75-77, numbers 29-30; Pope and others, *The Freer Chinese Bronzes*, volume 1, 79, plate 12; Hayashi, *In Shū seidōki sōran*, plate volume, 215-44.

3. See James C.Y. Watt and Barbara Brennan Ford, *East Asian Lacquer: The Florence and Herbert Irving Collection*, New York: Metropolitan Museum of Art, 40-43, numbers 1-2.

4. See Percival David Foundation, *Imperial Taste*, 24, number 4; 28-29, number 7; 37, number 13; 40, number 16.

5. A query from John D. Cosby of Niagara Falls NY, about the date and place of manufacture of two vases virtually identical to the Clague vessel appeared in a recent issue of *Arts of Asia*, along with illustrations of the pieces; a note from the editor indicated that readers' responses ranged from China to Japan and even to Korea as the country of origin, though no dates were proposed. See *Arts of Asia* (Hong Kong), volume 23, number 1, January-February 1993, 8.

6. Verbal communication of Yang Boda to Robert H. Clague on 7 June 1992 (as translated by Kelly Tan). On his visit to the Clague Collection, Mr Yang inspected this vase; he commented that although such pieces are difficult to date, an attri-bution to the Ming dynasty would be acceptable. When questioned about a more specific date, Mr Yang stated that due to lack of dated comparative material, a more precise attribution would be impos-sible at this time.

7. See The Arts Council of Great Britain and The Oriental Ceramic Society, *Chinese Jade Through-out the Ages*, London: Arts Council of Great Britain and Oriental Ceramic Society, 1975, number 438; Ip Yee, *Chinese Jade Carving* (The 8th Festival of

Asian Arts), Hong Kong: Urban Council, 1983, 237, number 211; 249, number 222; Watt, *Chinese Jade*, 124, number 132; 169, number 143.

8. Percival David Foundation, *Imperial Taste*, 46-47, numbers 21-22; 50-51, number 24; 54-55, number 27; Valenstein, *A Handbook of Chinese Ceramics*, 140, numbers 136; 182, number 179; 193, number 189; 217, number 208; 219, number 210; 223, number 215; 227, number 221; 263, number 267.

9. For a selection of Japanese bronze vases of the Edo period exhibiting characteristics discussed here, see Michael Goedhuis, *Chinese and Japanese Bronzes: AD 1100-1900*, London: Michael Goedhuis/Colnaghi Oriental, 1989, numbers 92-94, 96-97, 105.

10. See Goedhuis, *Chinese and Japanese Bronzes*, number 104.

11. Apparently headed for Japan, the Chinese merchant ship that sank off the coast of Korea in 1323 carried numerous items of bronze, silver, and ceramic ware, among others; see Ministry of Culture and Information, *Sinan haejŏ yumul*. For a selection of later Chinese bronzes preserved in Japan, see Nezu Museum, compiler, *Koro* (Censers), Tokyo: Nezu bijutsukan, 1972; Baba Ichiro editor, 'Ikebana' (Flower Arrangement), *Taiyō* (Tokyo), 1975, number 12; Tokyo National Museum compiler, *Cha no bijutsu: Tokubetsuten* (The Art of the Tea Ceremony), Tokyo: Tokyo kokuritsu hakubutsukan, 1980; Tokugawa Museum and Nezu Museum compilers, *Hanaike* (Flower Vases), Nagoya: Tokugawa bijutsukan, and Tokyo: Nezu bijutsukan, 1982.

11

1. See, Li and Watt, *The Chinese Scholar's Studio*, 74, number 7; National Palace Museum, compiler, *Wan Ming bianxing zhuyi huajia zuopin zhan* (Style Transformed: A Special Exhibition of Works by Five Late Ming Artists), Taipei: Guoli gugong bowuan, 1977, 93, number 010-02; 111, number 018. For a painting showing a small circular box with censer (but without vase, spoon, and tongs), see Ho and others, *Eight Dynasties of Chinese Painting*, 374, number 275. For a reconstructed set and for a detail of a set depicted on a late Ming bronze, see Gerard Tsang and Hugh Moss, *Chinese Metalwork of the Hu Wenming Group* (International Asian Antiques Fair, Hong Kong, catalog), Hong Kong: Andamans East International, 1984, 65, numbers 47-48. For an example in lacquer decoration, see Watt and Ford, *East Asian Lacquer*, 77, number 23.

2. For information on Hu Wenming, see Tsang and Moss, *Chinese Metalwork*, 33-68; R. Soame Jenyns and William Watson, *Chinese Art: The Minor Arts (Gold, Silver, Bronze, Cloisonné, Cantonese Enamel, Lacquer, Furniture, Wood)*, New York: Universe Books, 1963, 90-91; Kerr, *Later Chinese Bronzes*, 52; Li Fangwu, *Zhongguo yishujia zhenglüe* (An Introduction to Chinese Artists) (1911), reprinted as Li Juanyai, *Zhongguo yishujia zhenglüe*, Taipei: Taiwan zhonghua shuju, 1967, *juan* 1, 6 (verso and recto).

3. Songjiang had risen to prosperity at least by the Yuan and had produced a community of literati by the early Ming. Cao Zhao (flourished 1387-1399), the early Ming antiquarian and author of *Gegu yaolun*, an important work on the connoisseurship of Chinese antiquities, was a native of Songjiang, for example. By the late Ming, an important and highly influential circle of literati was active there, a circle that included Mo Shilong (1539?-1587), Dong Qichang (1555-1636), and Chen Jiru (1558-1639). A high government official, Dong Qichang was the preëminent figure of the late Ming, and his style and theories have shaped the course of Chinese painting down to the present. He was equally talented as a painter, calligrapher, connoisseur, theorist, critic, and art historian.

4. See Li and Watt, *The Chinese Scholar's Studio*, 118, number 62; Tsang and Moss, *Chinese Metalwork*, 63, numbers 43-44.

5. National Central Library, compiler, *Mingren juanji ziliao suoyin* (An Index of Ming Biographical Materials), Taipei: Guoli zhongyang tushuguan, 1965-66, volume 1, 343.

6. L. Carrington Goodrich, 'Ts'ao Chao' (Cao Zhao), in L. Carrington Goodrich and Chaoying Fang editors, *Dictionary of Ming Biography: 1368-1644*, New York and London: Columbia University Press, 1976, volume 2, 1297.

7. As reflected in an unpublished example in the Grenville L. Winthrop Collection at the Harvard University Art Museums (accession number 1943.52.78), Han-dynasty silver boxes typically have straight, vertical walls, squared corners, and lightly domed covers, the covers usually with a stylized floral motif composed of four heart-shaped leaves or petals; a free-turning ring for removing the cover often appears at the center of the floral motif.

8. See Bo Gyllensvärd, *Chinese Gold and Silver in the Carl Kempe Collection*, Stockholm: Carl Kempe, 1953, 95-96, numbers 39, 41; 145-46, numbers 91-92, 94; 170, number 112; 188, number 121; Kelley, *Chinese Gold and Silver*, 68-71, numbers 34-38; Jenyns and Watson, *Chinese Art: The Minor Arts*, 65, number 27.

9. See Gyllensvärd, *Chinese Gold and Silver*, 207, numbers 134-35.

10. See Satō Masahiko and Hasebe Gakuji, *Zui Tō* (Sui and Tang), volume 11 in *Sekai tōji zenshū* (Ceramic Art of the World), Tokyo: Shogagukan, 1976, 115, number 95; 152, number 141; 158, number 150; 160, numbers 152-53; 251, numbers 229 (left) and 230 (right); 262, numbers 240-41; William Watson, *Tang and Liao Ceramics*, New York: Rizzoli, 1984, 170, numbers 186-87.

11. See Hasebe, *Sō*, 62, number 51; 184, figures 45-48; 203, number 194; 275, number 271.

12. See Percival David Foundation, Imperial Taste, 33, number 10; Watson, *Tang and Liao Ceramics*, 77, number 48; 148, number 127; Hasebe, *Sō*, 62, number 51.

13. See Watt, *Chinese Jades*, 138-39, numbers 114-15.

14. See Bo Gyllensvärd and John Alexander Pope, *Chinese Art from the Collection of H. M. King Gustav Adolf of Sweden*, New York: Asia Society, 1966, 107, 125; Watt and Ford, *East Asian Lacquer*, 56, number 11; 60, number 14; 105-07, numbers 40-42.

15. See Rene-Yvon Lefebvre d'Argencé, 'Chinese Lacquerware of the Late Medieval Period,' *Apollo* (London), volume 112, number 221, August 1980, 11, figure 14. For an example with identical shape and with identical *leiwen* borders on its straight vertical sides but with figural decor on its broad flat face, see Watt and Ford, *East Asian Lacquer*, 107, number 42.

16. See d'Argencé, 'Chinese Lacquerware of the Late Medieval Period,' 11, figure 14; Watt and Ford, *East Asian Lacquer*, 105-06, numbers 40-41; Gyllensvärd and Pope, *Chinese Art*, 107, number 125; Watt, *Chinese Jades*, 138-39, numbers 114-15.

17. C.A.S. Williams, *Outlines of Chinese Symbolism and Art Motifs*, Shanghai: Kelly and Walsh, 1932, second, revised edition, 324-26 (Plant of Long Life).

18. See San Francisco Center of Asian Art and Culture compiler, *Osaka Exchange Exhibition: Paintings from the Abe Collection and Other Masterpieces of Chinese Art*, San Francisco: San Francisco Center of Asian Art and Culture, and Osaka: Osaka Municipal Museum of Fine Arts, 1970, 36, number 11; for information on Zheng Sixiao, see Chu-tsing Li, 'Cheng Ssu-hsiao' (Zheng Sixiao), in Herbert Franke editor, *Song Biographies: Painters*, Wiesbaden: Franz Steiner Verlag GMBH, 1976, 15-23.

19. See The National Palace Museum compiler, *Wupai hua jiushinian zhan* (Ninety Years of Wu School Painting), Taipei: Guoli gugong bowuyuan, 1974, 128, number 115; 173, number 155; 176, number 158; 222, number 198; Richard Edwards, *The Art of Wen Cheng-ming (1470-1559)*, Ann Arbor: University of Michigan, 1976, 183, number LIII A; National Palace Museum, *Wan Ming bianxing zhuyi huajia zuopin zhan*, 117, number 021.

20. See Kerr, *Later Chinese Bronzes*, 15, figure 1; 43, figure 31.

21. See Kuo, *Born of Earth and Fire*, 76, number 54.

22. See Watt, *Chinese Jades*, 139, number 115.

23. See Gyllensvärd and Pope, *Chinese Art*, 107, number 125; Watt and Ford, *East Asian Lacquer*, 100, number 36; 105, number 40.

24. See National Palace Museum, *Wan Ming bianxing zhuyi huajia zuopin zhan*, 448-49, number 085, especially detail on 448; 482-83, number 095, especially detail on 483.

25. In many ways, the broadening of the decorative palette associated with Ming bronzes parallels the expansion of the palette associated with contemporaneous porcelains; with porcelains, the palette was limited to underglaze cobalt-blue and copper-red at the beginning of the dynasty but came to include a full range of overglaze enamel colors by the end.

26. Because of its similarity in shape to the markings on the shell of a tortoise [see 44] – an auspicious animal in the realm of Chinese mythology and an emblem of the north in Chinese directional symbolism – the hexagon began to find favor as form in Song times. At least as early as the Yuan dynasty, hexagons were occasionally used for surface patterning in both bronze and architectural ornament, sometimes with simple internal embellishments, sometimes without; for an example in bronze, see Ministry of Culture and Information, *Sinan haejŏ yumul*, 130, number 164; for an example as architectural ornament in a painting, see Editorial Committee of the Joint Board of Directors of the National Palace Museum and National Central Museum, *Three Hundred Masterpieces of Chinese Painting*, volume 4, number 175. By the early sixteenth century, blue-and-white porcelain decoration occasionally included hexagonal diapers with single-Y markings on their interiors; see Palace Museum compiler, *Gugong bowuyuan cang ci xuanji* (The Palace Museum: Ceramics), Beijing: Wenwu chubanshe, 1962, number 60.

27. Compare Tsang and Moss, *Chinese Metalwork*, 46, numbers 9-10.

28. Wen Zhenheng, *Zhangwu zhi* (1637), in Deng Shi and Huang Binhong compilers, *Meishu congshu*, Taipei: Yiwen yinshuguan, photo reprint of 1947, fourth revised edition, volume 15, 3/9, *juan* 7, 198.

29. Wen Zhenheng, *Zhangwu zhi*, *juan* 7, 199.30. Tu Long, *Xiangjian* (not dated, but late sixteenth century), in Deng Shi and Huang Binhong compilers, *Meishu congshu*, Taipei: Yiwen yinshuguan, photo reprint of 1947, fourth revised edition, volume 10, 2/9, 159-60.

12

1. Literally, *feiyu* means 'flying fish' in Chinese. A fabulous creature of Chinese mythology and decidedly a member of the dragon family, the *feiyu* has a dragon's head and a scale-covered body that sometimes resembles that of a fish but that more commonly resembles that of a dragon (as usually depicted in Chinese art). The *feiyu* has a pair of wings – usually webbed, like those of a bat, but sometimes feathered like those of a bird – clearly setting it apart from the standard dragon (*long*); it typically has a fish tail, which also distinguishes it from the standard dragon. The *feiyu* is often, though not necessarily, horned, sometimes with one horn, other times with two. The *feiyu* may or may not have a pair of clawed legs; if it lacks legs, it may have a pair of caudal fins, though such do not always appear. It may also have a pair of ventral fins placed near the wings. For more information about the *feiyu* and other Ming fabulous beasts, see Schuyler Cammann, 'Some Strange Ming Beasts,' *Oriental Art* (London), new series volume 2, number 3, Autumn 1956, 94-102.

2. *Baize* and *bixie* defy ready translation into English, though both terms denote types of lion-like chimeras.

3. Compare Tsang and Moss, *Chinese Metalwork*, 46, numbers 9-10.

4. See Loehr, *Ritual Vessels*, 115, number 49; Delbanco, *Art from Ritual*, 83, number 29; 99-101, numbers 37-38; Hayashi, *In Shū seidōki sōran*, plate volume, 82-136.

5. See Yang Boda, *Zhongguo meishu quanji: Yuqi*, 145, number 259; Arts Council of Great Britain, *Chinese Jade Throughout the Ages*, 101-102, numbers 328-330; Li and Watt, *The Chinese Scholar's Studio*, 113, number 51.

6. See Mowry, *Handbook*, 67, number 1979.146; Hasebe, *Sō*, 229, figure 88; Palace Museum, *Gugong bowuyuan cang ci xuanji*, number 26; Percival David Foundation, *Imperial Taste*, 43, number 18; 45, number 20.

7. The often debated question of whether Hu Wenming studied original examples of archaic ritual bronze vessels or whether he had available only woodblock-printed illustrations in published catalogs of ancient bronzes can be raised but not settled here. Hu Wenming and other bronze casters of the Song, Yuan, Ming, and Qing periods were certainly familiar with such catalogs; at the same time, well known casters must have had access to original ancient bronzes through their clients (some of whom doubtless wanted archaistic vessels) and through antique dealers (some of whom likely commissioned high-quality fakes for sale as originals). In addition, since any claim to status in traditional China had, *de rigueur*, to be legitimized by knowledge (and preferably possession) of such antiquities as bronzes, jades, paintings, inkstones, and seals, it is entirely possible that a successful craftsman of Hu Wenming's fame and presumed means might have owned a small collection of antiques, especially of ancient bronzes. Under the circumstances, this author contends that most sophisticated foundrymen had access to both actual bronzes and illustrated catalogs, drawing upon one or the other as befitted the work at hand or, in the market economy of the late Ming, drawing upon whichever produced the most salable results.

8. Similar censers are known; see Tsang and Moss, *Chinese Metalwork*, 45-46, numbers 8-9; 63, number 44 (by Hu Wenming's son, Hu Guangyu); Goedhuis, *Chinese and Japanese Bronzes*, number 59; Sydney L. Moss Ltd compiler, *The Literati Mode: Chinese Scholar Paintings, Calligraphy and Desk Objects*, London: Sydney L. Moss Ltd, 1986, 291, number 145; 293, number 147 (by Hu Guangyu); Sydney L. Moss compiler, *The Second Bronze Age: Later Chinese Metalwork*, London: Sydney L. Moss Ltd, 1991, numbers 88-89 (both by Zhu Zhenming of Yunjian).

9. Cammann, 'Some Strange Ming Beasts,' 94.

10. See Ross E. Taggart, George L. McKenna, and Marc F. Wilson editors, *Handbook of the Collections in the William Rockhill Nelson Gallery of Art and Mary Atkins Museum of Fine Arts*, Kansas City MO: William Rockhill Nelson Gallery, 1973, fifth edition, volume 2, 91, number 50-10; Jan Fontein and Tung Wu, *Unearthing China's Past*, Boston: Museum of Fine Arts, 1973, 177, number 90; Robert D. Mowry, 'Koryŏ Celadons,' *Orientations* (Hong Kong), volume 17, number 5, May 1986, 34, figures 15-16.

11. See Mowry, 'Koryŏ Celadons,' 28, figure 6; 35, figure 18.

12. See Valenstein, *A Handbook of Chinese Ceramics*, color plate 11 and 80, number 72.

13. See Kerr, *Later Chinese Bronzes*, 43-44, plates 31-32; 58-59, plates 46-47.

14. The Tuancheng, or Round Fort, is a walled enclosure adjoining the Beihai, or North Lake, in Beijing. For illustrations of the massive wine bowl, see Yang Boda, *Zhongguo meishu quanji: Yuqi*, 148-49, numbers 264-66; S. Howard Hansford, *Chinese Jade Carving*, London: Lund Humphries, 1950, 74-78, and plate 28a; S. Howard Hansford, *Chinese Carved Jades*, London: Faber and Faber, 1968, 89, and plate 78; Zhou Nanquan and Wang Mingshi, 'Beijing Tuancheng nei Dushan Dayuhai kao' (Research on the Great Black-jade Wine Bowl in the Round Fort, Beijing), *Wenwu*, 1980, number 4, 23-26, and plate 7, figures 1-3; Watt, *Chinese Jades*, 22, figure 2.

15. See James C.Y. Watt assisted by Michael Knight, *Chinese Jades from the Collection of the Seattle Art Museum*, Seattle: Seattle Art Museum, 1989, 66, number 41 (and front cover). Set against an openwork ground of rocks, *lingzhi* fungi, and flowering plants, two related *feiyu* (misidentified as phoenixes) emblazon a Yuan to early Ming jade belt plaque in the British Museum, London. Probably of Yuan date, a jade pendant in the National Palace Museum, Taipei, has been worked in the form of a *feiyu* with feathered wings. See, respectively, Arts Council of Great Britain, *Chinese Jade Throughout the Ages*, 107, number 347; National Palace Museum compiler, *Gugong guyu tulu* (Illustrated Catalogue of Ancient Jade Artifacts in the National Palace Museum), Taipei: Guoli gugong bowuyuan, 1982, 189, number 350.

16. Watt, *Chinese Jades from the Collection of the Seattle Art Museum*, 66.

17. Addis, *Chinese Ceramics from Datable Tombs*, 70, number 33d. It should be noted that feathered wings continued to be used for a variety of mythical animals in the Ming dynasty, as revealed by two glazed tiles depicting rampant rams with feathered, bird-like wings from the Bao'en Pagoda, Nanjing, erected in 1412; see Addis, *Chinese Ceramics from Datable Tombs*, 78-79, numbers 34 e-f.

18. See A.D. Brankston, *Early Ming Wares of Chingtechen*, Beijing: Henri Vetch, 1938, plate 10b.

19. See Mowry, *Handbook*, 77, number 1979.173.

20. See Cammann, 'Some Strange Ming Beasts,' 96, figure 2.

21. See The Joint Board of Directors of The National Palace Museum and the National Central Museum compilers, *Blue-and-white Ware of the Ming Dynasty*, Hong Kong: Cafa Company, 1963, book 6, 64-65, plates 18-18e; City of Venice compiler, *Mostra d'Arte Cinese* (Exhibition of Chinese Art),

Venice: Alfieri Editore, 1954, 196, number 724.

22. See Sir Harry Garner, *Oriental Blue and White*, London: Faber and Faber, 1954, plate 59a; Sheila Riddell, *Dated Chinese Antiquities, 600-1650*, London and Boston: Faber and Faber, 1979, 106, number 87.

23. Watt, *Chinese Jades from the Collection of the Seattle Art Museum*, 66.

24. Cammann, 'Some Strange Ming Beasts,' 96.

25. See Delbanco, *Art from Ritual*, 93, number 34; Loehr, *Ritual Vessels*, 121, number 52.

26. See Tsang and Moss, *Chinese Metalwork*, 47-48, numbers 11-13; Li and Watt, *The Chinese Scholar's Studio*, 118, number 62.

27. The handles on Shang and early Western Zhou bronze *gui* usually take the form of a ring issuing from the mouth of a fabulous beast; nonrepresentational designs frequently enliven the ring's surfaces and a spur typically appears at its bottom. Bronze designers of the Ming apparently transformed the nonrepresentational surface designs on the handles of antique vessels into tufts of fur on their own. See Delbanco, *Art from Ritual*, 99, number 37; Loehr, *Ritual Vessels*, 115, number 49.

28. Compare, Tsang and Moss, *Chinese Metalwork*, 45, number 8.

29. Cammann, 'Some Strange Ming Beasts,' 100. Cammann notes that the *feiyu* was dropped from court and official insignia at the end of Ming and thus was not included among the symbols used to distinguish official rank in the Qing.

30. See Joint Board of Directors, *Blue-and-white Ware of the Ming Dynasty*, book 6, 64-65, plates 18-18e.

31. Mowry, 'Catalogue,' in Li and Watt, *The Chinese Scholar's Studio*, 179, number 66.

13

1. A young, or immature, dragon, the *chilong* typically has a broad, triangular face with flattened snout, a sinuous feline body, usually without scales, and thus different from other members of the dragon family, rounded paws with short claws, and a long tail that splits into two (or even three) tips that curl outward in opposite directions. Although encyclopaedias describe the *chilong* as hornless, since it is an immature dragon, it is often shown with a horn in the visual arts, as in this covered box. Despite its feline or salamander-like appearance, the *chilong* is definitely a member of the dragon family, a close relative of the *long* (three- or five-clawed conventional dragon), *mang* (four-clawed conventional dragon), and *yinglong* (five-clawed conventional dragon with a pair of outspread wings attached at the base of its head); it is also related to such lesser members of the dragon family as the *feiyu* (flying fish-dragon; see entry 12), and *douniu* (literally, 'dipper ox'), which has a conventional dragon's body, usually with three claws, but has two down-swept horns and a split tail that often supports a jewel. Although the

convention is not always observed, the *chilong*, *feiyu*, and *douniu* are not supposed to be shown in pursuit of the flaming pearl, a symbol reserved for the senior members of the dragon family. For additional information on these creatures, see Cammann, 'Some Strange Ming Beasts.'

2. See Watt, *Chinese Jades*, 138, number 114; Ip Yee, *Chinese Jade Carving*, 235, number 210.

3. See Watt and Ford, *East Asian Lacquer*, 105, number 40.

4. See, respectively, d'Argencé, 'Chinese Lacquerware of the Late Medieval Period,' cover illustration and 10, figures 11-12; Watt and Ford, *East Asian Lacquer*, 62-63, number 16.

5. See National Palace Museum compiler, *Masterpieces of Chinese Carved Lacquer Ware in the National Palace Museum*, Taipei: National Palace Museum, 1970, number 2; National Palace Museum compiler, *Gugong qiqi tezhan* (Catalogue of an Exhibition of Chinese Lacquer in the Palace Museum Collection), Taipei: Guoli gugong bowuyuan, 1981, number 11. Also compare Harry M. Garner, *Chinese and Associated Lacquer from the Garner Collection*, London: British Museum, 1973, plate 15, number 38.

6. See Loehr, *Ancient Chinese Jades*, 375-77, numbers 538-40; 395-97, numbers 572-74; 400, number 579; Watt, *Chinese Jades*, 180, number 156.

7. See Watt, *Chinese Jades*, 150, number 124; 195-96, numbers 187-88; 204, number 203; Li and Watt, *The Chinese Scholar's Studio*, 112, number 47; Cammann, 'Some Strange Ming Beasts,' 100, figure 6.

8. See Loehr, *Ancient Chinese Jades*, 302-303, numbers 441-43; 334, number 490.

9. See Fontein and Wu, *Unearthing China's Past*, 177, figure 92.

10. See, Watt, *Chinese Jades*, 64, number 44; 96, number 80; Yang Boda, *Zhongguo meishu quanji: Yuqi*, 142, number 254; Heilongjiang Cultural Management Team, 'Heilongjiang pan Suibin Zhongxing gucheng he Jindai muxun' (The Old City of Zhongxing, Suibin County, Heilongjiang, and a Group of Jin Dynasty Tombs), *Wenwu* (Beijing), 1977, number 4, 40-49, especially plate 7, figure 3.

11. See Watt, *Chinese Jades*, 70, number 52-53; 74, number 55; 99. 98-103, numbers 84-87, 89; 196, number 188; Li and Watt, *The Chinese Scholar's Studio*, 112, number 49; 114, number 52; Shanghai Museum, compiler, 'Shanghai Pudong Ming Lushi mu jishu' (A Description of the Lu-family Tomb from the Ming Dynasty in Pudong, Shanghai), *Kaogu* (Beijing), 1985, number 6, 540-49, illustration 54, and plate 1, figure 6.

12. See Li and Watt, *The Chinese Scholar's Studio*, 124, number 69e.

13. See d'Argencé, *Treasures from the Shanghai Museum*, 117, number 119 a-b.

14. See Mowry, *Handbook*, 68, number 1979.148.

15. See Tsang and Moss, *Chinese Metalwork*, 59, number 36; 67, diagram j.

14

1. An unpublished example appears in the Grenville L.Winthrop Collection at the Harvard University Art Museum (accession number 1943.52.78.); its inlaid volutes vaguely recall the so-called scrolling-cloud designs that first appeared on carved lacquers during the Song dynasty and rose to popularity during the Yuan and Ming, lacquers of a type better known in the West by the Japanese name *guri*.

2. See Delbanco, *Art from Ritual*, 119, 47; 122-23, 49; Jessica Rawson, *Chinese Bronzes: Art and Ritual*, London: British Museum Publications, 1987, 88, number 34; 92-93, numbers 39c, 40; Loehr, *Ancient Chinese Jades*, 300, number 438.

3. See Nancy Thompson, 'The Evolution of the T'ang Lion and Grapevine Mirror,' *Artibus Asiae* (Ascona, Switzerland), volume 29, number 1, 1967, 25-54; Alexander C. Soper, 'Addendum: The 'Jen Shou' Mirrors,' *Artibus Asiae* (Ascona, Switzerland), volume 29, number 1, 1967, 55-66.

4. See Taggart, McKenna, and Wilson, *Handbook of the Collections in the William Rockhill Nelson Gallery*, volume 2, 38, numbers 46-85.

5. See J.J. Lally and Company compiler, *Chinese Ceramics and Works of Art: Inaugural Exhibition*, New York: J.J. Lally and Company, 1986, number 34 and cover illustration.

6. See Fontein and Wu, *Unearthing China's Past*, 177, figure 92.

7. See Mino, *Freedom of Clay and Brush*, 148, figure 165; 149, number 62; Shanxi Provincial Work Committee, Houma Work Station compiler, 'Shanxi Xinjiangahai cun Yuan mu' (A Yuan Tomb at Xinjiangzhai, Shanxi Province), *Kaogu* (Beijing), 1966, number 1, 33-37, plate 8, figure 11.

8. See Editorial Committee of the Joint Board of Directors of the National Palace Museum and National Central Museum, *Three Hundred Masterpieces of Chinese Painting*, volume 3, number 131.

9. See Wen Fong, *Sung and Yuan Paintings*, New York: The Metropolitan Museum of Art, 1973, 69, number 12.

10. See Watt, *Chinese Jades*, 138, number 114.

11. See Garner, *Chinese and Associated Lacquer*, plates 26, figure 50; 27, figure 52; 28, figure 55; 29, figure 61.

12. See Watt, *Chinese Jades*, 205, number 205.

13. See Delbanco, *Art from Ritual*, 129, number 52; Loehr, *Ritual Vessels*, 155, number 69; 159-73, numbers 71-79; Chase, *Ancient Chinese Bronze Art*, 66-70, numbers 29-32.

14. See Li and Watt, *The Chinese Scholar's Studio*, 128, number 71.

15

1. *Xuande dingyi pu* (Catalogue of Xuande *Ding* and *Yi* Vessels) (composed 1428; date of first publication uncertain but perhaps sixteenth century), in Deng Shi and Huang Binhong compilers, *Meishu congshu*, Taipei: Yiwen yinshuguan, photo reprint of 1947, fourth revised edition, volume 7, 2/4, 111-244; Jenyns and Watson, *Chinese Art: The Minor Arts*, 87-90; Zhang Guangyuan (Chang Kuang-yüan), 'Da Ming Xuande lu' (Xuande Censers of the Ming Dynasty), *Gugong wenwu yuekan* (National Palace Museum Monthly of Chinese Art) (Taipei), number 32, November 1985, 4-16.

2. Jenyns and Watson, *Chinese Art: The Minor Arts*, 87; Zhang Guangyuan, 'Da Ming Xuande lu,' 8.

3. Published in 1626 with an erroneous attribution to the connoisseur-collector Xiang Yuanbian (1525-1590), *Xuanlu bolun* (A Discussion of Xuande Censers) notes that although genuine Xuande bronzes were rare already by late Ming times, forgeries were numerous, the rule of thumb being that nine out of ten purported Xuande bronzes were spurious. Xiang, Yuanbian, Xuanlu bolun (A Discussion of Xuande Censers) (1626), in Deng Shi and Huang Binhong compilers, *Meishu congshu*, Taipei: Yiwen yinshuguan, photo reprint of 1947, fourth revised edition, volume 7, 2/4, 245-49. Interest in Xuande censers and the problems surrounding their authenticity has continued to modern times. See also Chang Xiang, *Xuanlu gezhu* (Notes in Praise of Xuande Censers) (date uncertain, but Qing dynasty), in Deng Shi and Huang Binhong compilers, *Meishu congshu*, Taipei: Yiwen yinshuguan, photo reprint of 1947, fourth revised edition, volume 7, 2/4, 251-57.

4. Given that such fragile works of art as painting, calligraphy, lacquer, and porcelain have survived in some quantity from the Xuande period while the more durable bronzes have all disappeared, one is tempted to wonder whether there really were high quality Xuande bronzes or whether the phenomenon might be a complete hoax perpetrated by a later generation and unwittingly perpetuated by succeeding generations. One might even be tempted to question the authenticity of *Xuande dingyi pu* (Catalogue of Xuande *Ding* and *Yi* Vessels) (see note 1), since it does not appear in the *Ming shi* (Official Ming History) and since the *Ming shi* does not record even a mention of the casting of thousands of bronzes during the Xuande reign. Still, as William Watson notes, '...the official language and the arrangement of the report have the marks of authenticity, and anything approaching a travesty of an imperial decree and of so high-ranking a report so comparatively soon after the event is on general considerations improbable.' Jenyns and Watson, *Chinese Art: The Minor Arts*, 95, note 5. Chinese tradition remains firm in its conviction that Xuande bronzes existed and that they embraced the very highest level of quality. Under the circumstances, we must accept the historicity of Xuande bronzes but continue to ponder the mystery of their seemingly complete disappearance.

5. See Mowry, *Handbook*, 67, 1979.146; Percival David Foundation, *Imperial Taste*, 43, number 18;

45, number 20; Palace Museum, *Gugong bowuyuan cang ci xuanji*, number 26. See the fish-shaped handles on a Longquan celadon mallet vase in Valenstein, *A Handbook of Chinese Ceramics*, 106, number 100.

6. In the absence of identically shaped and certifiably genuine Xuande bronzes for comparison, it might be noted, by analogy, that fifteenth-century Longquan celadon vases sometimes have a squat body set on a narrow foot and surmounted by a long, attenuated neck, resulting in a streamlined form with an incongruously bulbous body, reminiscent of, though less exaggerated than, the effect seen in this censer. See Fujioka and Hasebe, *Min*, 234, number 228; The Joint Board of Directors of The National Palace Museum and the National Central Museum, compilers, *Lung-ch'üan Ware of the Sung Dynasty*, Hong Kong: Cafa Company, 1962, 40-41, number 7. The taste for such streamlined forms continued into the seventeenth and eighteenth centuries, as witnessed by examples in Kangxi and Yongzheng ceramics. See John Ayers and Satō Masahiko, *Shin* (Qing), volume 15 in *Sekai tōji zenshū*, Tokyo: Shogakukan, 1983, 39, number 31.

7. See *Xuande yiqi tupu* (Illustrated Catalogue of Xuande Sacral Vessels) (1526), in Tao Xiang, compiler, *Xiyongxuan congshu*, Beijing: Tao Xiang, 1930, *bingbian*, volume 2, *juan* 13, 2 recto; *juan* 19, 4 recto.

8. Xiang Yuanbian, *Xuanlu bolun*, 245-49; Chang Xiang, *Xuanlu gezhu*, 251-57; Jenyns and Watson, *Chinese Art: The Minor Arts*, 87-88; Zhang Guangyuan, 'Da Ming Xuande lu,' 10, 13.

9. As related by Zhang Guangyuan, 'Da Ming Xuande lu,' 13; 15, figure 21.

10. See National Palace Museum, compiler, *Ming Xuande ciqi tezhan mulu* (Catalog of a Special Exhibition of Ming Porcelains of the Xuande Era), Taipei: Guoli gugong bowuyuan, 1979.

11. See Zhang Guangyuan, 'Da Ming Xuande lu,' 5-6, figures 1-8.

16

1. See *Xuande yiqi tupu*, volume 2, *juan* 12, 7; *juan* 17, 11-12 (all pages recto).

2. See Loehr, *Ritual Vessels*, 63, number 23; 89, number 36; Delbanco, *Art from Ritual*, 81, number 28; Hayashi, *In Shū seidōki sōran*, plate volume, 137-49.

3. See Hayashi, *In Shū seidōki sōran*, plate volume, 145, number 81.

4. See The Joint Board of Directors of The National Palace Museum and the National Central Museum compilers, *Ju Ware of the Sung Dynasty*, Hong Kong: Cafa Company, 1961, 36-39, plates 6-9.

5. See The Joint Board of Directors of The National Palace Museum and the National Central Museum compilers, *Kuan Ware of the Sung Dynasty*, Hong Kong: Cafa Company, 1962, 47, plate 18.

6. See Loehr, *Ritual Vessels*, 131, number 57; 143-45, numbers 63-64; 151, number 67; 175, number 80; Delbanco, *Art from Ritual*, 116, number 46; 133-41, numbers 54-58.

7. See The Joint Board of Directors of The National Palace Museum and the National Central Museum, compilers, *Kuan Ware of the Southern Sung*, Hong Kong: Cafa Company, 1962, book 1, part 1, 82-83, plate 26; Hasebe, *Sō*, 71, numbers 61, 62; Palace Museum, *Gugong bowuyuan cang ci xuanji*, numbers 18, 19; Bo Gyllensvärd, *Chinese Gold, Silver, and Porcelain: The Kempe Collection*, New York: Asia Society, 1971, 107, number 111.

8. See Mowry, *Handbook*, 67, 1979.146; Percival David Foundation, *Imperial Taste*, 43, number 18; Palace Museum, *Gugong bowuyuan cang ci xuanji*, number 26.

9. See Watt, *Chinese Jades*, 208-15, numbers 209-13, 215-16.

10. See Ayers and Satō, *Shin*, 33, number 26; Margaret Medley, *Illustrated Catalogue of Ming and Ch'ing Monochrome in the Percival David Foundation of Chinese Art*, London: Percival David Foundation of Chinese Art, University of London, 1973, 25, number 580; plate 4, number 580; and cover.

11. See Goedhuis, *Chinese and Japanese Bronzes*, number 57.

12. See Rawson, *Chinese Bronzes*, color plate 5, number 5; Loehr, *Ritual Vessels*, 91, number 37; Delbanco, *Art from Ritual*, 49, number 12; 69, number 22.

13. See Jenyns and Watson, *Chinese Art: The Minor Arts*, 132-33, number 58.

14. Li Fangwu, *Zhongguo yishujia zhenglüe*, juan 1, 7, verso; Jenyns and Watson, *Chinese Art: The Minor Arts*, 91; Kerr, *Later Chinese Bronzes*, 65; The Oriental Ceramic Society of Hong Kong compiler, *Arts from the Scholar's Studio*, Hong Kong: Oriental Ceramic Society of Hong Kong, 1986, 178, number 157. The last-named work illustrates a small, inlaid bronze water vessel with a carved mark on the base including the cyclical date *xinchou*, which the authors interpret to be 1541 or 1601, but which might well be 1661, given Shisou's lack of mention in writings by such late Ming authors as Wen Zhenheng and Tu Long.

15. Rose Kerr's intriguing suggestion, based on analogy to medieval European craft production practices, that 'Shi Sou' may well have been the trade mark adopted by entrepreneur(s) who coordinated the work of a number of outworkers' seems out of keeping with Chinese custom which, until modern times, favored the individual or the anonymous collective, but not the named collective. Kerr, *Later Chinese Bronzes*, 65. Revealing as they can be, cross-cultural investigations must be approached within a rigorously defined methodological framework and the results of such investigations must be confirmed by hard evidence.

16. In his visit to the Clague Collection on 7 June 1992, Yang Boda, Deputy Director Emeritus of the Palace Museum, Beijing, remarked on the oddity of this combination. The combination of Shisou mark and Zhengde mark mentioned by Gerard Tsang and Hugh Moss has no more credibility than

the combination of Shisou mark and Xuande mark on this censer. See The Oriental Ceramic Society of Hong Kong, *Arts from the Scholar's Studio*, 178, number 157.

17. Technical analysis and comparison of the wire used for the Shisou mark and that used for the fine-line inlay might shed light on the problem. Differences in the composition of the alloys, especially differences in trace elements, would suggest that the mark was added at a later date. Similarities in the alloys would be less revealing, as they could indicate that the mark was inlaid at the same time or merely that the same recipe for alloy production was used over a long period of time.

18. During his visit to the Clague Collection on 7 June 1992, Yang Boda commented to Robert H. Clague that this is the working assumption of the specialists in the Palace Museum, Beijing.

19. See Tsang and Moss, *Chinese Metalwork*, 36, number 3.

20. See National Palace Museum, compiler, *Qing Kang, Yong, Qian mingci tezhan* (Catalogue of a Special Exhibition of Kangxi, Yongzheng, and Qianlong Porcelains from the Qing Dynasty in the National Palace Museum), Taipei: Guoli gugong bowuyuan, 1986, 123, number 107.

17

1. Visually powerful, the ancient clerical script (*lishu*) relies upon brushstrokes of modulated width for dramatic effect; since it loses much of its force when written with lines of even width, clerical script is not the most appropriate for silver-wire inlay. Interested in a variety of ancient scripts, scholars of the late Ming and Qing periods no doubt found the use of clerical script on articles for the studio to be charming, however.

2. See Wang Zhongshu, *Han Civilization*, New Haven and London: Yale University Press, 1982, 110, figure 124 (translated by K.C. Chang and others).

3. See Loehr, *Ritual Vessels*, 155-59, numbers 69-71.

4. See Watt and Ford, *East Asian Lacquer*, 138, number 62.

5. See Pope and others, *The Freer Chinese Bronzes*, volume 1, 229, number 40; The Freer Gallery of Art compiler, *The Freer Gallery of Art*, volume 1 China, Tokyo: Kodansha, not dated (but about 1972), 21, number 5.

6. See Gyllensvärd, *Chinese Gold and Silver*, 154-55, number 99.

7. See Goedhuis, *Chinese and Japanese Bronzes*, number 41.

8. See Mikami, *Ryō Kin Gen*, 62-63, numbers 49-51; Percival David Foundation, *Imperial Taste*, 54-55, number 27.

9. Mowry, 'Catalogue,' in Li and Watt, *The Chinese Scholar's Studio*, 179, number 66.

10. On his visit to the Clague Collection on 7 June 1992, Yang Boda, Deputy Director Emeritus of the Palace Museum, Beijing, commented to Robert H.

Clague that this is a standard Qing manifestation of the Shisou style.

11. See P.J. Donnelly, *Blanc de Chine: The Porcelain of Tehua in Fukien*, New York and Washington DC, 1969, plate 52b (center).

18

1. See, for example, Li and Watt, *The Chinese Scholar's Studio*, 140, number 88; Hasebe, *Sō*, 60, number 49; National Palace Museum, *Kuan Ware of the Sung Dynasty*, 39, plate 11.

2. See Hasebe, *Sō*, 77, number 67; 79, number 70; 91, number 82; 205, number 201; 208, numbers 207-10; National Palace Museum, *Ju Ware of the Sung Dynasty*, 30-33, plates 3-4; National Palace Museum, *Kuan Ware of the Southern Sung*, book 1, part 1, 70-71, plate 20.

3. See Ayers and Satō, *Shin*, 34-35, number 27; Valenstein, *A Handbook of Chinese Ceramics*, 237, numbers 231-38.

4. See Valenstein, *A Handbook of Chinese Ceramics*, 237, number 231; Ayers and Satō, *Shin*, 34, number 27 (right); Li Yihua editor, *Gugong zhencang Kang Yong Qian ciqi tulu* (Qing Porcelain of the Kangxi, Yongzheng, and Qianlong Periods from the Palace Museum Collection), Hong Kong: Forbidden City Publishing House and Woods Publishing Company, 1989, 137, number 120.

5. Mary Gardner Neill, 'The Flowering Plum in the Decorative Arts,' in Maggie Bickford and others, *Bones of Jade, Soul of Ice: The Flowering Plum in Chinese Art*, New Haven CT: Yale University Art Gallery, 1985, 206.

6. Mowry, 'Catalogue,' in Li and Watt, *The Chinese Scholar's Studio*, 155, number 20.

7. Mowry, 'Catalogue,' in Li and Watt, *The Chinese Scholar's Studio*, 155, number 20.

8. See Li Yihua, *Gugong zhencang Kang Yong Qian ciqi tulu*, 77; number 60; 108, number 91; Percival David Foundation, *Imperial Taste*, 118, figure 4; Michel Beurdeley and Guy Raindre, *Qing Porcelain: Famille Verte, Famille Rose*, London: Thames and Hudson, 1987, 112, number 160 (translated by Charlotte Chesney).

9. See Mowry, *Handbook*, 70, number 1979.153; Percival David Foundation, *Imperial Taste*, 62, number 32; Valenstein, *A Handbook of Chinese Ceramics*, color plate 22; Maggie Bickford and others, *Bones of Jade, Soul of Ice*, 208-13, numbers 94, 97-101.

10. See Kerr, *Later Chinese Bronzes*, 64, figure 50.

11. See Ayers and Satō, *Shin*, 50-51, numbers 41-42; 107, number 117; 183, number 233; Li Yihua, *Gugong zhencang Kang Yong Qian ciqi tulu*, 221, number 50; 330, number 11; 344, number 25; 360, number 41; 364, number 45; National Palace Museum, *Qing Kang, Yong, Qian*, 150, number 135; Margaret Medley, *Illustrated Catalogue of Ming Polychrome Wares*, London: Percival David Foundation of Chinese Art, University of London, 1978, 50, number 164; plate

13, number 164; Lady David, *Illustrated Catalogue of Ch'ing Enamelled Ware in the Percival David Foundation of Chinese Art*, London: Percival David Foundation of Chinese Art, University of London, 1973 revised reprint of the 1958 edition, 29, number A803, plate 9, number A803.

12. *Bianfu*, the two-syllable word used for 'bat' today, combines the syllable *fu* with *bian*, another one-syllable word meaning 'bat.' Through similar combinations of closely related terms, the majority of nouns in modern spoken Mandarin have become bisyllabic, thereby decreasing unintentional ambiguity of speech by decreasing the number of homonyms. *Fu*, meaning 'good fortune', is sometimes combined with *qi* or *ze*, yielding *fuqi* and *fuze*, to distinguish it from yet other words with the same basic pronunciation. Because Chinese characters are ideographic, the written language does not share the spoken language's problem of ambiguity resulting from an abundance of homonyms.

13. The all-over decoration of stylized bats suggests that the current attribution to the sixteenth-seventeenth century of a small, garlic-headed vase with Shisou mark in the Victoria and Albert Museum, London, will require further study. See Kerr, *Later Chinese Bronzes*, 64-65, figure 50. The Victoria and Albert piece is of interest here, because it has about its neck a series of three relief rings similar to those on the Clague vase. Separately cast, the neck was inserted into the body of the Victoria and Albert vase, supporting the suggestion above that the Clague piece may have been prepared in two parts fitted together after casting.

19

1. See Percival David Foundation, *Imperial Taste*, 37, figure 18; Terukazu Akiyama and others, *Arts of China*, volume 1: *Neolithic Cultures to the Tang Dynasty – Recent Discoveries*, Tokyo and Palo Alto CA: Kodansha, 1968, 99, plates 178-79.

2. See Percival David Foundation, *Imperial Taste*, 37, number 13.

3. See Watt and Ford, *East Asian Lacquer*, 42, number 2.

4. Watt and Ford, *East Asian Lacquer*, 42.

5. See Murata Jirō and Fujieda Akira editors, *Kyoyōkan* (Chü-yung-kuan; The Juyong Gate), Kyoto: Faculty of Engineering, Kyoto University, 1955, volume 2 (plates), plates 30, 47, 86-87, 104; Watt and Ford, *East Asian Lacquer*, 42, figure 13; Addis, *Chinese Ceramics from Datable Tombs*, 46, number 29e.

6. See, for example, Watt and Ford, *East Asian Lacquer*, 69-73, numbers 19-21. Terese Tse Bartholomew, Asian Art Museum, San Francisco, on a recent visit to the Clague collection, identified the blossom shape of the Clague piece as hibiscus, a member of the mallow family.

7. See Watt, *Chinese Jades*, 78-79, number 61; 134-35, number 111; 138-39, numbers 114-15.

8. See Garner, *Chinese and Associated Lacquer*, plate 29, number 61.

9. See Claudia Brown, *Chinese Cloisonné: The Clague Collection*, Phoenix AZ: Phoenix Art Museum, 1980, 52-53, number 18.

10. See Wang Zhongshu, *Han Civilization*, 70, figure 76; Lucy Lim and others, *Stories from China's Past: Han Dynasty Pictorial Tomb Reliefs and Archaeological Objects from Sichuan Province, People's Republic of China*, San Francisco: Chinese Culture Foundation of San Francisco, 1987, 86-87, plates 4, 5; 92-93, plate 9.

11. The Buddha once spoke of the lotus, commenting that in the same way it could grow in sullied waters yet put forth blossoms of great beauty and purity he could live in this world yet propound teachings of great truth and profundity. Thus, the lotus became one of the most important symbols of the Buddhist church.

12. See Yutaka Mino and Katherine R. Tsiang, *Ice and Green Clouds: Traditions of Chinese Celadon*, Indianapolis: Indianapolis Museum of Art, 1986, 91, number 30; 94-98, numbers 32-34.

13. See· Fontein and Wu, *Unearthing China's Past*, 177, number 90 and figure 91; Jenyns and Watson, *Chinese Art: The Minor Arts*, 59, number 21; 62-63, number 25; Gyllensvärd, *Chinese Gold and Silver*, 145, number 93; 168, number 111; 192, number 124.

14. See Kuo, *Born of Earth and Fire*, 79, number 58; Mowry, *Handbook*, 64, number 1979.139; Mino and Tsiang, *Ice and Green Clouds*, 153, number 58; 157, number 60.

15. See The Joint Board of Directors of The National Palace Museum and the National Central Museum compilers, *Blue-and-white Ware of the Ming Dynasty*, Hong Kong: Cafa Company, 1962, book 2, part 2, 146-49, numbers 59-60. John Carswell, *Blue and White: Chinese Porcelain and Its Impact on the Western World*, Chicago: David and Alfred Smart Gallery, University of Chicago, 1985, 76-77, 76-77, numbers 20-21; John A. Pope, *Chinese Porcelains from the Ardebil Shrine*, Washington DC: Freer Gallery of Art, Smithsonian Institution, 1956, 91-93, plates 30-31.

16. See Ho and others, *Eight Dynasties of Chinese Painting*, 223-25, number 177.

17. Zhang Qiande (Zhang Chou), *Pinghua pu* (A Treatise on Flower Arranging) (first half, seventeenth century), in Deng Shi and Huang Binhong compilers, *Meishu congshu*, Taipei: Yiwen yinshuguan, photo reprint of 1947, fourth revised edition, volume 10, 2/10, 118.

20

1. See Hayashi, *In Shū seidōki sōran*, plate volume, 36-46.

2. For a selection of Western Zhou *fangding* with rounded corners, see Hayashi, *In Shū seidōki sōran*, plate volume, 44, number 75; 45, 76, 82-84; 46, numbers 85-87.

3. *Xuande yiqi tupu*, volume 2, *juan* 19, 3 recto. The three *fangding* with angular corners are pictured in volume 1, *juan* 4, 2 recto; 5 recto; *juan* 5, 3 recto.

4. See *Xuande yiqi tupu*, volume 2, *juan* 9, 4-6.

5. See *Xuande yiqi tupu*, volume 2, *juan* 19, 6 recto.

6. See Valenstein, *A Handbook of Chinese Ceramics*, 15, number 14; William Watson, *Pre-Tang Ceramics of China: Chinese Pottery from 4000 BC to AD 600*, London and Boston: Faber and Faber, 1991, 70, number 31; Margaret Medley, *The Chinese Potter: A Practical History of Chinese Ceramics*, New York: Charles Scribner's Sons, 1976, 2, figure 1 (frontispiece); 25, figure 11.

7. See d'Argencé, *Treasures from the Shanghai Museum*, 77, number 21; Fong, *The Great Bronze Age*, 89, number 9; Loehr, *Ritual Vessels*, 49, number 16.

8. See Loehr, *Ritual Vessels*, 131, number 57; Hayashi, *In Shū seidōki sōran*, plate volume, 57, number 86; 65, number 45.

9. See Ministry of Culture and Information, *Sinan haejŏ yumul*, 48, number 49. Inspired by Chinese ceramics of the Song dynasty, Korean potters of the Koryŏ dynasty (918-1392) often incorporated twisted-rope or twisted-vine handles into their celadon wares, using them much more frequently than did their Chinese counterparts; see, for example, G.St.G.M. Gompertz, *Korean Celadon and Other Wares of the Koryŏ Period*, London: Faber and Faber, 1963; Choi Sun'u and Hasebe Gakuji, *Korai* (Koryŏ), volume 18 in *Sekai tōji zenshū*, Tokyo: Shogakukan, 1978.

10. See Ministry of Culture and Information, *Sinan haejŏ yumul*, 123-24, numbers 154, 156-57; 172, number 234.

11. See Brown, *Chinese Cloisonné*, 25, number 4; Helmut Brinker and Albert Lutz, *Chinese Cloisonné: The Pierre Uldry Collection*, New York: Asia Society Galleries, 1989, numbers 42, 53 (translated by Susanna Swoboda).

12. See James C.Y. Watt, *An Exhibition of Te Hua Porcelain*, Hong Kong: Art Gallery, Institute of Chinese Studies, Chinese University of Hong Kong, 1975, numbers 49-50.

13. See, d'Argencé, *Treasures from the Shanghai Museum*, 76, number 18; Li and Watt, *The Chinese Scholar's Studio*, 138, number 84; Fong, *The Great Bronze Age of China*, 39, figure 7; 92-93, number 11; 160-61, number 28; 228, number 54.

14. See d'Argencé, *Treasures from the Shanghai Museum*, 100, number 80; Valenstein, *A Handbook of Chinese Ceramics*, 147, number 142; Medley, *The Chinese Potter*, 120, figure 82.

15. See Ministry of Culture and Information, *Sinan haejŏ yumul*, 73, number 87.

16. See Zhou Lili, 'Ciqi bajixiangwen xintan,' (New Light on the *Bajixiang* Motif in Chinese Ceramics), *Shanghai bowuguan jikan* (Bulletin of the Shanghai Museum) (Shanghai), number 4, 1987, 324, number 24; Riddell, *Dated Chinese Antiquities*, 81, number 56; The Joint Board of Directors of The National Palace Museum and the National Central Museum,

compilers, *Blue-and-white Ware of the Ming Dynasty*, Hong Kong: Cafa Company, 1963, book 5, 60-61, plate 20.

17. Introduced into China during the Yuan dynasty, the *bajixiang*, or 'Eight Auspicious Emblems,' derive from Tibetan Buddhism and must be distinguished from the *babao*, or 'Eight Treasures,' sometimes translated as 'Eight Precious Objects,' which also ornament Chinese decorative arts of the Yuan, Ming, and Qing dynasties. A native answer to the foreign 'Eight Auspicious Emblems,' the 'Eight Treasures' feature objects long associated in China with wealth, culture, power, and well being; although not as rigidly standardized as the 'Eight Auspicious Emblems,' the 'Eight Treasures' typically comprise a selection of the following: a jewel (*zhu*), one or two coins (*qian*), one or two lozenges (*fangsheng*), a painting (*hua*), a musical stone chime (*qing*), one or two books (*shu*), one or two rhinoceros horns (*xijiao*), sometimes in the form of a horn-cup (*xijue*), a bronze mirror (*tongjing*), an auspicious cloud head (*xiangyun*), a maple leaf (*hongye*), a banana leaf (*jiaoye*), an artemisia or yarrow leaf (*aiye*), a *ding* tripod vessel (*ding*), a branch of *lingzhi* fungus (*lingzhi*), and an ingot of gold or silver (*yuanbao*). Both the 'Eight Auspicious Emblems' and the 'Eight Treasures' must also be distinguished from the 'Eight Attributes of the Scholar,' the 'Eight Musical Instruments,' and the attributes of the Eight Immortals; since the last three categories are only infrequently represented in the decorative arts, they are not enumerated here. For further information see Zhou Lili, 'Ciqi bajixiangwen xintan,' 312-13; Williams, *Outlines of Chinese Symbolism and Art Motifs*, 155 (Eight Treasures); Brinker and Lutz, *Chinese Cloisonné: The Pierre Uldry Collection*, figures 73-84.

18. See Zhou Lili, 'Ciqi bajixiangwen xintan,' 321, number 3; 323, number 18; 324, 19-21; d'Argencé, *Treasures from the Shanghai Museum*, 50, color plate 30.

19. See Brown, *Chinese Cloisonné*, 111, number 48; National Palace Museum, *Masterpieces of Chinese Tibetan Buddhist Altar Fittings in the National Palace Museum*, Taipei: National Palace Museum, 1971, number 19; Marylin M. Rhie and Robert A.F. Thurman, *Wisdom and Compassion: The Sacred Art of Tibet*, San Francisco: Asian Art Museum of San Francisco and New York: Tibet House in association with Harry N. Abrams Inc, 1991, 280-81, number 103; 338-40, number 134; 382, number 159; Zhou Lili, 'Ciqi bajixiangwen xintan,' 329, number 46; Hemmi Baiei, *Chūgoku Ramakyō bijutsu taikan* (An Overview of Chinese Lamaist Art), Tokyo: Tokyo bijutsu, 1975, volume 1, 452, numbers 894-95.

20. See, for example, d'Argencé, *Treasures from the Shanghai Museum*, 50, color plate 30; 163-64, number 92, which pictures a fourteenth-century molded blue-and-white plate decorated with the 'Eight Auspicious Emblems' motif, including conch shell, flower, wish-granting jewel, cloud head,

lotus blossom, endless knot, branch of coral, and a jewel of another type.

21. Zhou Lili, 'Ciqi bajixiangwen xintan,' 314-16; Brinker and Lutz, *Chinese Cloisonné: The Pierre Uldry Collection*, figure 73; d'Argencé, *Treasures from the Shanghai Museum*, 171, number 111.

22. See Zhou Lili, 'Ciqi bajixiangwen xintan,' 325, number 26; 331, diagram.

23. See Zhou Lili, 'Ciqi bajixiangwen xintan,' 327, number 37.

24. See Zhou Lili, 'Ciqi bajixiangwen xintan,' 332, diagram.

25. *Xuande dingyi pu, juan* 8, 235.

26. See *Xuande yiqi tupu*, volume 2, *juan* 17, 6 recto and verso; 7 verso; 8 recto.

27. See Zhou Lili, 'Ciqi bajixiangwen xintan,' 324, number 23; National Palace Museum, *Blue-and-white Ware of the Ming Dynasty*, book 2, part 2, 104-05, plate 33; 108-09, plate 35; 124-25, plate 45.

28. Wen Zhenheng, *Zhangwu zhi, juan* 7, 198.

21

1. See *Xuande yiqi tupu*, volume 2, *juan* 16, 3 recto; *juan* 19, 3, 5 recto.

2. See *Xuande yiqi tupu*, volume 2, *juan* 15, 2-3 recto; *juan* 19, 3 recto.

3. See Hayashi, *In Shū seidōki sōran*, plate volume, 151-156.

4. See Hayashi, *In Shū seidōki sōran*, plate volume, 151, number 5.

5. See Brinker and Lutz, *Chinese Cloisonné: The Pierre Uldry Collection*, figure 271.

6. See Brankston, *Early Ming Wares of Chingtchen*, plate 10b; National Palace Museum, *Blue-and-white Ware of the Ming Dynasty*, book 2, part 2, 130-31, plate 51; Percival David Foundation, *Imperial Taste*, 63, number 33.

7. See Mowry, *Handbook*, 75, number 1979.167; 77, number 1979.173.

8. Such monuments include the Juyong Gate outside Beijing. See Murata and Fujieda, *Kyoyōkan*, volume 2 (plates), plates 69-72, 93.

9. See Percival David Foundation, *Imperial Taste*, 54, number 27; 56-57, number 28 and figures 27-29; Medley, *The Chinese Potter*, 173, figure 127; 179, figure 131; 183, figure 134; 185, figures 136-37; 187, figure 138; plate 5.

10. See Machida International Print Museum, *Chūgoku kodai hanga ten*, 92, number 22; Heather Karmay, *Early Sino-Tibetan Art*, Warminster, England: Aris and Phillips Ltd, 1975, 47, numbers 26-28; 50, numbers 29-30.

11. See Karmay, *Early Sino-Tibetan Art*, 85-91, numbers 50, 52-54, 56, 58, 60, 62-63.

12. See Machida International Print Museum, *Chūgoku kodai hanga ten*, 94, number 2; Karmay, *Early Sino-Tibetan Art*, 85, number 49.

13. See Mowry, *Handbook*, 70, number 1979.153; 75-76, 1979.168, 1979.170; Percival David Foundation, *Imperial Taste*, 58, number 29; Valenstein, *A Hand-*

book of Chinese Ceramics, 155, number 150.

14. See Watt and Ford, *East Asian Lacquer*, 103-04, number 38.

15. See, for example, Rhie and Thurman, *Wisdom and Compassion*, 278-79, number 102; 287, number 106; 295, number 111.

16. See, for example, Valenstein, *A Handbook of Chinese Ceramics*, 260, number 262.

17. See Watt, *Chinese Jades*, 122-23, number 104.

22

1. See *Xuande yiqi tupu*, volume 2, *juan* 19, 6 recto.

2. See, for example, Rhie and Thurman, *Wisdom and Compassion*, 287, number 106; 295, number 111; 339, numbers 134.1-2.

3. See d'Argencé, *Treasures from the Shanghai Museum*, 100, number 80.

4. See Ministry of Culture and Information, *Sinan haejō yumul*, 73, number 87.

5. See Zhou Lili, 'Ciqi bajixiangwen xintan,' 329, number 41; 332, diagram.

6. Williams, *Outlines of Chinese Symbolism and Art Motifs*, 155 (Eight Treasures).

7. See Mino and Tsiang, *Ice and Green Clouds*, 124-25, number 45; 129, number 47; 132-35, numbers 49-50.

8. See Mowry, *Handbook*, 62-63, 1979.131-36; Percival David Foundation, *Imperial Taste*, 33, number 10; Mino and Tsiang, *Ice and Green Clouds*, 138-57, numbers 52-60.

23

1. See *Xuande yiqi tupu*, volume 2, *juan* 15, 4 recto.

2. See Valenstein, *A Handbook of Chinese Ceramics*, 230, number 224.

3. See Valenstein, *A Handbook of Chinese Ceramics*, 240, number 243.

4. An unpublished Kangxi-period porcelain vase in the collection of the Harvard University Art Museums (accession number 1942.148) has the same shape as the vases indicated in notes 2 and 3, above, but it has decoration in gold over a 'mirror-black' glaze.

5. See Watt, *An Exhibition of Te Hua Porcelain*, number 49; Donnelly, *Blanc de Chine*, plate 12 (top); plate 20 (top left).

6. K.C. Chang, 'Ancient China,' in K.C. Chang editor, *Food in Chinese Culture*, New Haven and London: Yale University Press, 1977, 34.

7. See Hayashi, *In Shū seidōki sōran*, plate volume, 1-35.

8. Sir Percival David editor and translator, *Chinese Connoisseurship: The Ko Ku Yao Lun. The Essential Criteria of Antiquities*, New York and Washington DC: Praeger, 1971, 12; for Chinese text, see 338, 7a.

24

1. See *Xuande yiqi tupu*, volume 2, *juan* 14, 3 recto.

2. *Xuande yiqi tupu*, volume 2, *juan* 14, 3 verso. Comments following the illustrations in *Xuande yiqi*

tupu indicate that a number of Xuande bronzes were outfitted with stands and covers in fine hardwoods, the covers usually with white-jade knob in the form of a *chilong*. In his *Zhangwu zhi* of 1637, Wen Zhenheng states that 'in olden times sacral vessels had stands and covers. People of today use wood (for the stands and covers); ebony (*wumu*) is best; *zitan* (*Pterocarpus indicus*) and *huali* (*Dalbergia odorifera*) woods must be avoided. Ones in the form of a mallow flower (*kuihua*) or water caltrop blossom (*linghua*) are vulgar. Song jade hat ornaments and carvings of *jiaoduan* (a mythical beast) and sea creatures (*haishou*) can be used for the cover's knob so long as they are appropriately matched with the censer in size. Antique (pieces of carved) agate, rock crystal, and such can also be used.' Wen Zhenheng, *Zhangwu zhi*, *juan* 7, 198. For information on fine and rare woods traditionally used in China, see Wang Shixiang, *Classic Chinese Furniture: Ming and Early Qing Dynasties*, San Francisco: China Books and Periodicals and Hong Kong: Joint Publishing Company, 1986, 16-18.

3. I am grateful to Lan-ying Tseng for her assistance in ascertaining the origin and meaning of this name.

4. Kong Yingda editor, *Zhouyi zhengyi* (Annotations to the Book of Changes), *Wuqiubeizhai Yijing jicheng ben* edition, Taipei: Chengwen chubanshe, 1976, *juan* 2, 2 verso; Ban Gu, *Hanshu* (History of Han), *Wang Xianqian buzhu ben* edition, Taipei: Shangwu yinshuguan, *Lülizhi* section, *diyishang*, 1678.

5. Kong Yingda, *Zhouyi zhengyi, juan* 11, 6 recto.

6. Kong Yingda, *Zhouyi zhengyi, juan* 11, 6 recto.

7. See Mowry, *Handbook*, 52, number 1979.107; Freer Gallery of Art, *The Freer Gallery of Art*, volume 1 *China*, 44, number 31; Pope and others, *The Freer Chinese Bronzes*, volume 1, 611, number 121.

8. See Loehr, *Ritual Vessels*, 175, number 80; Pope and others, *The Freer Chinese Bronzes*, volume 1, 617, number 122.

9. See Satō and Hasebe, *Zui Tō*, 63, number 46; 235, number 50; Watson, *Tang and Liao Ceramics*, 152, number 132.

10. See Kelley, *Chinese Gold and Silver*, 77, number 44.

11. See Hasebe, *Sō*, 71, number 62; Palace Museum, *Gugong bowuyuan cang ci xuanji*, number 18.

12. See Gyllensvärd, *Chinese Gold, Silver, and Porcelain*, 107, number 111; Feng Xianming editor, *Dingyao* (Ding Ware), volume 9 in *Zhongguo taoci* (Chinese Ceramics), Shanghai: Shanghai Renmin chubanshe, 1983, plate 84.

13. See National Palace Museum, *Kuan Ware of the Southern Sung*, book 1, part 1, 82-83, plate 26.

14. See Sydney L. Moss, *The Second Bronze Age*, number 66; Miranda Rothschild, *Miranda Rothschild: Chinese Works of Art and Buddhist Bronzes at Ormonde Gallery* (exhibition brochure), London, not dated (but about 1991), back cover.

25

1. For examples of such Arabic-inscribed sets in cloisonné enamel, see Brinker and Lutz, *Chinese Cloisonné: The Pierre Uldry Collection*, figure 340; Brown, *Chinese Cloisonné*, 165, number 77.

2. Transliteration and translation from Carswell, *Blue and White*, 97.

3. Carswell, *Blue and White*, 97

4. Several publications discuss the question of Chinese bronzes with Arabic/Persian inscriptions, but none resolves the issue, let alone proposes a credible scheme of dating: Stephen W. Bushell, *Chinese Art*, London: Victoria and Albert Museum, 1924, volume 1, 57-58; Berthold Laufer, 'Chinese Muhammedan Bronzes,' *Ars Islamica* (Ann Arbor MI), volume 1, part 2, 1934, 133-47; Jenyns and Watson, *Chinese Art: The Minor Arts*, 91; 134-35, number 59; Carswell, *Blue and White*, 95-97, numbers 39-40. See also, Sir Harry Garner, 'Blue and White of the Middle Ming Period,' *Transactions of the Oriental Ceramic Society*, 1951 (London), 1954, 61-72.

5. Jenyns and Watson, *Chinese Art: The Minor Arts*, 91.

6. A large fourteenth-century blue-and-white plate with peacock decoration given to the Harvard University Art Museums by Richard C. Hobart in 1961, for example, has two syllables of Persian incorporated into the relief floral sprays that ornament its cavetto (accession number 1961.112); see The Arts Council of Great Britain and The Oriental Ceramic Society, *The Ceramic Art of China*, London: Oriental Ceramic Society, 1971, plate 98; Sherman E. Lee and Wai-kam Ho, *Chinese Art Under the Mongols: The Yüan Dynasty (1279-1368)*, Cleveland: Cleveland Museum of Art, 1968, plate 150.

7. See Fujioka and Hasebe, *Min*, 193, figure 49; The Joint Board of Directors of The National Palace Museum and the National Central Museum compilers, *Blue-and-white Ware of the Ming Dynasty*, Hong Kong: Cafa, 1963, book 4, 44-49, numbers 1-3; Pope, *Chinese Porcelains from the Ardebil Shrine*, plates 75-77; Carswell, *Blue and White*, 94-95, numbers 37-38; Medley, *The Chinese Potter*, 218-19, figures 161-62; Valenstein, *A Handbook of Chinese Ceramics*, 168, number 163.

8. See Fujioka and Hasebe, *Min*, 206, number 213.

9. See Donnelly, *Blanc de Chine*, plate 19a.

10. See Claudia Brown and Donald Rabiner, *Clear as Crystal, Red as Flame: Later Chinese Glass*, New York: China Institute in America, 1990, 63, number 27.

11. See Brinker and Lutz, *Chinese Cloisonné: The Pierre Uldry Collection*, figure 340; Brown, *Chinese Cloisonné*, 165, number 77.

12. See Donnelly, *Blanc de Chine*, plate 18d.

13. John Carswell has attributed to the sixteenth century a porcelain censer in the Ashmolean Museum, Oxford, that boasts three Arabic inscriptions whose wording is identical to that on the Clague censer and whose ogival panels are similar. (The catalog does not specify the type of ware, though

from the illustration it appears to be Dehua porcelain.) See Carswell, *Blue and White*, 96-97, number 40. Carswell's attribution to the sixteenth century rests on the use of Arabic inscriptions as decoration and on the similarity of the censer's shape and decoration to those of several bronze censers with marks dated to 1430 and 1431; although he doubts their Xuande-period origins, Carswell leans toward a sixteenth-century date for the bronzes, noting, however, that they might be later. For reasons explained in this entry, the present author believes that the Clague bronze and the related ones cited by Carswell date to the nineteenth century (or to the second half of the eighteenth century at the very earliest). If the Ashmolean porcelain censer is indeed related to this group of bronzes, then it too must have been made in the eighteenth or nineteenth century. Although it possesses a handsome and satisfying form, the Ashmolean censer exhibits poor craftsmanship, at least it seems so in the illustration, which would argue for a nineteenth-century date of manufacture: the ogival panel is not centered over the leg; the top point of the panel is off-center so that it does not appear directly over the corresponding indentation in the lower border; the panel is slightly irregular in shape, which disturbs the symmetry that is ordinarily considered a cardinal element of such a design; and the top portion of the cabriole leg is lumpy. In addition, in having an indentation rather than a downward-pointing barb at the center of the lower border, the decorative panel resembles in shape those on nineteenth-century cloisonné enamels with Arabic inscriptions; compare Brinker and Lutz, *Chinese Cloisonné: The Pierre Uldry Collection*, figure 340.

14. Zhengde-period blue-and-white porcelain brushrests in the form of five mountain peaks, for example, typically have inscriptions in Persian reading *khama dan*, which might be translated 'pen holder' or 'brush rest.' An unpublished example was given to the Harvard University Art Museum by Mr and Mrs Samuel B. Grimson in 1983. For other examples, see Valenstein, *A Handbook of Chinese Ceramics*, 168, number 163; Medley, *The Chinese Potter*, 218, figure 161.

15. The six-character marks recorded in *Xuande yiqi tupu* invariably end with the character *zhi*; *Xuande yiqi tupu* does not record any marks on Xuande bronzes with *zao* as the final character. In addition, genuine marks on Xuande porcelains always end with the character *zhi*; see National Palace Museum, *Ming Xuande ciqi tezhan mulu*.

16. *Xuande yiqi tupu*, volume 1, *juan* 6, 4-10 (all recto).

17. See Hayashi, *In Shū seidōki sōran*, plate volume, 1-35.

18. See National Palace Museum, *Kuan Ware of the Sung Dynasty*, 50-51, plates 20-21.

19. See *Ritual Vessels*, 131, number 57.

20. Compare Brown and Rabiner, *Clear as Crystal,*

Red as Flame, 70, number 34.

21. See Brinker and Lutz, *Chinese Cloisonné: The Pierre Uldry Collection*, figure 340.

22. The reason for the reliance on cold working remains unknown; it may be simply that foundries preferred to produce a number of virtually identical blanks that could be decorated quickly to fit a client's specifications.

23. See Carswell, *Blue and White*, 96, figure 34.

26

1. See Pope, *Chinese Porcelains from the Ardebil Shrine*, plate 98, number 29.436; National Palace Museum, *Blue-and-white Ware of the Ming Dynasty*, book 6, 36-37, plate 4.

2. See Beurdeley and Raindre, *Qing Porcelain*, 75, plate 105, ewer at right.

3. See Gyllensvärd, *Chinese Gold, Silver, and Porcelain*, 64, number 67; Gyllensvärd, *Chinese Gold and Silver*, 230-31, number 151.

4. See Fujioka and Hasebe, *Min*, 92-93, numbers 97-98; Seizo Hayashiya, Henry Trubner and others, *Chinese Ceramics from Japanese Collections: T'ang Through Ming Dynasties*, New York: Asia Society in association with John Weatherhill Inc, 1977, 94, number 50; 97, number 53; Medley, *Ming and Ch'ing Monochrome*, 37, number A560; plate 8, number A560; Pope, *Chinese Porcelains from the Ardebil Shrine*, plate 98, number 29.433.

5. See Watt, *Chinese Jades from the Collection of the Seattle Art Museum*, 114, number 96.

6. See Tokyo National Museum, compiler, *Tōyō no shikkō gei: Tokubetsu ten* (Oriental Lacquer Arts: A Special Exhibition), Tokyo: Tōkyō kokuritsu hakubutsukan, 1977, number 526.

7. See Fujioka and Hasebe, *Min*, 92, number 97; Hayashiya, Trubner and others, *Chinese Ceramics from Japanese Collections*, 97, number 53.

8. See Fujioka and Hasebe, *Min*, 93, number 98; Hayashiya, Trubner and others, *Chinese Ceramics from Japanese Collections*, 94, number 50.

9. See Gyllensvärd, *Chinese Gold, Silver, and Porcelain*, 64, number 67; Gyllensvärd, *Chinese Gold and Silver*, 230-31, number 151.

10. See Fujioka and Hasebe, *Min*, 93, number 98; Hayashiya, Trubner and others, *Chinese Ceramics from Japanese Collections*, 94, number 50.

11. See Fujioka and Hasebe, *Min*, 93, number 98; Hayashiya, Trubner and others, *Chinese Ceramics from Japanese Collections*, 94, number 50.

12. See Mikami, *Ryō Kin Gen*, 97, number 79; Fujioka and Hasebe, *Min*, 9, number 1; 14, number 7; 163, number 143; Mowry, *Handbook*, 71, number 1979.155; Percival David Foundation, *Imperial Taste*, 58, number 29; Pope, *Chinese Porcelains from the Ardebil Shrine*, plate 54.

13. See Fujioka and Hasebe, *Min*, 127, number 129.

14. See Assadullah Souren Melikian-Chirvani, *Islamic Metalwork from the Iranian World, 8th-18th*

Centuries: Victoria and Albert Museum Catalogue, London: Her Majesty's Stationery Office, 1982, 297, number 129.

15. See Jenyns and Watson, Chinese Art: The Minor Arts, 73, number 32.

16. See Gyllensvärd, Chinese Gold, Silver, and Porcelain, 100, number 98; 111, number 118. Inspired by Chinese ceramics of the Song dynasty, Korean potters of the Koryŏ dynasty (918-1392) often placed a tiny loop at the top of the handles on their celadon-glazed ewers, using them much more frequently than did their Chinese counterparts; see, for example, Gompertz, Korean Celadon; Choi and Hasebe, Korai.

17. See Valenstein, A Handbook of Chinese Ceramics, 78, number 72a; Mino and Tsiang, Ice and Green Clouds, 139, number 52.

18. See Fujioka and Hasebe, Min, 127, number 129. This ogival panel shape persisted into the seventeenth and eighteenth century, but in altered form; see, respectively, Beurdeley and Raindre, Qing Porcelain, 75, plate 105, ewer at right; Brown and Rabiner, Clear as Crystal, Red as Flame, 63, number 27.

19. In this context, it should be noted that a version of the ewer with flattened pear shape continued to be made into Qianlong times, sometimes in gold. Such mid-Qing ewers are more organically unified in shape and are more heavily decorated; in addition, their covers seldom have the high domes of late Ming and early Qing examples and their footrings are generally short and splayed. See Gyllensvärd, Chinese Gold, Silver, and Porcelain, 39, number 29; Royal Academy of Arts, Catalogue of the International Exhibition of Chinese Art, 1935-36, London: Royal Academy of Arts, 1935, 195, number 2089.

27

1. Contrast the relatively flat covers of Kangxi-period, 'peachbloom-glazed,' seal-paste boxes (of the type that appear among the 'eight objects for the writing table'), for example; see Valenstein, A Handbook of Chinese Ceramics, 237, number 237; Ayers and Satō, Shin, 35, number 27; 195, number 254.

2. See Arts Council of Great Britain, Chinese Jade Throughout the Ages, number 458; Watt, Chinese Jades, 140, number 116.

3. See Valenstein, A Handbook of Chinese Ceramics, 267, number 276; 271, number 280.

4. See Donnelly, Blanc de Chine, plate 54b; Watt, Te Hua Porcelain, number 25.

5. See Percival David Foundation, Imperial Taste, 56, figure 27; 57, number 28; Medley, The Chinese Potter, plate 5 (opposite 192); Valenstein, A Handbook of Chinese Ceramics, 145, number 140; Mikami, Ryō Kin Gen, 65, number 52; Margaret Medley, Yuan Porcelain and Stoneware, London: Pitman Publishing, 1974, plate 48.

6. See Fujioka and Hasebe, Min, 127, number 129.

7. For information on the tree peony, see Maggie Keswick, The Chinese Garden: History, Art and Architecture, London: Academy Editions and New York: St Martin's Press, 2nd revised edition, 1986, 181-83.

8. See Ho and others, Eight Dynasties of Chinese Painting, 327-29, numbers 242-43.

9. See Percival David Foundation, Imperial Taste, 83, number 51; Medley, The Chinese Potter, 249, figure 198; Mowry, Handbook, 82, number 1979.187.1-2.

10. Williams, Outlines of Chinese Symbolism and Art Motifs, 317.

11. The flowers associated with the twelve months of the Chinese lunar calendar are plum, peach, peony, cherry, magnolia, pomegranate, lotus, pear, mallow, chrysanthemum, gardenia, and poppy.

12. Although it translates literally as 'jade hall honor [and] riches,' yutang fugui translates idiomatically as 'May you enjoy wealth and honor,' since yutang (jade hall) is a polite substitute for 'you.'

13. See Watt, Chinese Jades, 209, number 210.

14. Williams, Outlines of Chinese Symbolism and Art Motifs, 312-13.

15. For examples of eighteenth-century porcelains decorated with peaches, see Mowry, Handbook, 82, number 1979.188; Percival David Foundation, Imperial Taste, 78, number 47; 84, number 52; Li Yihua, Gugong zhencang Kang Yong Qian ciqi tulu, 210, number 39; 335, number 16; 344, number 25; Ayers and Satō, Shin, 176, number 203; 177, number 207; 181, numbers 226-27.

16. See Percival David Foundation, Imperial Taste, 67, number 37; Medley, The Chinese Potter, 223, figure 171.

17. Li Yihua, Gugong zhencang Kang Yong Qian ciqi tulu, 96-97, numbers 79-80.

18. Li Yihua, Gugong zhencang Kang Yong Qian ciqi tulu, 92-95, numbers 75-78; Oriental Ceramic Society, The Ceramic Art of China, plate 142, number 206a; Valenstein, A Handbook of Chinese Ceramics, 240, number 243.

19. Wujin refers to an evenly distributed, dark black color, be it in ink, metal, ceramic glaze, or ink rubbing. According to vanGulik, 'The term wu-chin (wujin) belongs to metallurgy where it stands for a mixture of about 9 parts copper and 1 part gold, which is said to have a dark, purplish lustre. Hence the term is used also with reference to the lustre of good ink.' Robert H. vanGulik, Chinese Pictorial Art as Viewed by the Connoisseur, Rome: Istituto Italiano per il Medio ed Estremo Oriente, 1958, reprinted New York: Hacker Art Books, 1981, 87, note 1; Mowry, 'Catalogue' in Li and Watt, The Chinese Scholar's Studio, 163, number 29; 204, note 29/2.

20. An unpublished Kangxi-period porcelain vase in the collection of the Harvard University Art Museums has a mirror-black glaze with decoration in overglaze gilding (accession number 1942.148). Also see Beurdeley and Raindre, Qing Porcelain, 160, plate 223; Ayers and Satō, Shin, 41, number 33; 194, number 251; Oriental Ceramic Society, The Ceramic Art of China, plate 166, number 241.

21. Li Yihua, *Gugong zhencang Kang Yong Qian ciqi tulu*, 244, number 73.

22. Li Yihua, *Gugong zhencang Kang Yong Qian ciqi tulu*, 393-99, numbers 74-80.

28

1. During the Tang and Song periods, tea was commonly prepared by beating dry, powdered tea and hot water to a froth in a tea bowl with a bamboo whisk, in a manner preserved today in the Japanese tea ceremony. Ewers for hot water were thus needed for preparing tea at the table, though the teapot *per se* had not yet come into being. The Chinese most likely invented steeped tea, prepared by pouring boiling water over whole tea leaves, in the Yuan or early Ming period; not long thereafter Chinese potters began to produce ceramic pots specially designed for brewing tea.

2. See Hasebe, *Sō*, 34, number 27; 175, figures, 32-33.

3. See Machida International Print Museum, *Chūgoku kodai hanga ten*, 51, illustration second from left at top of page.

4. Bennet Bronson and Ho Chuimei, 'Chinese Pewter Tea Wares,' *Arts of Asia* (Hong Kong), volume 18, number 6, November-December 1988, 106-16.

5. Verbal comment to Robert H. Clague on 7 June 1992 (as translated by Kelly Tan).

6. Inspired by Chinese ceramics of the Song dynasty, Korean potters of the Koryŏ dynasty (918-1392) often incorporated handles segmented to resemble a section of bamboo stalk into their celadon wares, in addition to handles shaped to resemble twisted rope or twisted vine, using them much more frequently than did their Chinese counterparts; see, for example, Gompertz, *Korean Celadon*; Choi, Sun'u and Hasebe, *Gakuji, Korai*.

7. See Watt and Ford, *East Asian Lacquer*, 90-91, number 31.

8. Williams, *Outlines of Chinese Symbolism and Art Motifs*, 326-28.

9. Keswick, *The Chinese Garden*, 178-87; Williams, *Outlines of Chinese Symbolism and Art Motifs*, 68-69.

10. Bickford, *Bones of Jade, Soul of Ice*, 206; Williams, *Outlines of Chinese Symbolism and Art Motifs*, 32-33.

11. See Li Yihua, *Gugong zhencang Kang Yong Qian ciqi tulu*, 352, number 33.

12. See Valenstein, *A Handbook of Chinese Ceramics*, 257, number 260.

29

1. See *Xuande yiqi tupu*, volume 1, juan 9, 4-6, recto.

2. See National Palace Museum, *Kuan Ware of the Sung Dynasty*, 48-49, plate 19.

3. See Hasebe, *Sō*, 210, number 214.

4. See Loehr, *Ritual Vessels*, 123, number 53; 131, number 57.

5. Keswick, *The Chinese Garden*, 187-88; Williams, *Outline of Chinese Symbolism and Art Motifs*, 298.

6. See San Francisco Center of Asian Art and Culture, *Osaka Exchange Exhibition*, 36, number 11; for information on Zheng Sixiao, see Li, 'Cheng Ssu-hsiao,' in Franke, *Song Biographies: Painters*, 15-23.

7. See Ju-hsi Chou and Claudia Brown, *The Elegant Brush: Chinese Painting Under the Qianlong Emperor, 1735-1795*, Phoenix AZ: Phoenix Art Museum, 1985, 168-73, numbers 54-55; 251-53, number 79.

8. See Mowry, *Handbook*, 83, number 1979.189; Sherman E. Lee, *Asian Art: Selections from the Collection of Mr and Mrs John D. Rockefeller Third Collection, Part II*, New York: Asia Society, 1975, 60, number 43.

9. See Li Yihua, *Gugong zhencang Kang Yong Qian ciqi tulu*, 376, number 57; 380, number 61.

30

1. Wen Zhenheng, *Zhangwu zhi, juan* 7, 211-12; David, *Chinese Connoisseurship*, 13, for Chinese text, see 338/7a; Mowry, 'Catalogue,' in Li and Watt, *The Chinese Scholar's Studio*, 189-90, number 82.

2. See Loehr, *Ritual Vessels*, 75-77, numbers 29-30; Delbanco, *Art from Ritual*, 43-49, numbers 9-12; Pope and others, *The Freer Chinese Bronzes*, volume 1, 79, number 12.

3. See Suzanne G. Valenstein, *Ming Porcelains: A Retrospective*, New York: China Institute in America, 1970, 85, number 57.

4. See Watt, *Te Hua Porcelain*, not paginated, text figure.

5. See Watt, *Te Hua Porcelain*, number 24; Donnelly, *Blanc de Chine*, plate 48 B.

6. Herbert A. Giles editor and translator, *Chuang Tzu: Taoist Philosopher and Chinese Mystic*, London: George Allen and Unwin, second revised edition, 1926, reprinted 1961, 47.

7. Williams, *Outline of Chinese Symbolism and Art Motifs*, 50-51.

8. Osvald Sirén, *Chinese Painting: Leading Masters and Principles*, London: Lund, Humphries, and Company, 1956 and 1958, reprinted by New York: Hacker Art Books, 1973, volume 2, 76-77.

9. See Percival David Foundation, *Imperial Taste*, 72, number 41.

10. See Ayers and Satō, *Shin*, 169, number 167; Palace Museum, *Gugong bowuyuan cang ci xuanji*, number 74.

11. See Ayers and Satō, *Shin*, 177, number 206; Palace Museum, *Gugong bowuyuan cang ci xuanji*, number 74; Li Yihua, *Gugong zhencang Kang Yong Qian ciqi tulu*, 219, number 48; Hugh Moss, *By Imperial Command: An Introduction to Ch'ing Imperial Painted Enamels*, Hong Kong: Hibiya, 1976, plate volume, plate 62.

12. See Chou and Brown, *The Elegant Brush*, 247-48, number 77.

13. Sydney L. Moss, *The Second Bronze Age*, number 98.

31

1. See Li Yihua, *Gugong zhencang Kang Yong Qian ciqi tulu*, 20, number 3; Valenstein, *A Handbook of Chinese Ceramics*, 219, number 210.

2. See Li Yihua, *Gugong zhencang Kang Yong Qian ciqi tulu*, 53, number 36; Ayers and Satō, *Shin*, 13, number 3; 146, number 138; Valenstein, *A Handbook of Chinese Ceramics*, 227, number 221.

3. See Watt and Ford, *East Asian Lacquer*, 90-91, number 31; Sir Harry Garner, *Chinese Lacquer*, London and Boston: Faber and Faber, 1979, 135, number 73.

4. Unpublished; Field Museum of Natural History catalogue number 117647.

5. See Christies New York, 3 June 1993, sale number 7688, lot 28.

6. For information on bamboo carving, see Wang Shixiang and Wan-go Weng, *Bamboo Carving of China*, New York: China Institute in America, 1983; Ip Yee and Laurence C.S. Tam, *Chinese Bamboo Carving*, 2 volumes, Hong Kong: The Urban Council and the Hong Kong Museum of Art, volume 1, 1978, volume 2, 1982.

7. Mowry, 'Catalogue' in Li and Watt, *The Chinese Scholar's Studio*, 175, number 58.

8. The stroke was always deleted from the character during the Xuande era, as the Emperor himself omitted it in writing his reign title (for reasons that, though much debated, remain unknown). Painted by the Xuande Emperor, a hanging scroll in the Nelson-Atkins Museum of Art, Kansas City, includes a signature with the Xuande reign title as written by the Emperor himself, as does an album leaf in the Harvard University Art Museums, Cambridge. See, respectively, Ho and others, *Eight Dynasties of Chinese Painting*, 145, number 120; Richard M. Barnhart, *Painters of the Great Ming: The Imperial Court and the Zhe School*, Dallas TX: The Dallas Museum of Art, 1993, 54, number 15.

32

1. See Loehr, *Ritual Vessels*, 21, number 2; 43, number 13; Delbanco, *Art from Ritual*, 39-41, numbers 7-8; Chase, *Ancient Chinese Bronze Art*, 47-48, numbers 9-10; Pope and others, *The Freer Chinese Bronzes*, volume 1, 59, number 8.

2. See Percival David Foundation, *Imperial Taste*, 46, number 21.

3. See Li Yihua, *Gugong zhencang Kang Yong Qian ciqi tulu*, 151, number 134; 158, number 141.

4. Valenstein, *A Handbook of Chinese Ceramics*, 263, number 267; 277, number 286.

5. See Watt, *Chinese Jades*, 210-12, numbers 211-13; 215, number 216.

6. See Herold, 'A Family of Post-Han Ritual Bronze Vessels,' 264, figure 13b (vessel in center); 266, 16c.

7. See Addis, *Chinese Ceramics from Datable Tombs*, 29, number 19c.

8. See Mikami, *Ryō Kin Gen*, 127, number 102; 186, number 168 (piece in upper right corner of illustration); 205, number 180; 207, number 188 (two pieces at left of illustration); Ministry of Culture and Information, *Sinan haejŏ yumul*, 40, number 33; 86-87, numbers 103-108.

9. See, for example, Barnhart, *Painters of the Great Ming*, 178, number 25a; Machida International Print Museum, *Chūgoku kodai hanga ten*, 170, number 41.

10. See Rolf A. Stein, *The World in Miniature: Container Gardens and Dwellings in Far Eastern Religious Thought*, Stanford CA: Stanford University Press, 1990, 74, figure 33 (translated by Phyllis Brooks). This illustration comes from the *Suyuan shipu* of 1613.

11. See Li Yihua, *Gugong zhencang Kang Yong Qian ciqi tulu*, 268, number 97.

12. See Sydney L. Moss Ltd, *The Second Bronze Age*, numbers 47-49.

13. See Zhang Guangyuan, 'Da Ming Xuande lu,' 8, number 13.

33

1. See Hasebe, *Sō*, 60, number 49; Percival David Foundation, *Imperial Taste*, 41, number 17; Mino and Tsiang, *Ice and Green Clouds*, 169, number 66; Kuo, *Born of Earth and Fire*, 78, number 57.

2. See Kelley, *Chinese Gold and Silver*, 81-82, numbers 49-50.

3. See Nezu Institute of Fine Arts, compiler, *Tōji: Hakuji, seiji, sansai* (Tang Pottery and Porcelain), Tokyo: Nezu bijutsukan, 1988, 56, number 61 (right).

4. See Watson, *Tang and Liao Ceramics*, 96, number 62; Valenstein, *A Handbook of Chinese Ceramics*, 56, number 49; 58, number 52; Nezu Institute of Fine Arts, *Tōji*, 26, number 12; 35, number 27; 45, number 41.

5. See Fontein and Wu, *Unearthing China's Past*, 198, number 105; 199, figure 110; Lee and Ho, *Chinese Art Under the Mongols*, number 33d; Jenyns and Watson, *Chinese Art: The Minor Arts*, 77, number 34a.

6. See Mikami, *Ryō Kin Gen*, 76-77, numbers 59-60; 95, number 78; 212-13, numbers 207-10, 214; Lee and Ho, *Chinese Art Under the Mongols*, numbers 142-44.

7. See Mikami, *Ryō Kin Gen*, 53, number 40.

8. See, for example, Percival David Foundation, *Imperial Taste*, 59, number 30; 67, number 37; 72, number 41; Mowry, *Handbook*, 73, number 1979.162; 74, number 1979.165; 75, numbers 1979.166, 1979.168; 76, numbers 1979.169, 1979.171; 77, number 1979.172; 80, number 1979.181.

9. See, for example, Watt and Ford, *East Asian Lacquer*, 73-75, numbers 21-22; 91, number 31; 101-02, numbers 36-37; 105, number 31; Garner, *Chinese and Associated Lacquer*, plates 26, number 50; 27, number 52; 28, number 55; 29, numbers 61-63.

10. See Mowry, *Handbook*, 83, number 1979.189; Lee, *Asian Art*, 60, number 43; Percival David Foundation,

Imperial Taste, 83, number 51; 87, number 54.

11. See Mowry, *Handbook*, 73, numbers 1979.160.
1979.162; 75, number 1979.168; 1979.169; Percival David
Foundation, *Imperial Taste*, 58-61, numbers 29-31;

12. See Mowry, *Handbook*, 82-83, numbers 1979.186,
1979.187, 1979.188, 1979.189; Percival David Foundation, *Imperial Taste*, 76-77, numbers 45-46; 82-89,
numbers 50-56.

13. See Mowry, *Handbook*, 83, number 1979.189;
Lee, *Asian Art*, 60, number 43; Percival David Foundation, *Imperial Taste*, 83-89, numbers 51-56.

34

1. Traditional interpretation recounted by Yang
Boda, Deputy Director Emeritus of the Palace Museum, Beijing, during his visit to the Clague Collection
on 7 June 1992 (as translated by Kelly Tan).

2. So-termed because they appear in Tang tombs
in such abundance, occurring more than vessels of
any other vessel shape.

3. See Satō and Hasebe, *Zui Tō*, 35, number 21;
67-71, numbers 48-51; 108, number 85; 119, number
98; Watson, *Tang and Liao Ceramics*, 39, number
15; 74, number 45; 78, number 50; 110-12, numbers
79-82; 164-65, numbers 152-57; Valenstein, *A Handbook of Chinese Ceramics*, 71, number 65; Medley,
The Chinese Potter, 83, number 55; 91, number 63;
Nezu Institute of Fine Arts, *Tōji*, 30, number 19; 41,
number 36; 44, number 37; 51 number 50.

4. See Valenstein, *A Handbook of Chinese Ceramics*,
129, number 123.

5. See Mino and Tsiang, *Ice and Green Clouds*,
199, number 80; Mikami, *Ryō Kin Gen*, 52-53, numbers 39-40; 188, numbers 176-77.

6. The iron-brown splashes on *qingbai* ware were
no doubt inspired by those on Longquan celadon
ware. Long associated with the celadon tradition,
iron-brown spots were first used on fourth- and
fifth-century celadons from the Yue kilns, sometimes as touches of descriptive local color, to darken
the eyes of a ram-shaped vessel, for example, and
at other times as decorative elements in their own
right. Seldom used during the Northern Song period,
iron spots perhaps appeared on Longquan celadon,
the inheritors of the Yue tradition, under the influence of late Northern Song and Jin-period purple-
splashed Jun ware. For examples of early Yue wares
with iron-brown splashes, see Okazaki, *Chūgoku
kodai*, 107, number 95; 227, number 230; Medley, *The
Chinese Potter*, 69, number 45; d'Argencé, *Treasures
from the Shanghai Museum*, 158, number 57.

7. It is well recorded that late in the Koryŏ dynasty
(918-1392), the rulers of Korea shipped celadons with
overglaze gilt decoration to Beijing as tribute to the
Mongol emperors of China's Yuan dynasty. Few
examples of Koryŏ celadons with gilding remain, so
it is impossible to determine the appearance of
the gilt decoration; it has always been assumed,
however, that gilding was used in combination

with inlaid decoration, the gilding emphasizing the
outlines and other features of the inlaid decoration. Though unlikely, it is not impossible that
Korean celadons with overglaze gilding could have
played some role in the creation of early Ming
bronzes with gold-splashed decoration. For information on Koryo celadons with gilt decoration, see
Gompertz, *Korean Celadon and Other Wares of
the Koryŏ Period*.

8. See *Xuande yiqi tupu*, volume 2, juan 13, 2-3
both recto.

9. *Xuande yiqi tupu*, volume 2, juan 13, 2-3 both verso.

10. See Watson, *Tang and Liao Ceramics*, 164, number 153; Nezu Institute of Fine Arts, *Tōji*, 102, number
80. See also an unpublished eighth-century Tang
sancai jar with a blue-splashed white glaze in the
Hofer Collection at the Harvard University Art
Museums (accession number 1967.44).

11. See Li Yihua, *Gugong zhencang Kang Yong
Qian ciqi tulu*, 126, number 109.

12. See Li Yihua, *Gugong zhencang Kang Yong
Qian ciqi tulu*, 312, number 141.

13. See Li Yihua, *Gugong zhencang Kang Yong
Qian ciqi tulu*, 266, number 95.

14. Some gold splashes are unusually thick, for
example, indicating the possibility of repeated
applications. In addition, the large splashes appear
to adhere directly to the brassy metal fabric but a
number of smaller ones seem to appear over the
chemically altered brown surface, suggesting that
the splashes may have been applied in a series of
gold-mercury amalgam applications.

35

1. See Kelley, *Chinese Gold and Silver*, 64, number 30; Jenyns and Watson, *Chinese Art: The Minor
Arts*, 64, number 26.

2. See Watson, *Tang and Liao Ceramics*, 18, number 8; Satō and Hasebe, *Zui Tō*, 101, number 77;
103, number 79; Satō Masahiko, *Hakuji* (White Ware),
volume 37 in *Tōji taikei* (A Compendium of Ceramics),
Tokyo: Heibonsha, 1975, plate 38; Henry Trubner,
The Arts of the Tang Dynasty, Los Angeles: Los
Angeles County Museum of Art, 1957, number 263.

3. A related porcelain bowl in the Percival David
Foundation, London, bears a mark dated to 1672, indicating that bowls of such shape were produced
during the Kangxi era. The David bowl has a pair of
relief bands about its midsection, recalling the ridge
encircling the Clague censer; differing from the present piece, the David bowl has a flaring lip, expanding
walls, and squatter proportions. See Medley, *Illustrated Catalogue of Ming and Ch'ing Monochrome*,
34, number A532; plate VI, number A532.

4. It should be emphasized that although they
trace their lineage to Tang gold and silver, the
small, covered incense boxes [numbers 11, 13, and
14] popular throughout the Ming and Qing are the
products of a tradition that continued its evolution

from the Tang through the Qing; this censer and the previous jar, by contrast, represent the revival of forms that had not been seen, let alone produced, since the Tang or Five Dynasties.

5. See *Xuande yiqi tupu*, volume 2, *juan* 13, 2-3, both recto.

6. See *Xuande yiqi tupu*, volume 2, *juan* 13, 4 recto.

7. See Mowry, *Handbook*, 52, number 1979.109; Valenstein, *A Handbook of Chinese Ceramics*, 38, number 39.

8. See Kelley, *Chinese Gold and Silver*, 80, number 48; Gyllensvärd, *Chinese Gold and Silver*, 148-149, number 96; Gyllensvärd, *Chinese Gold, Silver and Porcelain*, 49, number 44.

9. Spherical censers with openwork designs continued to be produced into the Song; for a Song example in bronze with reticulated designs of boys playing amidst floral scrolls, see J.J. Lally and Company, compiler, *Arts of Ancient China*, New York: J.J. Lally and Company, 1990, number 34.

10. See Watson, *Tang and Liao Ceramics*, 256, number 306; Gyllensvärd, *Chinese Gold, Silver and Porcelain*, 95, number 89.

11. See Thomas Lawton, *Chinese Art of the Warring States Period: Change and Continuity, 480-222 BC*, Washington DC: Freer Gallery of Art, Smithsonian Institution, 1982, 86, number 40.

36

1. See Pope and others, *The Freer Chinese Bronzes*, volume 1, 597, number 118.

2. See Okazaki, *Chūgoku kodai*, 212, number 197.

3. See Hasebe, *Sō*, 76-78, number 67-69; 89, number 81; 206, numbers 202-03; Kuo, *Born of Earth and Fire*, 87, number 68; Ministry of Culture and Information, *Sinan haejŏ yumul*, 109-10, numbers 139 a-b.

4. See Joint Board of Directors of the National Palace Museum and National Central Museum compiler, *Blue-and-White Ware of the Ming Dynasty*, Hong Kong: Cafa, 1963, volume 2, part 1, 34-37, numbers 7-8.

5. See Beurdeley and Raindre, *Qing Porcelain*, 75, plate 105; Li Yihua, *Gugong zhencang Kang Yong Qian ciqi tulu*, 117, number 100; Lady David, *Illustrated Catalogue of Ch'ing Enamelled Ware*, 10, number 811; 13, number 819; plates 1, number 811; 2, 819.

6. See Li Yihua, *Gugong zhencang Kang Yong Qian ciqi tulu*, 53, number 36.

7. See Zhou Lili, 'Ciqi bajixiangwen xintan', 328, number 43; 332, top row of diagram.

8. Chase, *Ancient Chinese Bronze Art*, 28.

37

1. See Goedhuis, *Chinese and Japanese Bronzes*, number 71. The Clague vase is published: Sydney L. Moss Ltd, *The Second Bronze Age*, number 68.

2. Large bronze *ding*-shaped censers are known, some measuring more than eighteen inches in height. See, for example, Goedhuis, *Chinese and Japanese*

Bronzes, numbers 67, 71-72.

3. See Percival David Foundation, *Imperial Taste*, 54-55, number 27; Medley, *The Chinese Potter*, 179, figure 131; Mikami, *Ryō Kin Gen*, 62-63, numbers 49-51.

4. Percival David Foundation, *Imperial Taste*, 55.

5. See, for example, Garner, *Oriental Blue and White*, plate 47.

6. Satō and Ayers, *Shin*, 15, number 4.

7. See Robert D. Mowry, 'Chinese Ceramics' in Jeffrey H. Munger and others, *The Forsyth Wickes Collection in the Museum of Fine Arts, Boston*, Boston: Museum of Fine Arts, 1992, 292, number 264.

8. See Beurdeley and Raindre, *Qing Porcelain*, 106, number 152.

9. See Watt, *Chinese Jades*, 209, number 210.

10. See Watt and Ford, *East Asian Lacquer*, 110-11, number 45.

38

1. Buddhist paintings and woodblock-printed illustrations from the Tang and Northern Song periods often show altars furnished with a censer flanked by two offering bowls laden with fruit or with brass balls probably intended to represent *cintāmaṇi* (Chinese, *ruyi baozhu*), talismanic jewels that symbolize transcendent wisdom and that are said to be capable of granting every wish.

2. See Machida International Print Museum, *Chūgoku kodai hanga ten*, 251. It should be noted that, in using both red and black inks, this illustration to a Yuan-dynasty Commentary on the Diamond Sutra (*Jingangjing zhu*) is the world's earliest known example of color printing.

3. See Machida International Print Museum, *Chūgoku kodai hanga ten*, 251; Shanghai Museum facsimile edition of a Chenghua-period woodblock-reprint of *Xinbian shuochang Bao Long tu gongan duanwai wupen zhuan*, not paginated but lower illustration on the front side of the thirtieth page, and Shanghai Museum facsimile edition of a Chenghua-period woodblock-reprint of *Quanxiang shuochang Shiguan Shouqi Liu Dusai shangyuan shiwu ye kandeng zhuan*, not paginated but upper illustration on the front side of the twenty-second page, volumes 5 and 9, respectively, in *Ming Chenghua shuochang cihua congkan: Shiliu zhong fu baitu ji chuanqi yi zhong*, Shanghai: Shanghaishiwenwu baoguan weiyuanhui and Shanghai bowuguan, 1973.

4. See Zhongguo Diyi Lishi Danganguan (Chinese First Historical Archives) compiler, *Qingdai diwang lingqin* (The Imperial Mausoleums of the Qing Dynasty), Beijing: Dangan chubanshe, 1982, 12, 33, 65; Gugong bowuyuan (The Palace Museum) and Zhongguo lyou chubanshe (China Travel Publishers), compiler, *Zijincheng dihou shenghuo* (Imperial Life in the Forbidden City), Beijing: Zhongguo lyou chubanshe, 1983, 113.

5. Zhang Guangyuan, 'Dingxingqi di fangwei yu mingwen weizhi di guanxi,' 67-87.

6. See Delbanco, *Art from Ritual*, 107, number 41.

7. See Loehr, *Ritual Vessels*, 143, number 63.

8. See same sources as in note 3 above.

9. See Goedhuis, *Chinese and Japanese Bronzes*, number 71.

10. See Goedhuis, *Chinese and Japanese Bronzes*, number 67; Galerie Zacke, compiler, *Bronzen aus der Ming-Dynastie (1368-1644)*, Vienna: Galerie Zacke, 1987, number 48; *Xuande yiqi tupu*, volume 2, *juan* 14, 4 recto.

11. See Mikami, *Ryō Kin Gen*, 217, number 229.

12. See Sichuansheng wenwu guanli weiyuanhui, Deyangxian wenwu guanli suo (Sichuan Provincial Committee for Antiquities Administration, Deyang County Division for Antiquities Administration), compilers, 'Sichuan Deyangxian faxian Songdai jiaocang' (A Song-dynasty Storage Cellar Discovered in Deyang County, Sichuan Province), *Wenwu* (Bejing), 1984, number 7, 82-84 (84, numbers 9-10).

13. See Ministry of Culture and Information, *Sinan haejō yumul*, 126-27, numbers 160-61; 176-78, numbers 240-41.

14. See Shanghai Museum facsimile edition of a Chenghua-period woodblock-reprint of *Xinbian shuochang Bao Long tu gongan duanwai wupen zhuan*, not paginated, lower illustration on the front side of the thirtieth page, and Shanghai Museum facsimile edition of a Chenghua-period woodblock-reprint of *Quanxiang shuochang Shiguan Shouqi Liu Dusai shangyuan shiwu ye kandeng zhuan*, not paginated, upper illustration on the front side of the twenty-second page.

15. See Machida International Print Museum, *Chūgoku kodai hanga ten*, 251.

16. See Joint Board of Directors, *Blue-and-White Ware of the Ming Dynasty*, book 6, 50-51, number 11.

17. See Brown, *Chinese Cloisonné*, 145, number 67; Brinker and Lutz, *Chinese Cloisonné*, numbers 193-194; 250.

18. See National Palace Museum, *Blue-and-white Ware of the Ch'ing Dynasty*, Hong Kong: Cafa, 1968, book 2, 66-67, number 23

19. See Shanghai Museum facsimile edition of a 1478 woodblock-reprint of *Xinbian quanxiang shuochang zuben Hua Guan Suo chushen zhuan deng si zhong*, not paginated, illustrations on back of first page and on front of last page.

20. See Brown, *Chinese Cloisonné*, 145.

21. See The Oriental Art Gallery compiler, *Oriental Works of Art*, London: Oriental Art Gallery, 1993, number 76.

22. William Edward Soothill, *A Dictionary of Chinese Buddhist Terms*, London: Kegan Paul, Trench, Trubner, and Company, 1937, 211.

23. See Lim and others, *Stories from China's Past*, 174, plate 68; 180, plate 70 D.

24. See Lee and Ho, *Chinese Art Under the Mongols*, number 59; Valenstein, *A Handbook of Chinese Ceramics*, 149, number 144; Mikami, *Ryō Kin Gen*, 183, number 154; 247, number 294.

25. The frontal dragon first appeared in the mid-sixteenth century; the Qianlong elements of style thus relate to the arrangement of the dragon's body, the pattern of its scales, the shape and rhythm of its spinal barbs, and the configuration of its claws, rather than to its frontal presentation.

26. See, for example, Li Yihua, *Gugong zhencang Kang Yong Qian ciqi tulu*, 329, number 10; Oriental Art Gallery, *Oriental Works of Art*, number 106.

27. See Goedhuis, *Chinese and Japanese Bronzes*, number 72.

28. See Goedhuis, *Chinese and Japanese Bronzes*, number 72.

29. The censer was integrally cast with its decoration but its handles were separately cast and affixed with tenons and pins. The candlesticks were cast in at least four parts – base, drip tray, column, and saucer-shaped candle mount – that are held together by a long pin that extends downward from the bottom of the candle mount through the other parts; the flattened end of the pin is visible inside the base. The vases were integrally cast except for their c-form handles and moveable rings and for their base plates, all of which were separately prepared and secured into place with molten metal.

39

1. See Watt and Ford, *East Asian Lacquer*, 108, number 43.

2. See Valenstein, *A Handbook of Chinese Ceramics*, 130, number 124.

3. See Watt and Ford, *East Asian Lacquer*, 54-55, number 10; Lee Yu-kuan, *Oriental Lacquer Art*, New York and Tokyo: Weatherhill, 1971, 134-135, number 68; 162, number 96.

4. See Valenstein, *Ming Porcelains*, 86, number 58; d'Argencé, *Treasures from the Shanghai Museum*, 172, number 113 and color plate 37; Medley, *The Chinese Potter*, 231, figure 179; Li Yihua, *Gugong zhencang Kang Yong Qian ciqi tulu*, 241, number 70; 329, number 10;.

5. See Brown, *Chinese Cloisonné*, 73, number 28; Brinker and Lutz, *Chinese Cloisonné*, numbers 190-91.

6. See Valenstein, *A Handbook of Chinese Ceramics*, 149, number 144; Mikami, *Ryō Kin Gen*, 247, number 294.

7. See Valenstein, *A Handbook of Chinese Ceramics*, 189, number 185; Hayashiya, Trubner and others, *Chinese Ceramics from Japanese Collections*, 100, number 56; Medley, *Illustrated Catalogue of Ming Polychrome Wares*, 33, number 92 and plate 9, number 92.

8. A small boss in the outer relief line bordering the *leiwen* band around the central medallion raises the possibility that elements of the design, the *leiwen* band, for example, might have been soldered into place. Until resolved, this suggestion will necessarily remain speculation; such speculation is useful, however, in pointing the way for future research and laboratory analysis.

40

1. See Brown, *Chinese Cloisonné*, 118-19, number 52; Brinker and Lutz, *Chinese Cloisonné*, number 265. The Clague bronze is published: Spink and Son Ltd, compiler, *Octagon* (London), volume 24, number 2, June 1987, 5.

2. See Claudia Brown and Donald Rabiner, *Chinese Glass of the Qing Dynasty: The Robert H. Clague Collection*, Phoenix AZ: Phoenix Art Museum, 1987, 18, number 2; 22-24, numbers 9-14; 27, number 18; 32, number 28; 36, number 35; 40, number 40.

3. During his visit to the Clague Collection on 7 June 1992, Yang Boda, Deputy Director Emeritus of the Palace Museum, Beijing, noted that this vase is identical to ones still in the Palace collection, indicating that it must have come from one of the palaces.

4. See Li Yihua, *Gugong zhencang Kang Yong Qian ciqi tulu*, 375, number 56; 378, number 59; 397, number 78

5. See d'Argencé, *Treasures from the Shanghai Museum*, 101, number 83; Li and Watt, *The Chinese Scholar's Studio*, 140, number 88.

6. See Joint Board of Directors, *Kuan Ware of the Sung Dynasty*, 39, number 11.

7. See Loehr, *Ritual Vessels*, 139, number 61; 161-65, numbers 72-74.

8. See Watt, *Chinese Jades*, 209-215, numbers 210-13, 215-16.

9. One was formerly in the Robert H. Clague collection, now donated to the Phoenix Art Museum (accession number 91.204); published: Spink and Son Ltd, compiler, *The Minor Arts of China III*, London, 1987, 78, number 97. The other one, in the Uldry collection, is published in Brinker and Lutz, *Chinese Cloisonné*, number 304.

10. See Jenyns and Watson, *Chinese Art: The Minor Arts*, 117, number 50.

41

1. For background information on the use of hand warmers, see Ulrich Hausmann, 'Keeping Warm in a Cold Study: The Warmer' in Sydney L. Moss Ltd, compiler, *The Literati Mode: Chinese Scholar Paintings, Calligraphy and Desk Objects*, London: Sydney L. Moss Ltd, 1986, 311-15.

2. Wen Zhenheng, *Zhangwu zhi, juan 7*, 200.

3. See Li Yihua, *Gugong zhencang Kang Yong Qian ciqi tulu*, 161, number 144.

4. See Tsang and Moss, *Chinese Metalwork*, 57-59, numbers 32-35; Sydney L. Moss Ltd, *The Second Bronze Age*, numbers 84-85; Sydney L. Moss Ltd compiler, *In Scholar's Taste: Documentary Chinese Works of Art*, London: Sydney L. Moss Ltd., 1983, 227, numbers 159; Sydney L. Moss Ltd, compiler, *Emperor, Scholar, Artisan, Monk: The Creative Personality in Chinese Works of Art*, London: Sydney L. Moss Ltd, 1984, 271, numbers 125.

5. Wen Zhenheng, *Zhangwu zhi, juan 7*, 200.

6. See James C.Y. Watt, *The Sumptuous Basket: Chinese Lacquer with Basketry Panels*, New York: China Institute in America, 1985, 33, plate 2.

7. See Mowry, *Handbook*, 83, numbers 1979.189; Lee, *Asian Art*, 60, number 43; Percival David Foundation, *Imperial Taste*, 83, number 51; 87, number 54.

8. See Li Yihua, *Gugong zhencang Kang Yong Qian ciqi tulu*, 355, number 36.

9. See Li Yihua, *Gugong zhencang Kang Yong Qian ciqi tulu*, 323-25, numbers 4-6; 389-90, numbers 70-71; 395-96, numbers 76-77; 398-99, numbers 79-80.

10. Two related hand warmers have recently been published, one with a mark reading *Pan Xiangfeng zhi* (Made by Pan Xiangfeng) and the other with a mark reading *Pan Xiangli zhi* (Made by Pan Xiangli). Paul Moss, the author who published the two pieces, read both marks as *Pan Xiangli zhi*; although similarly written, *feng* and *li* are different characters and they are clearly and correctly differentiated in the marks. Given the Chinese custom of assigning the same character to all paternally related, male family members of the same generation, that is, brothers and their male first cousins on the father's side, as the first syllable of the given name, it is more reasonable to conclude that Pan Xiangfeng and Pan Xiangli were brothers or first cousins than it is to conclude that they are the same person, a person who wrote both marks mentioned above, but wrote his own name incorrectly in one of them. Since their names and their artistic styles are similar, it is likely that Pan Xiangfeng and Pan Xiangli were two closely related members of the same family of metalsmiths. For the mark reading *Pan Xiangfeng zhi*, see Sydney L. Moss Ltd, *The Second Bronze Age*, numbers 79; for the mark reading *Pan Xiangli*, see Sydney L. Moss Ltd, *The Literati Mode*, 309-10, numbers 163.

11. See Sydney L. Moss Ltd, *The Second Bronze Age*, numbers 79.

12. Most hand warmers lack a separately articulated foot; instead, the walls turn sharply inward at something approximating a ninety-degree angle at the bottom of the container to form a flat base.

13. See Brinker and Lutz, *Chinese Cloisonné*, numbers 236, 249-50, 253, 260, 263, 268-69.

42

1. See Loehr, *Ritual Vessels*, 161-63, numbers 72-74; Delbanco, *Art from Ritual*, 129, number 52.

2. See Wang, *Han Civilization*, 108, numbers 116-18; 110, number 123.

3. See Jenyns and Watson, *Chinese Art: The Minor Arts*, 101-03, numbers 40-41; 107, number 43; 128, number 56; Kerr, *Later Chinese Bronzes*, 17, number 4; 23, number 13; Goedhuis, *Chinese and Japanese Bronzes*, numbers 77, 80-81.

4. Some late Ming and Qing bronzes inlaid in

Song fashion reveal their later date by their use of 'eyes' in the center of inlaid sheets of gold or silver, the circular apertures fitting over small bronze posts that serve a decorative function as well as the very practical one of helping to hold the inlays in place [compare 30]. See Goedhuis, *Chinese and Japanese Bronzes*, number 82.

5. See Jenyns and Watson, *Chinese Art: The Minor Arts*, 111, number 46; Kerr, *Later Chinese Bronzes*, 53, number 41; Goedhuis, *Chinese and Japanese Bronzes*, numbers 84-89; Tsang and Moss, *Chinese Metalwork*, 34-35, numbers 1-2.

6. See Li and Watt, *The Chinese Scholar's Studio*, 120, number 67; Jenyns and Watson, *Chinese Art: The Minor Arts*, 153, number 70.

7. Since it requires less gold and silver than traditional inlay and can be accomplished more quickly and easily than traditional inlay, damascening enabled bronze craftsmen to produce finished vessels at less cost than did inlay. Since damascened vessels were no doubt sold as inlaid vessels, at inlaid-vessel prices, profits must have risen commensurately, with none the wiser, save the artisan and a few discerning connoisseurs. Such economy of material and labor is a feature of Chinese crafts of the nineteenth century, from bronze to jade to lacquer; it mirrors the general decline of both empire and national economy.

8. Compare Li Yihua, *Gugong zhencang Kang Yong Qian ciqi tulu*, 386, number 67; Watt, *Chinese Jades*, 216, number 218.

9. A thermoluminescence (TL) test performed at the Research Laboratory for Archaeology and the History of Art, Oxford University, on a sample of casting core removed from under the footring confirmed the jar's antiquity. The test certificate, dated 26 October 1990 and bearing the signature of Doreen Stoneham, indicates that the sample (number 566k7) was last fired between one hundred and two hundred years ago.

10. Because virtually all of the gold and silver is intact, it is impossible to discern whether the surface was scored in preparation for damascening through integral casting or through cold work. Those areas embellished with silver lines show less wear than the ones ornamented with gold and silver sheets because the wire used for the lines is much thicker than the sheets.

43

1. For information on the scholar's studio and its appointments, see Li and Watt, *The Chinese Scholar's Studio*.

2. See Watt, *Chinese Jades*, 73, number 54.

3. See Watt, *Chinese Jades*, 71, number 49.

4. See *Xuande yiqi tupu*, volume 2, *juan* 12, 7; *juan* 15, 4; *juan* 19, 6, all pages recto.

5. See Watt, *Chinese Jades*, 59, number 36; 60, numbers 37-38.

6. Despite its ferocity and seeming naturalism, this lion relies more on conceptual presentation than realistic modeling, as the head is too large for the body, the ribs extend too far back on the torso, the right hind paw is impossibly positioned in relation to the leg, and the left rear leg has been entirely omitted. Such traits also argue for the early date of this vessel, since mid- and late Ming jade and bronze animals, whether hollow vessels or solid sculptures, generally indicate more anatomical completeness (though not necessarily accuracy), and their bases usually have at least a cursory representation of the animal's underside, if not a detailed description.

44

1. For information on ink and inkstones, see Mowry, 'Catalogue' in Li and Watt, *The Chinese Scholar's Studio*, 184-187.

2. See Li and Watt, *The Chinese Scholar's Studio*, 139, number 86; Desmond Gure, 'An Early Jade Animal Vessel and Some Parallels,' *Transactions of the Oriental Ceramic Society, 1957-59* (London), volume 31, 1959, 75-82, plates 26-27; Brian Morgan, *Dr Newton's Zoo: A Study of Post-Archaic Small Jade Carvings*, London: Bluett and Sons Ltd, 1981, 12, number 10; Ōsaka shiritsu bijutsukan (Osaka Municipal Museum) compiler, *Rokuchō no bijutsu (Arts of the Six Dynasties)*, Tokyo: Heibonsha, 1976, 292, number 159. (Although Gure and others have argued that vessels of this shape were lamps, the consensus today is that they were water droppers.)

3. Wen Zhenheng, *Zhangwu zhi*, *juan* 7, 204.

4. See Loehr, *Ancient Chinese Jades*, 354-57, number 522; Lawton, *Chinese Art of the Warring States Period*, 155, number 102; 181-83, numbers 134-35; Arts Council of Great Britain, *Chinese Jade Throughout the Ages*, 64, numbers 173-74; Wang Zhongshu, *Han Civilization*, 95, number 105; 98-99, numbers 111, 115; Jenyns and Watson, *Chinese Art: The Minor Arts*, 291, numbers 129-30; Watt and Ford, *East Asian Lacquer*, 17, number 3; 19, number 6.

5. See Lim and others, *Stories from China's Past*, 179, plate 70 C.

6. Chai and Chai, *Li Chi: Book of Rites*, volume 1, 384.

7. Later pieces tend to be more fanciful, turning the tortoise's head slightly, intertwining the snake's tail with that of the tortoise, eliminating the cup's handles, and even embellishing the underside of the tortoise with scrolling floral motifs. See Brinker and Lutz, *Chinese Cloisonné*, number 259.

45, 46, 47

1. Mowry, 'Catalogue' in Li and Watt, *The Chinese Scholar's Studio*, 181, number 69; Watt, *Chinese Jades*, 143, number 119.

2. Morgan, *Dr Newton's Zoo*, 2.

3. Wen Zhenheng, *Zhangwu zhi*, *juan* 7, 205. On the same page, Wen further noted that Xuande-

period bronze horses, oxen, felines, gibbons, lions, and other wild animals make especially elegant paper weights. The list of Xuande forms is limited to actual animals but the list of other bronzes, presumably late Ming ones, also includes several mythical ones; the significance, if any, of this distinction remains unclear, though it would be tempting to infer from it that a greater number of mythical animal sculptures was produced in the late Ming.

4. Perhaps an importation from Persia, the horned *bixie* chimera, an imaginary creature resembling a winged lion, rose to prominence in the arts of the Han dynasty. The typical Han *bixie* is a fully self-assured beast that strides forward proudly, its head held high, its mouth open and growling, its tail curled with nervous energy. Large sculptures of *bixie* chimeras were associated with the royal tombs of the Southern Dynasties during the Six Dynasties period. Their exact meaning remains unclear, but their ferocious demeanor suggests a tutelary function. Depicting them with wisps of flame but without wings, Ming artists tended to present these creatures more as docile, semi-domesticated pets than as ferocious guardians. In fact, the combination of bulging, staring eyes with closed mouth and passive posture makes the Ming examples seem, by contrast, timid and diffident. Mowry, 'Catalogue' in Li and Watt, *The Chinese Scholar's Studio*, 172; Robert D. Mowry, 'Chinese Jades from Han to Qing,' *Archaeology* (New York), volume 34, number 1, January-February 1981, 52-55.

5. One of the *siling*, or four intelligent creatures, mentioned in the Zhou-dynasty *Liji* (Book of Rites), the mythical *qilin* stands alongside the dragon, phoenix, and tortoise as a creature of good omen; according to Chinese legend, the *qilin* appears only during the reign of exceptionally virtuous and enlightened emperors. Sometimes called a unicorn in English, it is a symbol of longevity, grandeur, felicity, illustrious offspring, and wise administration. Descriptions of the *qilin* vary widely, but it is usually said to resemble a large stag in its general form. Combining the body of the musk deer with the tail of an ox, it supposedly has the hooves of a horse and the forehead of a wolf, from which grows a single horn; its belly is yellow and its skin of five colors, red, yellow, blue, white, and black. The *qilin's* voice is melodious, like the sound of bells and other musical instruments. Other descriptions state that the *qilin* has two horns, that it has the body of a horse, and that it is covered with scales like a fish. Although typically shown as a deer-like creature, the *qilin* often looks more like a cloven-hoofed horse in those representations portraying it as a fully scaled beast, especially if called by its alternative name, *longma*, or dragon horse. For more information on the *qilin/longma*, see Williams, *Outline of Chinese Symbolism and Art Motifs*, 409-11 (Unicorn). Gerard Tsang and Hugh Moss suggest a resemblance to a sheep or goat in their discussion

of a similar piece, commenting especially on the animal's beard; while the sculpture admittedly bears some superficial resemblance to a sheep, the long, slender head with its broad muzzle, prominent jaw, and small, erect ears looks more like that of a horse than that of a sheep or goat, at least to this author. Given that the *qilin/longma* typically has spindly legs with cloven hooves, often has both a scale-covered body and a beard, and sometimes has selected features of a horse, the tentative identification of this creature as a *qilin* seems the more rational. For the similar sculpture and for its identification as a sheep or goat, see Oriental Ceramic Society of Hong Kong, *Arts from the Scholar's Studio*, 214-14, number 194. For a deer-like *qilin* with a beard on its lower jaw, see Mowry, *Handbook*, 69, number 1979.151. Attributed to the sixteenth century and termed a *qilin*, a third sculpture of the type represented by number 47 is published in Michael Goedhuis compiler, *Michael Goedhuis/ Colnaghi Oriental* (exhibition brochure), London: Michael Goedhuis/ Colnaghi Oriental, not dated, not paginated. Called a lion or chimera but not attributed in time, another small sculpture of the type represented by number 45 depicting a recumbent animal scratching its ear is published in Galerie Zacke, *Bronzen aus der Ming-Dynastie*, number 27.

6. In many ways, the decoration of Ming small bronze sculptures parallels that of contemporaneous vessels: early Ming vessels [number 7] and sculptures [number 43] both have integrally cast decoration with little, if any, cold working; in addition, they contrast plain surfaces with textured ones and they incorporate numerous spirals, whether curled manes or coiled *leiwen*, into the design. Late Ming vessels [11, 13] and sculptures [numbers 45-47] rely heavily on cold working for finishing details and they show a preference for all-over decoration.

48, 49

1. See John Hay, *Kernels of Energy, Bones of Earth: The Rock in Chinese Art*, New York: China Institute in America, 1985. The Clague brushrest is published: Sydney L. Moss Ltd, *The Second Bronze Age*, number 28.

2. He notes that the rocks most preferred for brushrests were of Ying and Lingbi stone, which, not coincidentally, were the same ones most highly prized as so-called 'scholar's rocks' – exquisitely shaped, usually igneous, rocks that scholars collected as abstract sculpture for appreciation in their studios. For information on scholar's rocks, see Nancy Berliner, 'The Rosenblum Collection of Chinese Rocks,' *Orientations* (Hong Kong), volume 21, number 11, November 1990, 68-75.

3. Wen Zhenheng, *Zhangwu zhi, juan* 7, 201.

4. Representing the four quarters surrounding the center, the Wuyue, or Five Sacred Mountains are Mounts Tai, in Shandong province (representing

East); Heng, in Hunan (South); Hua, in Shaanxi (West); Heng, in Hebei (North); and Song, in Henan (Center). For information on the sacred peaks, see E.T.C. Werner, *A Dictionary of Chinese Mythology*, New York: Julian Press, 1961, 578-80 (Wu Yo); Kiyohiko Munakata, *Sacred Mountains in Chinese Art*, Urbana-Champaign: Krannert Art Museum, University of Illinois, 1991.

5. Yang Boda, Deputy Director Emeritus of the Palace Museum, Beijing, confirmed this interpretation during his visit to the Clague Collection on 7 June 1992. Although Paul Moss' interpretation of the scene as an entrance to a Daoist paradise in the Isles of the Immortals might have some validity as a secondary meaning, the primary meaning is clearly that stated in the text above. See Sydney L. Moss, *The Second Bronze Age*, number 28.

6. See Satō and Hasebe, *Zui Tō*, 99, number 76; 223, number 181.

7. An unpublished, Zhengde-period blue-and-white porcelain brushrest was given to the Harvard University Art Museums by Mr and Mrs Samuel B. Grimson in 1983 (accession number 1983.49). For other examples, see Valenstein, *A Handbook of Chinese Ceramics*, 168, number 163; Medley, *The Chinese Potter*, 218, figure 161.

8. See Sothebys London, 10 December 1985, sale number 3441A, lot 42; Goedhuis, *Chinese and Japanese Bronzes*, number 30.

9. See Li and Watt, *The Chinese Scholar's Studio*, 109, number 43. An unpublished late Ming enameled-porcelain brushrest in the form of three mountains in the collection of the Harvard University Art Museums has dragons striding among the mountains and stylized waves lapping at their bases (accession number 1940.278).

10. Mowry, 'Catalogue' in Li and Watt, *The Chinese Scholar's Studio*, 179, number 66.

11. The results of a thermoluminescence (TL) test performed at the Research Laboratory for Archaeology and the History of Art, Oxford University, on a sample of casting core removed from inside two of the peaks are consistent with the attribution proposed here. The test certificate, dated 7 June 1991 and bearing the signature of Doreen Stoneham, indicates that the sample (number 566s2) was last fired between four hundred and seven hundred years ago.

12. Wen Zhenheng, *Zhangwu zhi, juan* 7, 201.

13. Reportedly excavated in the Philippines, an unpublished Yuan-period *qingbai* porcelain water dropper in the form of a silver ingot with an openwork *chilong* handle is in the collection of the Harvard University Art Museums (accession number 1972.324). For a related handle on a Yuan-period *qingbai* porcelain cup, see Lee and Ho, *Chinese Art Under the Mongols*, number 110; Gyllensvärd, *Chinese Gold, Silver and Porcelain*, 115, number 124.

14. See Li and Watt, *The Chinese Scholar's Studio*, 119; number 63; Kerr, *Later Chinese Bronzes*, 42,

number 29; Ayers, 'Blanc-de-Chine: Some Reflections,' 23.

15. See Oriental Ceramic Society of Hong Kong, *Arts from the Scholar's Studio*, 179, number 156.

16. See Tokugawa bijutsukan (Tokugawa Museum), compiler, *Bunbōqu* (Scholars' Desk Materials from the Libraries of the Daimyō), *Zōhinchō* 4 (Collection Catalogue 4), Nagoya: Tokugawa bijutsukan, 1988, 63, number 135; 115, number 135; vii, number 135; Sydney L. Moss Ltd, *The Second Bronze Age*, number 29

50

1. The inscription translates:
On the auspicious twenty-second day of the sixth [lunar] month of the eleventh year of Jiajing [1532], the surviving son Wang Shi, together with the second son Wang Baoyou, [along with] Wang Guantian and Wang Haoxi, dedicated this sculpture, made in East Street, Ningling xian, Henan province, to honor the spirits of their deceased father and mother, Xin, the third concubine, Weigu of the Zhu clan.

This translation is a revised and modified version of that provided by Professor Ju-hsi Chou of Arizona State University, Tempe, in his letter of 2 March 1988 to Robert H. Clague. I am grateful for Professor Chou's assistance.

2. See National Palace Museum, *Three Hundred Masterpieces of Chinese Painting*, volume 6, number 295; Machida International Print Museum, *Chūgoku kodai hanga ten*, 101, number 14; for information on Chinese portraiture, see Richard Ellis Vinograd, *Boundaries of the Self: Chinese Portraits, AD 1600-1900*, Cambridge and New York: Cambridge University Press, 1992.

3. See Goedhuis, *Chinese and Japanese Bronzes*, number 1.

4. See Machida International Print Museum, *Chūgoku kodai hanga ten*, 90, number 14; 99, number 11.

5. That is, separately cast in advance and set into the main mold with its tenon, so that in casting the body, molten metal surrounded the neck and tenon, securing them in place by interlock and perhaps by partial fusion. For information on casting-on, see Chase, *Ancient Chinese Bronze Art*, 28.

51

1. For information on Guandi, see Giles, *A Chinese Biographical Dictionary*, 383-84 (Kuan Yü); Werner, *A Dictionary of Chinese Mythology*, 227-30 (Kuan Yü).

2. See Oriental Ceramic Society compiler, *Chinese Ivories from the Shang to the Qing*, London: Oriental Ceramic Society jointly with the British Museum, 1984, 102-03, numbers 110, 112; 107, number 119,

3. See Oriental Ceramic Society, *Chinese Ivories*, 105, number 116.

4. See Oriental Ceramic Society, *Chinese Ivories*, 70-71, numbers 52-53; 81, number 72; 85, number 78; 105, number 116.

52

1. Published: Sydney L. Moss, *The Second Bronze Age*, number 8.

2. In addition, those Tang horses with a molded groove along the upper part of the spine and a circular perforation in place of a tail are thought to have been outfitted with manes and tails made from horse hair.

3. See Oriental Ceramic Society, *Chinese Ivories*, 34, number 15; 99, number 105.

4. See Goedhuis, *Chinese and Japanese Bronzes*, number 3.

5. Yang Boda mentioned the unpublished piece and its attribution during his visit to the Clague Collection on 7 June 1992.

53

1. Published: Sydney L. Moss, *The Second Bronze Age*, number 9.

2. Although it has been suggested that they represent the figure's name, *Xiao Han*, the last two characters should more probably be read as a noun, *xiaohan*, a reference to the heavens; reading the characters as a name destroys the symmetry of the two lines of linked verse. See Sydney L. Moss, *The Second Bronze Age*, number 9.

3. Sydney L. Moss, *The Second Bronze Age*, number 9.

4. For a painting, now in the Metropolitan Museum of Art, New York, by Qiu Ying (1494/95-1552) representing 'The Five Star Gods and the Twenty-eight Constellations,' see Sothebys New York, 5 December 1985; sale number 5406, lot 86.

5. See Ho and others, *Eight Dynasties of Chinese Painting*, 7, number 5; Thomas Lawton, *Chinese Figure Painting* (volume 2 of *Freer Gallery of Art Fiftieth Anniversary Exhibition*), Washington DC: Smithsonian Institution, 1973, 156-59, number 38.

6. See Sothebys, New York, 1 December 1992, sale number 6370, lot 219; Oriental Ceramic Society, *Chinese Ivories*, 102-03, numbers 110, 112; 106-07, numbers 118-19; Donnelly, *Blanc de Chine*, plates 147d and 157 (lower right).

7. See Machida International Print Museum, *Chūgoku kodai hanga ten*, 77; 94, number 1; 205, number 22; 218, numbers 8-9.

8. Unpublished; Field Museum of Natural History catalogue number 120151.

54

1. Medley, *The Chinese Potter*, 223, figure 169.

2. See Kerr, *Later Chinese Bronzes*, 81, number 63.

3. See Goedhuis, *Chinese and Japanese Bronzes*, number 4.

4. See Ho and others, *Eight Dynasties of Chinese Painting*, 9, number 6; Lawton, *Chinese Figure Painting*, 200, 203, number 51; National Palace Museum, *Three Hundred Masterpieces of Chinese Painting*, volume 5, number 204.

5. See Lim and others, *Stories from China's Past*, 138, figure 9; 141, number 47; 144, number 49.

6. See Li and Watt, *The Chinese Scholar's Studio*, 97, number 28; Lawton, *Chinese Figure Painting*, 84, number 15.

7. See Goedhuis, *Chinese and Japanese Bronzes*, numbers 1, 4.

8. See Kerr, *Later Chinese Bronzes*, 81, number 63; Goedhuis, number 25; Sydney L. Moss, *The Second Bronze Age*, numbers 10-11, 18, 19.

55

1. Published: Skinner Inc, compiler, *Oriental Works of Art* (catalog of an auction held in Bolton MA, on Friday 22 February 1991; sale number 1366), Bolton MA: Skinner Inc, 1991, lot 240.

2. Benevolent Buddhist deities, bodhisattvas (Chinese, *pusa*) are enlightened beings who have postponed entry into final nirvana in order to assist other sentient beings in attaining enlightenment. Hallmarks of Mahayana Buddhism, bodhisattvas are usually presented in the guise of an Indian prince, since the Historical Buddha, Śakyamuni, was born a crown prince and lived in a royal palace in the foothills of the Himalayas before taking up the religious life. Bodhisattvas typically wear an array of silken scarves over the chest and an ankle-length *dhoti* of rich brocade about the waist and legs; they usually have long hair arranged in an elaborate coiffure and they often wear a wealth of jewelry, from crowns and hair ornaments to necklaces and earrings to bracelets and anklets. For information on the White-robed Guanyin, see: John M. Rosenfield and Elizabeth ten Grotenhuis, *Journey of the Three Jewels: Japanese Buddhist Paintings from Western Collections*, New York: The Asia Society in association with John Weatherhill Inc, 1979, 175-79, numbers 52-53; Ho and others, *Eight Dynasties of Chinese Painting*, 84-85, number 66; Jan Fontein and Money L. Hickman, *Zen Painting and Calligraphy*, Boston: Museum of Fine Arts, 1970, 47-49, number 19; 79-87, numbers 35-36; Jan Fontein, *The Pilgrimage of Sudhana*, The Hague: E.J. Brill, 1966. The thirty-three manifestations of Guanyin are described in the *Gandha-vyuha* (Chinese, *Huayan jing*), a principal text of the Avatamsaka (Chinese, Huayan) sect of Buddhism.

3. The *ūrnā* (Chinese, *guanghao*) is an auspicious mark that appears on the forehead of deities and is variously interpreted as a tuft of hair or as a third eye; it is one of the thirty-two major signs of a Buddha, though it appears on the foreheads of Buddhist deities other than Buddhas.

4. Ho and others, *Eight Dynasties of Chinese Painting*, 84, number 66.

5. Rosenfield and ten Grotenhuis, *Journey of the Three Jewels*, 175, number 52.

6. Rosenfield and ten Grotenhuis, *Journey of the Three Jewels*, 175, number 52.

7. See Ho and others, *Eight Dynasties of Chinese Painting*, 84, number 66.

8. See Oriental Ceramic Society, *Chinese Ivories*, 53, figure 15; 54-62, numbers 17-37; Donnelly, *Blanc de Chine*, plates 71a, 72 a and c, 75, 79b, 81, 82, 84, 85 a-c.

9. See Ho and others, *Eight Dynasties of Chinese Painting*, 258-59, number 202.

10. Mowry, 'Catalogue' in Li and Watt, *The Chinese Scholar's Studio*, 175, number 59. See Claudia Brown and Ju-hsi Chou, *Heritage of the Brush: The Roy and Marilyn Papp Collection of Chinese Painting*, Phoenix AZ: Phoenix Art Museum, 122, number 44c.

11. See Donnelly, *Blanc de Chine*, plate 82a. Shisou-marked sculptures and Dehua porcelain figurines often show strong similarities, though the nature of the relationship remains unknown, as does the direction of influence, if, indeed, one group influenced the other. One Shisou-type bronze sculpture of a standing Guanyin bears an inlaid mark of He Chaozong, a Dehua potter well known for his molded porcelain figurines; whether the mark is genuine or apocryphal, whether He Chaozong the porcelain sculptor and He Chaozong the purported bronze sculptor are the same person or are two different people, whether the mark, if genuine, appears as a maker's mark or as a tribute honoring a He Chaozong porcelain figurine replicated in bronze, all are questions that await study and resolution. See Goedhuis, *Chinese and Japanese Bronzes*, number 7.

56

1. A number of small casting flaws were expertly corrected during manufacture by excising the defective areas and filling them with new bronze. Such repairs are most visible in the smooth areas - around the lips of the larger fish, for example, and on the face of the smaller one. Well finished, the fills are square or rectangular in form and differ subtly in color from the bronze matrix into which they are set.

2. For information on the fish and its symbolism, see Williams, *Outlines of Chinese Symbolism and Art Motifs*, 181-84.

3. Zhou Lili, 'Ciqi bajixiangwen xintan,' 312-32.

4. See Arts Council of Great Britain, *Chinese Jade Throughout the Ages*, 128, number 420.

5. See Watson, *Tang and Liao Ceramics*, 160, number 142; Percival David Foundation, *Imperial Taste*, 18, number 1; 19, figures 1-3.

6. See Mowry, 'Chinese Ceramics' in Munger and others, *The Forsyth Wickes Collection in the Museum of Fine Arts, Boston*, 293, number 265.

7. See Li Yihua, *Gugong zhencang Kang Yong Qian ciqi tulu*, 312, number 141.

57

1. According to Werner, the popular tradition was inspired by a line in the text of *Sanqin ji* stating, 'The fish from the rivers and seas gather together below Lung Men [Longmen]. Those who can pass on upstream turn into dragons, while those who cannot, bump their heads and bruise their cheeks.' Werner, *A Dictionary of Chinese Mythology*, 287.

2. See Arts Council of Great Britain, *Chinese Jade Throughout the Ages*, 128, number 421.

58

1. Published: Sothebys London, 30 October 1987, sale number 3031, lot 413.

2. Chai and Chai, *Li Chi: Book of Rites*, volume 1, 384.

3. For more information on the *qilin*, see Williams, *Outline of Chinese Symbolism and Art Motifs*, 409-411 (Unicorn).

4. *Xuande yiqi tupu*, volume 1, *juan* 3, 6 recto and verso; volume 2, *juan* 11, 3-4 recto and verso for both pages. The texts record that the lion and jiaoduan were fitted with octagonal stands of *xiangmu* and *zitan* woods, respectively. With the reliance of Xuande bronze censers on Song ceramics, it is also possible that such early Ming animal-shaped censers could have been inspired by the covers of Song ceramic censers which sometimes take the form of lions, ducks, and other animals; for examples, see Hasebe, *Sō*, 46-47, numbers 38-39; Pearlstein and Ulak, *Asian Art in The Art Institute of Chicago*, 60; Gyllensvärd, *Chinese Gold, Silver and Porcelain*, 97, number 90.

5. For a Ming jade example, see Yang Boda, *Zhongguo meishu quanji: Yuqi*, 170, number 294. *Qilin* and other animal-shaped censers may have been categorized as *xunlu* rather than *xianglu*. The character *xun* (fragrant or perfume) implies sensuous pleasure and carries hedonistic, even erotic, overtones. *Xunlu*, clearly censers not for religious use, were used in rooms of the house other than the studio where scholars would have used either archaic bronzes or censers inspired by them that were part of matched sets.

6. See Oriental Ceramic Society of Hong Kong, *Arts from the Scholar's Studio*, 241, number 232; Sothebys Hong Kong, 15 May 1990, lot 365; Sothebys New York, 1 December 1992, sale number 6370, lot 203.

7. See Sothebys Hong Kong, 15 May 1990, lot 352.

8. See Ip Yee and Laurence C.S. Tam, *Chinese Bamboo Carving*, Hong Kong: The Urban Council and the Hong Kong Museum of Art, volume 1, 1978, 178, plate 26.

9. James Roberts, a conservator of arts and antiquities, examined this censer in March 1988; he noted the following in his condition report, dated 12 March 1988: '*Manufacture*: The tail was cast separately; it is attached to the body in two places with copper

pins and soldered to the body below the proper-right rear haunch. A corroding iron rod, approximately 1/4 inch in diameter, juts inside the sculpture from the ... shank of the proper right rear leg. Tests with a magnet reveal that the iron rod extended through the haunch into the shank. Due to the fact of iron corrosion and metallic structure of the solid cast shank, this iron rod was in place during the original casting of the sculpture. Tests with the magnet were inconclusive if another iron rod is cast into the proper left rear leg. Radiography of the sculpture could reveal the structure if necessary. Portions of the casting core remain inside the sculpture. The modeling is well executed and highly articulated. The surface has been well chased. There are some small casting flaws in the form of tiny air pockets visible along the ear, mouth, and chest of the Kylin (*qilin*). Some flaws continue through the metal as small holes visible from the inside when the sculpture is held near a strong light. *Surface*: The patina is a rich brown, olive underneath golden highlights in the body areas. This patina appears to be from age rather than chemically induced. The gilded areas appear to be a 'fire' or mercury gilding. The mane and tail were not gilded originally.'

10. Oriental Ceramic Society of Hong Kong, *Arts from the Scholar's Studio*, 240, number 232.